Inclusions and Exclusions in European Societies

European social development over the last century has been characterized by an increasing inclusion of people into the expanding collectivities of the nation state, the European Union and welfare entitlement pools. Yet recent empirical data indicates increasing disparities in income in many places. Within European physical borders there is greater cultural and ethnic heterogeneity than ever before. Processes of inclusion/exclusion are thus intricately linked.

Inclusions and Exclusions in European Societies features the work of eminent contributors from across Europe who address the contradictions and paradoxes created by this link. Among the topics discussed are:

- how to theoretically frame the relations between exclusion and inclusion through the concepts of citizenship and belonging;
- how exclusions and inclusions have changed work and welfare and the relevance of classical concepts of inequality for European societies facing transformation through integration and globalization;
- how considerations of inclusions/exclusions stretch beyond the nation state, relating Europe to the world.

This book provides a unique reflection on central empirical and theoretical questions about the nature of social belonging in European societies today.

Alison Woodward is Professor in Social Sciences at Vesalius College, the Free University of Brussels.

Martin Kohli is Professor of Sociology at the Free University of Berlin.

Routledge/European Sociological Association Studies in
European Societies
Series editors: Alison Woodward, Thomas P. Boje, Martin Kohli
and Max Haller

Inclusions and Exclusions in European Societies

Edited by
Alison Woodward and Martin Kohli

London and New York

First published 2001 by Routledge
11 New Fetter Lane, London EC4P 4EE

Simultaneously published in the USA and Canada
by Routledge
29 West 35th Street, New York, NY 10001

Routledge is an imprint of the Taylor & Francis Group

Typeset in Goudy by Wearset, Boldon, Tyne and Wear
Printed and bound in Great Britain by Biddles Ltd, Guildford and
King's Lynn

British Library Cataloguing in Publication Data
A catalogue record for this book is available from the British Library

Library of Congress Cataloging in Publication Data
A record for this book has been requested

ISBN 0-415-26023-X ✓

Contents

Illustrations

Contributors

Rainer Bauböck trained in sociology and political science, is now Senior Researcher at the Austrian Academy of Sciences, Research Unit for Institutional Change and European Integration and lectures at the Universities of Vienna and Innsbruck. He was previously Assistant Professor at the Institute for Advanced Studies in Vienna. In 1998–9 he was a Member of the School of Social Science at the Institute for Advanced Study in Princeton and an Honorary Fellow at the Center for Human Values at Princeton University. In 2000–1 he was Willy Brandt Professor in International Migration and Ethnic Relations at the University of Malmö. Recently he has pursued his interests in normative political theory and issues of citizenship, migration, ethnicity and nationalism, resulting in publications such as *Transnational Citizenship, Membership and Rights in International Migration* (1994). He edited *From Aliens to Citizens: Redefining the Legal Status of Immigrants in Europe* (1994) and *The Challenge of Diversity: Integration and Pluralism in Societies of Immigration* (1996, with A. Heller and A. Zolberg) as well as *Blurred Boundaries. Migration, Ethnicity, Citizenship* (1998, with J. Rundell).

Volker Bornschier is Director of the Sociological Institute of the University of Zürich and Professor of Sociology there. He was president of the World Society Foundation sponsoring social science research world-wide from 1983–96. Among his twelve books and numerous articles, the following are especially relevant for his work on European processes and globalization: *Western Societies in Transition* (1996) and the two forthcoming volumes *The Future of Hegemonic Rivalry* (with C. Chase-Dunn) and *Statebuilding in Europe: The Revitalization of the Integration in the 1980s*, which builds on his team's research on European integration, as well as 'Zivilisierung der Weltgesellschaft trotz Hegemonie der Marktgesellschaft?' in *Frieden machen* (1997, D. Senghaas, ed.).

Martin Kohli is Professor of Sociology at the Freie Universität Berlin, where he directs the Research Group on Aging and the Life Course, and chairs the Graduate School on Comparative Social Research. He has been a Fellow at the Institute for Advanced Study (Princeton), at the Collegium Budapest and at the Hanse Institute for Advanced Study (Delmenhorst/Bremen), and a Visiting Professor at Harvard University. His most recent books are *Die zweite Lebenshälfte* (2000, ed. with H. Künemund), *Generationen in Familie und Gesellschaft* (2000, ed. with M. Szydlik), and *Will Europe Work?* (2001, ed. with M. Novak). His research interests centre on generations and the life course and on the institutions that shape them: families, labour markets and welfare states. He was President of the European Sociological Association from 1997–9.

Carlos Machado is a political scientist (University Complutense of Madrid), but also has a Master's degree in European Science, Society and Technology (ESST) from the University of East London and the Vrije Universiteit Brussel. In 1998 he joined the Vrije Universiteit Brussel as a collaborator in two European projects (SEDEC and INPART) within the TESA (Research Centre for Socio-Economic Changes and Labour Relations). Together with other research members of TESA he has been co-author of several articles in journals in the specific area of social inclusion policies.

Karl Ulrich Mayer is Director of the Centre of Sociology and the Study of the Life Course at the Max-Planck-Institut für Bildungsforschung in Berlin and Honorary Professor of Sociology at the Freie Universität Berlin. Educated in Germany and the United States, he received his Habilitation from the University of Mannheim and has held research and teaching positions at Konstanz, Frankfurt, Oxford, Mannheim, Zurich, and Harvard as well as the Institutes of Advanced Studies in Vienna and Stanford University. In 1996–7 he was Research Scholar at the Robert Schuman Centre of the European University Institute in Florence. His research focuses on social stratification and mobility, the sociology of the life course and the comparative analysis of social structures. His editorial and writing activities include co-editorship of the *Kölner Zeitschrift für Soziologie und Sozialpsychologie*, and works such as *Kollektiv und Eigensinn. Lebensverläufe in der DDR und danach* (1995, with J. Huinink *et al.*), *The Berlin Aging Study* (1999, ed. with P.B. Baltes), 'Notes on a Comparative Economy of Life Courses' in *Comparative Social Research* (1997) and 'Transitions to Post-Communism in East Germany: Worklife Mobility of Women and Men between 1989 and 1993' in *Acta Sociologica* (1999 with M. Diewald and H. Solga).

Alberto Melucci (PhD Sociology, PhD Clinical Psychology) is Professor of Cultural Sociology at the University of Milan and Professor of Clinical Psychology at the Post-Graduate School of Clinical Psychology. He has taught extensively in Europe and the US, has been an invited lecturer in Latin America and East Asia and has contributed to international journals and readers. He is the author of fifteen books on social movements, cultural change, personal and collective identity, including *Nomads of the Present* (1989), *The Playing Self* (1996) and *Challenging Codes* (1996).

Zdravko Mlinar studied law and sociology at the University of Ljubljana where he is now Professor Emeritus of Sociology and a member of the Slovenian Academy of Science and Arts. He has pursued specialization courses in the United Kingdom and the United States and as professor, researcher and consultant, has been active at universities in Europe, the United States and India. Active in professional associations, he has been president of a Research Committee in the ISA and was co-founder of the Thematic Group on the Sociology of Local–Global Relations. His publication list includes several award-winning books. Among his more recent works as author or editor are *Individuation and Globalization in Space* (1994), *Globalization and Territorial Identities* (1992), *Autonomy and Connectedness in the European Space* (1995) and *Local Responses to Global Change* (1995).

Birgitta Nedelmann is Professor (Emerita) of Sociology at the Johannes Gutenberg University in Mainz, Germany and was member of the Council of Academia Europaea. She studied in Munich and Berlin and received her habilitation from the University of Mannheim. Her teaching career spans universities in Lund, Cologne, Freiburg, European University Institute in Florence, and La Sapienza in Rome, and she has been a Fellow at the Wissenschaftskolleg Berlin. With her interests in political sociology and the general theory of sociology she has published a wide variety of books including *Sociology in Europe: In Search of Identity* (1993, ed. with P. Sztompka) and *Political Institutions in Change* (1995) and articles such as 'Between National Socialism and Real Socialism: Political Sociology in the Federal Republic of Germany' in *Current Sociology* (1997) and 'The Continuing Relevance of Georg Simmel: Staking Out Anew the Field of Sociology' in *Handbook of Sociology* (2001, G. Ritzer and B. Smart, eds.).

Mojca Novak was educated at the University of Ljubljana in Slovenia, and is Professor at the Faculty of Social Sciences, and also teaches in the School of Social Work at the same university. Since 1997, she has headed the Social Protection Institute of the Republic of Slovenia. She recently spent time as a Fellow at the Netherlands Institute for Advanced Study in the Humanities and Social Sciences. Her research interests focus on planning processes, social structure and quality of life, and poverty and social security, as well as the development of the welfare state in comparative perspective. Recent publications include the books *Late Coming Pattern Mix: Slovenia at the European Periphery* (1991) and *Good Morning, Poverty: Evidence, Approaches and Policies* (1994) both in Slovenian, plus chapters in journals and books such as *Poverty: A Global Review* (1996, edited by E. Oyen, S.M. Miller and S.A. Samad).

John Scott has been Professor of Sociology at the University of Essex since 1994. Previously he was Professor at the University of Leicester. He is particularly interested in social stratification, business organisation and sociological theory but has published also on quantitative and historical methods. His books include *Corporations, Classes and Capitalism* (1985), *A Matter of Record: Documentary Sources in Social Research* (1990), *Who Rules Britain?* (1991), *Social Network Analysis* (1991, rev. ed. 2000), *Poverty and Wealth* (1994), *Sociological Theory* (1995), *Stratification and Power* (1996), *Corporate Business and Capitalist Classes* (1997), and *Social Structure* (2000, with José López). He is co-editor of *Sociology Review* and is on the editorial board of the *British Journal of Sociology* and the *European Journal of Social Theory*.

Jacques Vilrokx is Professor of Sociology and, since 1998, Dean of the Faculty of Economics, Social and Political Sciences and Solvay Management School at the Vrije Universiteit Brussel. Director of the Study Group in Technological, Economic and Social Change and Labour Market Research (TESA), he conducts research on labour market structure, organizational flexibility, individual and collective labour relations and citizens' income. Some of his research is covered under European framework projects (e.g. TSER). An author of numerous articles and publications, he co-edited in 1996 *The Challenges to Trade Unions in Europe: Innovation and Adaptation*. Among his latest work is 'Towards the denaturing of class relations? The political economy of the firm in global capitalism' in *Globalization and Labour Relations* (1999, P. Leisink, ed.).

Alison Woodward is Professor and Chair of the International Affairs Faculty at Vesalius College of the Free University of Brussels (VUB), and co-director of the Centre for Women's Studies. Her central research concerns the relations between public policy and societal ambitions in European societies. Her publications focus particularly on energy, housing and gender policies and include the books *Going for Gender Balance* (2001) and *Municipal Entrepreneurship: A Five Nation Study of Energy Politics, Innovation and Social Change* (1994, with J. Ellig and T. Burns). As a member of the Executive of the European Sociological Association, she served as Vice President for Programme from 1995–7 and is a co-editor of the book series *European Societies*.

Nira Yuval-Davis is Professor in Gender and Ethnic Studies and Post-Graduate Director at Greenwich University in London. She has written extensively on issues of nationalism, racism, fundamentalism and gender relations. Among her recent books are *Racialised Boundaries* (1992, with F. Antias), *Refusing Holy Orders: Women and Fundamentalism in Britain* (1992, with G. Fahgal), *Cross Fires: Nationalism, Racism and Gender Relations in Europe* (1995, with H. Lutz and A. Phoenix), *Unsettling Settler Societies* (1995, with B. Stasiulis) and *Gender and Nation* (1997).

Preface and acknowledgments

The changing patterns of social inclusions and exclusions were a main characteristic of the last century. For its 3rd International Conference held at the University of Essex in August 1997, the European Sociological Association (ESA) chose to highlight this with a title theme of *20th Century Europe: Inclusions/Exclusions*. The conference explored how issues of gender, ethnicity, class and age coloured the restructuring of European societies throughout this century and the role of sociology in the understanding of inclusionary and exclusionary changes. The plenary speakers – whether dealing with the issue of the continuing relevance of classical theory, the relation of work to welfare, globalization, European processes of integration, or inequalities both new and old – found a number of common meeting places and shared many reference points on the changing nature of citizenship and inclusion in Europe.

The chapters in this book are a partial mirror of the process of thinking set in motion at the conference. Here you will find the thoughts of some of the main speakers complemented by one commissioned offering. All the authors have substantially revised their contributions in light of the insights resulting from the conference. They have helped us enormously in our aim of providing not just a record of the conference, but a more cohesive reflection on the issues. This ended up being a lengthy process. The patience of the authors who have followed this project through to its end is worthy of special praise and we thank them for all their effort.

Envisioning the theme and bringing together these international collaborators was a collective effort and our thanks go to the inspirational work of our team in the ESA Program Committee for the Essex Conference which included Thomas Boje, Daniel Bertaux, Janusz Mucha, Katrin Paadam, Bart van Steenbergen, and Sylvia Walby as well as to the other members of the first Executive Board. We especially acknowledge the support of SISWO (The Netherlands Institute for the Social Sciences) which not only ensured the launch and survival of the fledgling association, but also hosted some of the Executive Board meetings that allowed an editorship to go on in the welcoming Amsterdam atmosphere. Bernard Kruithof's never ceasing effort to help us locate people and have smooth gatherings was crucial. The University of Essex's local organizing committee's energy and dedication to making a complicated international conference a real success has also been important for the quality of this book and we thank all the members of the committee under the dynamic direction of Joan Busfield and including Nigel Short, Stina Lyon, Lydia Morris, Carlo Ruzza, John Scott, Maggie French and many others.

Mari Shullaw of Routledge was key to the first steps of the ESA's book series and has played a central role in supporting the publication of thematic conference books. We appreciate her undertakings on behalf of the publication activities of the Association very much.

Martin Kohli is indebted to the Hanse Institute for Advanced Study (Delmenhorst/Bremen) for providing the intellectual ambiente and leisure in which editing could be completed. Alison Woodward has a life-time debt to Johan van der Auwera for his professional example and personal support and to the Latin Americanos for their sunshine.

1 European societies

Inclusions/exclusions?

Alison Woodward and Martin Kohli

Inclusions and exclusions are not necessarily opposites. In sociological terms the two are intricately linked, leading to contradictions and paradoxes. Twentieth-century European social development has been characterized by an increasing inclusion of its people into the expanding collectivities of nationally based welfare entitlement pools and political bodies, and ultimately European-wide citizenships. At the same time, some countries have demonstrated growing income gaps and cultural cleavages, and increasing numbers of people have been threatened by poverty, excluding them from economic and social well-being. At the level of differences among countries, similar contradictions can be noted. Socio-economic conditions have greatly improved for some of the newer members of the European Union such as Ireland, Greece, Portugal and Spain, while the drama of transformation in Eastern Europe has resulted in massive losses. Inclusion in the European process does not necessarily lead to an expansion of internal social inclusions; in countries such as Sweden and Finland it has been paralleled by a retrenchment of welfare rights. Where inclusion in the European process has raised the material well-being of a country, it may paradoxically exacerbate perceived differences. The frame of reference is no longer restricted to one's own country but is widened to include the other European countries as well.

Many of the processes of inclusion have thus been accompanied by exclusion and creation of new borders of resources, rights and identities. Within the expanding physical space of 'Europe' there is greater awareness of economic, cultural and ethnic heterogeneity than ever before and a higher mobility of people from an increasingly global pool. One consequence of greater contact and awareness may be backlashing border building, as reflected in the rise of Far Right parties in countries such as Austria or Belgium and in the tensions around the enlargement of Europe and its openness to including non-European Union citizens.

In this introductory chapter we consider some of the problems raised by the terms 'exclusion' and 'inclusion', relating them to more general issues in sociological theory and to the main lines of development in European societies in the last century. We then ask how the terms can stimulate thinking on current social change and how the contributions to this book respond to its challenge.

Inclusion/exclusion: the concepts

The concepts of inclusion and exclusion seem particularly appropriate to catch the contradictory and ambivalent nature of this change. Yet on closer inspection they turn out to be highly ambivalent themselves, and in need of clarification. We review here three of the concerns and discourses that have shaped the conceptualization of exclusion/inclusion: the discourse of social problems and inequalities, of social integration and order, and finally of institutional mechanisms of social membership (such as citizenship).

Exclusion

'Social exclusion' is a term that takes its inspiration from the discourse on social problems. It promises to address most or all of the social ills that our modern sensibilities deplore (cf. Goodin 1996): unemployment, discrimination, isolation, material deprivation and poverty – social suffering and 'misery' in all its forms (Bourdieu 1993). In France the term came to be used in this sense in the 1970s and then increasingly in the 1980s and 1990s (for an overview cf. Paugam 1996). From France, it crept into other national discourses, and most significantly, into the official discourse of the European Union where, since the mid-1990s, 'social exclusion' has virtually superseded 'poverty' as the key programmatic term on the socio-political agenda (Commission 1993, Byrne 1999, cf. Leisering and Leibfried 1999: 8, Percy-Smith 2000).

The intellectual attractiveness of the concept of social exclusion is due to its new perspective on social ills such as unemployment or poverty: it views them not as clearly delimited social problems but as part of the most basic social relation – that of belonging or not belonging to one's society. It posits that marginalization in the labor market increasingly coincides with social isolation (Kronauer 1999: 60f). This implies a shift in the lines of social inequality: the traditional vertical model of class cleavages centered around labor market position is giving way to a polarization between 'in' and 'out'. The concept thus emphasizes the dynamic interaction of structural factors with variables of social disadvantage (Percy-Smith 2000: 5).

For Europe, the concept has 'the strategic advantage of drawing from the social policy traditions of both social democracy and social catholicism. It resonates equally with social democratic concern[s] about inequality and equal opportunity and social catholic concern[s] for social ties in the family and community' (Chamberlayne and Rustin 1999: 33). Given its diverse origins, the concept is still coded very differently in the various national traditions of sociology in Europe. By stressing the dichotomy between in and out, it also articulates with the concept of the 'underclass' as developed in the US (Wilson 1996) and with the concerns of communitarianism.[1]

As with other broadly suggestive and fashionable terms, however, 'social exclusion' pays the price of conceptual vagueness. If exclusion is defined by criteria such as unemployment, poverty or social isolation, it remains to be clarified how these criteria are descriptively and causally related to each other and to further possible criteria such as gender, ethnicity or citizenship rights (Kohli 1999a, Littlewood and Herkommer 1999). To simply speak of exclusion as a 'multi-dimensional' and 'cumulative' process begs the question of which criteria are linked in what ways. At heart are issues of cause, effect and measurement. As an example, social isolation – in the sense of the dissolution of social networks or of their reduction to other marginalized people – is sometimes seen as an independent dimension of exclusion, sometimes as the consequence of marginalization in other dimensions such as from the labor market which would then be its primary cause. Similarly, poverty can be seen as one of a multitude of dimensions of exclusion, or as a consequence of being excluded from the labor market, or as the one criterion by which exclusion manifests itself most clearly and which should therefore be the primary target of remedial intervention. The last view is that of the European Commission, whose *Observatory on National Policies to Combat Social Exclusion* is, in reality, an Observatory on Poverty (Huster 1997; see the chapter by Machedo and Vilrokx in this book).

These diverse views are not simply reflections of interest to theoreticians but refer to – and sometimes divert from – a basic controversy on the present-day dynamics of social inequality. The question is to what extent social disadvantage is (still) mostly the result of labor market position and experience – in other words, whether inequality is (still) to be conceptualized in the traditional terms of class or whether this has indeed been replaced by new forms of inequality according to the major categories of social ascription such as gender, age, ethnicity/'race' or political membership (see the chapter by John Scott in this volume; also Korpi 2001). It may be argued (e.g., Castel 1995) that speaking of the social exclusion of marginalized groups diverts our attention from what is occurring in the center of our societies and which is its primary agent, namely, the destruction of the wage-earning contract and of the welfare regime based on it. A related controversy centers around the proposed novelty of present-day inequalities and deprivations in the labor market itself. Here again, some doubts may be in order. In what ways, for example, is the 'new' unemployment different from the old one, except that there is more of it – and even so, is this not the case everywhere? And finally, the robustness of exclusion in terms of sustained duration is also open to debate. The new 'dynamic' understanding of poverty or unemployment has shown that a cross-sectional one-moment-in-time perspective is highly misleading. Social and economic deprivation has to be seen as temporalized. It is a status that will apply to many more persons during their life course than can be ascertained at any one point in time, but which for most will not be a chronic condition (Kohli 1999a, Leisering and Leibfried 1999; see the chapter by Karl Ulrich Mayer). We may thus conclude that the concept of social exclusion promises to offer insight into some important current societal dynamics. But to be a meaningful term, it must be accompanied by a clear delineation of its dimensions and it must address the underlying theoretical issues.

Inclusion

The same effort is required for the concept of inclusion. It is often treated simply as the flip side of the coin of exclusion. But it is important to go beyond the emphasis on social problems that has shaped the discourse on exclusion. Inclusion should be viewed as a concept of its own that refers to a broader theoretical context: that of social integration and order, and that of the institutions of social membership. Inclusion has become a key term in the functionalist and system theoretical approaches to social integration, where it stands for a basic component of modernization. For example, Luhmann (1995) sees the transformation from traditional segmentary or stratified societies to modern functionally differentiated ones in terms of a transformation from a logic of partial inclusion to one of all-inclusiveness (cf. Kronauer 1999: 62). We will not pursue this issue except to note that the concept of inclusion as developed in systems theory does not fit easily with the perspective on exclusion/inclusion in terms of social problems, and is not able to make much theoretical sense of the current empirical phenomena of exclusion. More relevant for our purposes is another argument linked to Simmel's view of the new place of the individual in social order (see the chapter by Birgitta Nedelmann). Individualization raises the question of how individuals are integrated into the social whole while maintaining some measure of autonomy, which, in turn, is a necessary precondition for social integration in a functionally differentiated society. The relation between individual and society is therefore one of simultaneous inclusion and exclusion – a basic motive of Simmel's thought to which we will return below. A second context relevant to the concept of inclusion is that of the institutions of social membership. Here we may usefully distinguish between three basic dimensions of membership or inclusion – political, economic and civic inclusion – corresponding to the three societal subsystems or 'sectors' that today make up the portfolio of resources for well-being and social participation: state, market and civil society.[2] The contradictions, linkages and cumulations between these sectors and the individual 'membership mixes' that derive from them are critical for the overall patterns of inclusion.

Dimensions of inclusion

Political

The most obvious inclusionary movement in European societies has been that of political inclusions at both the territorial and individual level. The European territory was constructed, destroyed and reconstructed in the course of the last two centuries in a process which first involved the inclusion of many different political entities within the boundaries of the nation state. Today it has become a place of tense stability where varieties of culturally forged groups are politically cemented into place within state political borders – borders that, in many instances, are still highly contested (O'Dowd 2001). Since the middle of the last century, a new process of inclusion into a larger entity commenced with the construction of the European Communities and later European Union. Another part of this process was the drama of inclusion/exclusion originating in Eastern Europe since the late 1980s. The transformation from communist rule led to large groups being cast out of political spaces, wide-spread migratory movements and struggles for collective rights and identities (Brubaker 1996).

At the individual level, citizenship rights have become more and more inclusive, expanding from rights of freedom through those of political participation to social rights. Since Marshall's (1950) path-breaking work, this has become a well-known and widely-shared story, even though some of its finer points remain open to debate (cf. Goodin 1996). The concept and practice of citizenship in Europe expanded from a political citizenship for male property owners only, to political rights for males from all social classes and extended later to women. By 1950 all adult citizens, both men and women, could vote in almost every European country (save Switzerland). With the construction of the welfare state another expansion took place, from a political into a social citizenship. By the end of the century, the fact that citizenship is also a category that excludes had once again become paramount. Growing populations of non-citizens either born within a polity or with long records of residence (see the chapter by Rainer Baubock) challenge the basis of access to political and social rights. Migration has become the model case for conflicting views of citizenship, both in terms of the politics of membership and in terms of the practical salience of different kinds of rights. As to the latter issue, Soysal (1994) argues that national citizenship is losing some of its weight because of the development of supra-national rights and because social rights are mostly not restricted to those with full political membership, even if others remain skeptical about the extent of this shift (e.g., Koopmans and Statham 1998). Further fundamental questions of how included in the polity the 'included' actually are have arisen as many countries suffered crises of political legitimacy (Dogan 2000). Sometimes these crises were based on the lack of inclusiveness in representation in terms of gender (Phillips 1991, Saraceno 2001) or other interests, but the European process has also raised the ways that region or locality is represented (Scharpf 1999; for a general discussion, see Kymlicka 1995).

Inclusion as political actors has led to claims for inclusion as recipients of social rights and thus the processes of inclusion through social rights merit some special consideration. The development of the European welfare state is one of the fundamental social inventions of the last century. The large systems of social security in the domains of old age, health, family and unemployment have 'normalized' individual biographies by protecting individuals from the material deprivation following from labor market risks, illness, or family formation. Inclusion in a safety net from 'cradle to grave' became a reality in the advanced European societies by the 1960s. Social security has redistributed resources between the periods of the life course spent in and out of employment, and also between persons and groups, thereby reshaping the structure as well as the politics of social inequality. Democraticization of education is another institutional process that has helped reshape the configurations and fluidity of the class structure by introducing new possibilities of social mobility (Erikson and Goldthorpe 1992). Yet it can be argued that the very process of educational democratization leads groups who cannot take advantage of education or achieve advanced literacy to a firmer exclusion from the mainstream social community. Educational skills 'provided' by the state are seen as a requirement for belonging. Employment success increasingly depends on education, so that those who fail in education also have a harder time on the labor market.

Economic

The developments of social inclusion in the welfare state cannot be analyzed separately from the developments involving economic inclusion (Leibfried and Pierson 1995, Esping-Andersen 1996, Lister 1997). If the argument that inclusions are linked with exclusions is relevant anywhere, then it is in the changing nature of economic participation and its meaning for rights and identity. In many polities, social rights are directly related to economic participation with the concept of the 'citizen of the work society'. In the other ones where public welfare is universalized, one's welfare position is heavily dependent on participation in occupational security schemes, so that, for example, in the UK one speaks of the 'Two Nations' of welfare – the first with additional resources based on labor market position, the second restricted to the relatively meager public provisions only. During the boom decades of the 1950s and 1960s – variously called the 'Golden Age' or (in France) the 'Trente glorieuses' – Western European societies perfected their model of the work society based on full (male) employment and a redistributive welfare state. But economic participation has not followed a linear course. It has been inflated or deflated across the years. The example of the inclusion of women as full economic citizens is illustrative. Women did not make even progress into the economy, but were alternately included and excluded: their roles as war workers included them, while after war marriage bars excluded them. It is only during the last three decades that the inclusion of women into the labor market has proceeded more regularly, now including the quickly modernizing countries of Europe's southern and western periphery. Another example is the inclusion and exclusion of non-national labor power which also changed direction over the years, beginning with the labor migration of Southern Europeans and moving through the various post-colonial situations to the dissolution of communist Eastern Europe and global labor migration. A more uni-directional story can be told about age. Paradoxically, the growing normalization of formal employment for men (and now also for women) in their middle years has been accompanied by a growing exclusion or liberation of the early and later life phases (cf. Kohli 2000). Europe has eliminated child labor and has greatly extended the period before entering the labor market. At the other end, the institutionalization of retirement has freed the old from work; and, in spite of growing life expectancy, the mean age of exit from the labor force over the last decades has decreased substantially, creating additional burdens for the public pension systems.

Has this predominantly increasing inclusion in political, social and eco-nomic citizenship led to a lessening of social inequalities and exclusions in Europe? The answers are far from clear. While many know welfare that would have been unimaginable a century ago and is undreamed of in most parts of the globe today, some of the distances within and between advanced countries seem to be growing. Comparative data from the Luxembourg Income Study show a growth in European poverty in the 1980s and 1990s (Haataja 1998: 17). The distance between the top groups, in societies of the 'liberal' welfare regime type such as the United Kingdom, and the rest in terms of their income and wealth shares is growing (Jäntti and Danziger 1998). Across all welfare regimes, the rights to be included from cradle to grave are no longer self-evident. The long-term unemployed are struck from the social security rolls and referred to basic means-tested provisions (Yérez del Castillo 1994, Vranken *et al.* 1996). The transformation in Eastern Europe has created massive new inequalities within and between countries which have proven to be much more durable than originally expected or hoped. This dynamic drama of inclusion and exclusion takes place in a global context and may indeed be partly driven by transnational factors.

The risks of exclusion are compounded by the fact that, today, the European social model of the 'work society' has come under increasing pressure. However, while it clearly needs to be re-examined and redesigned, some of its basic prin-ciples remain critical for the future of Europe as a relatively unified polity and society (Kohli and Novak 2001). Whether the welfare state contributes to or restricts economic growth is open to debate, but the fact that it is needed as a buffer to protect those at risk of being marginalized and excluded has not changed. Without such a buffer, the legitimacy of opening the economy to international competition could wane, and be replaced by growing popular support for protectionism and isolationism. Public welfare is needed as a resource for social pacification and integration just as strongly as before. But the conditions for it have become more difficult on both sides. From the demand side there is an increasing number of those at risk through unemployment or under-employment, and an increasing burden on the welfare state posed by its use as a means of assuring the integration of disadvantaged regions.[3] From the supply side there is a decreasing tax and contribution base available for redistri-bution. In addition, there are other challenges posed by major societal changes now under way. One is the demographic challenge of ageing populations common (in somewhat varying degrees) to all European societies, which is by now well known but whose possible solutions are highly contended. A second challenge is that of changing work participation and organization, especially through the inclusion of women into the labor force, and through the changing work career patterns towards what some observers see as the demise of the 'normal work biography' (even though its extent is under dispute).

Even more than the old welfare regime, the new model is predicated upon ability for and access to work. The welfare state can no longer operate as 'poli-tics against markets' (Esping-Andersen 1985); it has to be reconceptualized – in the words of Streeck (2001) – as politics within and with the markets. The link between political and economic inclusion is thus reaffirmed in a new way.

Civic

A third aspect of inclusion that needs to be distinguished is civic inclusion in and by civil society. If one shares the diagnosis of an inexorably decreasing inclusionary potential of the employment system and of welfare rights based on it, inclusion through 'active citizenship participation' in the associational life of civil society becomes all the more important (see the chapter by Machado and Vilrokx). It is clear, however, that left to itself the 'third sector' would not be a viable alternative to the first two. In order to provide the economic resources needed for any social participation worth this name, it would need to be grounded in a redefinition of welfare rights towards universal claims of citizenship beyond the sphere of paid employment, i.e., in making the inclusionary mechanisms of the state respond more to the civil society than to the market. As noted above, the same applies to the 'fourth sector' of the family and other primary ties. This traditional domain of membership is still highly salient today. But in order to remain viable, it increasingly depends on the support by public provisions.

Oppositions and linkages

Exclusion and inclusion are often seen as opposites: the more there is of the former, the less of the latter. This is, of course, too simple. Exclusion of individuals in some dimensions may go together and even be causally linked with inclusion in others; inclusion of some groups may reinforce exclusion of others. But while taking this into account, the customary view of social exclusion in terms of social problems does tend to construct such an opposition. Exclusion is seen as a cumulative process of deprivation, up to the point where society is polarized into a majority of insiders and an increasingly walled-off minority of outcasts – *les exclus* or the *underclass*.

A similar dichotomy may play itself out at society's external borders. Since inclusion into a given society or social unit logically presupposes a membership boundary, it necessarily implies exclusion of those outside that boundary. People thus again find themselves either in or out.

If one accepts this view, a case can be made for making societies less exclusive by making them less inclusive (Goodin 1996); in other words, for restricting the legitimate demands for membership that societies can impose on their citizens and the claims that the latter can raise towards their societies. This corresponds to the liberal project of multiple memberships and weak states. In liberal thought, as Volker Bornschier reminds us in his chapter, inclusion by the state is seen as intrusion, and individuals have always strived to remain excluded from that intrusion.

But, as many of our arguments and examples have shown – and this will be taken up throughout the book – inclusion and exclusion are not necessarily opposed to each other. This is valid on the functional level of social integration. In Durkheimian functionalist thought, exclusion serves to reinforce inclusion: by excluding the deviant groups, society stabilizes itself. It is valid on the level of individuals as well. As noted above, in a basic sense modern individuals are both in and out of their society. In some instances, this condition is heightened. The model case for how inclusion and exclusion are intertwined is the 'stranger'. In Simmel's analysis (see the chapter by Birgitta Nedelmann; also Kronauer 1999: 64f), the stranger is both included (as a guest) and excluded (as one not belonging to the group). Social exclusion is a meaningful concept only insofar as those who are excluded are also in some way related to the group – the possible inhabitants of an unknown planet are not 'strangers' because they are in no relation to us. Simmel parallels the role of the stranger to that of the poor (1908: 352f; cf. Kronauer 1999: 65). The poor are excluded from the group but remain linked to it in a reciprocal relation: by being the object of exclusion and thus of the reproduction of social inequality. Being inside and outside is not logically opposed but part of the same process of sociation.

The sociological perspective

The model of the stranger has often been applied to sociology itself (e.g., Schütz 1964) by pointing out that the acuity of the sociological observer is heightened if he or she is not fully included into the community under study but remains on the threshold – in that specific situation of the stranger, simultaneously included and excluded.

The position of the stranger is especially productive when trying to identify the broad structural transformations that have created our societies and keep them in motion. Sociology's strong suit has been the study of social change, more so than its neighboring disciplines (Schelkle *et al.* 2000). If one can say that it has been born as a child of the great transformation from the *ancien régime* to modern capitalist industrialism and (more or less) democratic nation states, it is equally true that it owes its critical perspective to having been an illegitimate rather than a legitimate child. Since then, sociology has maintained its original concern with the long-term dynamics of societal construction, and European sociologists have been at the forefront in developing concepts, explanations and policy applications to contend with the causes and effects of these dynamics (Aron 1983, Boudon 1993, Münch 1993, Giddens 1996, Therborn 2000). They have also been highly concerned with describing and explaining the dynamics of social inequality. On the other hand, sociology has been slow to address the European process as such, with its institutional patterns beyond the nation state, and has only recently come to focus its attention on the specificities of European societies and European society in the contemporary world (Kaelble 1987, Therborn 1995, Crouch 1999; cf. Kohli and Novak 2001). The questions around inclusion/exclusion are well suited to take the analytical strengths of sociology to the European level.

We have emphasized that inclusion and exclusion are not opposite or mutually exclusive processes but in various ways intertwined. This needs to be taken into account when focusing on the current challenges to a society aiming at more integration and inclusion. They comprise, among other elements, the rising ethnic heterogeneity of populations, the changing position of women, a growing population of non-employed, including the elderly, and a shortage of young people. The continuing dynamics of European integration also press the internal and external borders of inclusion. Finally, the technological change towards an information economy and the globalization of organizations and markets also test the ability of European societies to remain inclusive on a local basis.

European policy makers and the public are increasingly concerned with the problems of exclusion, as witnessed by the number of projects in the last few years dealing with its social contours and costs.[4] Eliminating social exclusion is a broad policy objective for programs such as the European Structural Funds. But in order to eliminate exclusion, it is not enough to put it on the political agenda. There is a need for improved conceptualization in the debate (such as better articulation of exclusion with the classic and new dividers of class, gender, age, ethnicity and citizenship) and for more sustained empirical analysis and comparison. As Zdravko Mlinar notes in this collection, sociology is the most general and generalizing social science. By its design, it aims to encompass all spheres of social life in all periods of time. Thus it offers the most suitable starting-point for study of the transformation of Europe in an emerging world society.

How does sociology address the problems of inclusions and exclusions as they affect European societies today? Leading sociologists from all areas of Europe were asked to confront this issue.[5] They took three major tacks. A first group focuses on the need to reconceptualize the bases for inclusion in collective identities and the institutions of citizenship. A second group challenges sociologists to rethink their interpretation of the European social model of work and welfare in the light of new empirical developments. Finally a third group confronts the necessity to see European societies in the context of European integration and globalization.

The contributions

Framing inclusions and identities in Europe

The book is accordingly divided into three sections. The first section develops theoretical perspectives on citizenship and belonging. The four chapters provide a framework for looking at aspects of inclusion by rethinking the notions of citizenship and of collective and individual identities. To what extent does sociological theory in its classical forms passed down from the nineteenth century have the potential for elucidating the paradoxes of inclusion? Here Georg Simmel provides a useful point of departure. How will the supposedly 'inclusionary' institution of citizenship take account of social and demographic changes in Europe? Reviewing the ideas about citizenship that have developed in Europe are essential for facing up to these challenges. And how will the construction of identities evolve in an increasingly supra-national and even global context? This asks for an examination of boundary-making activities around identities.

Birgitta Nedelmann opens the section with a novel reflection on how sociology at the turn of the twentieth century engaged with questions of inclusion through a discussion of some of the work of Georg Simmel. The chapter itself is a demonstration of Simmelian style, as it takes a small point of departure to reach conclusions of broad sociological relevance. The essay treated is 'The Picture Frame' which opens up a specific way of thinking about what is 'in' and what is 'out'. The frame in some significant sense is an 'inclusive' mechanism, but it also works as a mediator between the picture and the world of social life. Nedelmann goes beyond Simmel to consider the issue of the individual 'framed' and mediated by culture. She considers the risk that the potential of human beings may be paralyzed due to failed mediation between individuals and culture.

Rainer Bauböck also tackles the relevance of older conceptualizations for present day inclusions, this time in the framework of citizenship. This concept lies at the heart of many of the debates around inclusion confronting European societies today. Bauböck discusses the positions outlined in political theory and contrasts them with current social developments. He organizes the conceptions of citizenship on a continuum from the 'thin' position of legal positivism to the 'thick' position of nationalism, where membership based on cultural identity is taken for granted. Given the challenges of migration and supra-national unification, ideals of homogeneity ought to be abandoned in favor of acknowledging multiplicity of membership.

Nira Yuval-Davis examines the role of cultural identities in citizenship inclusion from another angle. She puts the issues of culture and ethnicity at the center and focuses on the construction of identities being carried out by groups who create racial, gendered and ethnic borders. At the core is the paradoxical relationship between people's needs to culturally mark off their uniqueness and the need to transgress borders between human beings for social action. Davis addresses the range of social change in Europe and suggests that transversal dialog may be a way to go beyond the homogeneous assimilated universalism envisioned in earlier thinking about 'national' citizenship and yet escape the particularistic relativism of identity politics.

Finally, *Alberto Melucci* takes up the tension between the structural mechanisms of society and processes of individuation. He argues that the various forms of identity politics are a response to a search for meaning in European societies unable to provide forms of membership that meet the needs of individuals for self-realization and recognition. People are members, citizens, persons and through these different ways of belonging act on the borders of different systems. In these societies, inclusion and exclusion are redefined according to new forms of inequality which relate to the production and distribution of resources for individualization. Becoming a person is a matter of capacities, rights and responsibilities which are unequally shared. Melucci goes beyond the nation state and Europe to put identity construction in a planetary perspective, an issue which is raised again in the concluding chapters by Mlinar and Bornschier.

Exclusions and inclusions in work and welfare

The second section of the book turns from the conceptualization of inclusion and exclusion to an examination of its mechanisms and results in the domain of work and welfare. Here the focus is on the twentieth-century development of a 'work society', with a social citizenship contract based on participation in the labor market, and its eventual partial refutation. The chapters in this section focus on the inclusionary and exclusionary implications of formal work and of the welfare state constructed around it, offering measured assessments of similarities and differences among European societies, and of their continuities and transformations.

Karl Ulrich Mayer looks at the ways the advanced societies of Europe and North America have constructed their institutions in the domains of the family, education, the labor market and the welfare state that together make up what may be termed their life course regimes. He traces the institutionalization of the life course through the successive stages of modernization and asks whether European societies are converging towards a common pattern or whether diversity will continue to flourish. On the one hand, there is a widely-shared belief that global social change creates a set of similar pressures and challenges that will allow or force similar responses. On the other hand, there is an equally strong belief that historical differences among societies in their institutional configurations still matter to the degree that, in future, their developments will be highly path-dependent. Mayer uses a new comparative data set to examine these conflicting views and concludes that one can expect divergent rather than convergent life course regimes.

Mojca Novak expands the discussion to the welfare states of Eastern Europe. She also takes a historical approach to examine the roots of variation in the kinds of welfare provisions and inclusions that later had implications for the programs under state socialism. Novak demonstrates that it is incorrect to see Eastern Europe under state socialism as one homogeneous welfare regime, and anticipates that diversities in inclusions will continue. Traditions and class-coalitions count the most in explaining the various patterns of inclusion. Even though the welfare state is now under threat in Eastern Europe, Novak argues that it shows remarkable tenacity and has the potential to help integrate these states into a larger European community.

Have the recent transformations of European societies led to a shift from a class-based stratification system to one based on other grounds, and thus to a transformation of the mechanisms of social exclusion? *John Scott* reasserts the inspiration of classical sociological thinking for this controversy, and refuses to agree with those who argue that class is dead. While claims about the importance of class have in the past often been inflated, denying any independent explanatory power to other sources of social division and exclusion, the present rejection of class is misguided. Tackling literature from the 1950s frequently overlooked by the proponents of the death of class, Scott confronts the heart of the British debate on class – a debate that still may have a model function for other European societies as well. He reinterprets Weber's classical distinctions to propose a theoretical frame that includes not only the economic, but also the communal and authoritarian spheres of social life and power. Using this frame of analysis, he maintains, will show that most European societies remain class societies today, and that this remains critical for social exclusion.

But where can we go in the future, if the system of wage labor is an increasingly less successful institution for including all into European societies? In the final contribution to this section, *Carlos Macheda and Jacques Vilrokx* argue that inclusions and exclusions can be radically transformed if citizenship is constructed on other bases than formal work, such as through active citizenship participation. In the past, work has been central in defining social citizenship and social rights. Those not connected to the labor process are in many ways also not included as full citizens, and thus much social policy has been directed at putting people to work. Now, Macheda and Vilrokx contend, we need new ways of conceptualizing exclusion in order to develop a more comprehensive vision of an inclusive society. Drawing on data from comparative research into the social economy, they argue that third sector organization may be a way to expand citizenship rights beyond waged employment and enable a wider social participation.

Inclusions and exclusions beyond the nation state: Europe and the world

The final section of the book moves beyond national societies as isolated cases and pleads for sociology's place in thinking about inclusion and exclusion on the levels of Europe and the world. During the last decades, European unification has been a challenge to all European societies, whether members or not. Equally, developments in technology and the political economy have placed all European societies on the globe in a far different way than in the days of colonial imperialism. The chapters in this section address the specificity of the inclusive processes of European integration, and ask to what extent sociology can provide perspectives on Europe as a world region.

Zdravko Mlinar approaches the paradox of the simultaneous growth of individualization and globalization from the point of view of spatial geographies. He moves the focus from the European level to the place of Europe on the global map. He reintroduces the discussion of the relevance of classical sociology by providing an analytic tool for delineating village communities from global societies which echoes both Durkheim's and Tönnies' work, and returns to some of Melucci's concerns. With a 'global society' the chances to free oneself by exiting a closed system or to escape responsibility will dissolve, just as the drive towards individuation is at its peak. But with dialectical understanding we can better conceive of how ever smaller units may have a voice within an ever larger territorial context.

Volker Bornschier reminds us that the European Process has been neither smooth nor gradual, and that it has been strongly influenced by earlier European structures and ideologies. Bornschier notes that much in the process of integration has been a matter of compromise and sometimes paradox. He puts the integration of European societies in a longer historical panorama of inclusive projects throughout European history. European societies are forced, on the one hand, to respond to questions of regional and ethnic identifications, and on the other hand to surrender their sovereignty to the institutions of the New Europe. A special focus is the conflict between the nation state and nationalism (with their roots in the Absolutist state) on the one hand, and the forces of individualism (as expressed in classical liberalism) and of the market in driving European integration on the other. Individual citizens have struggled to remain free from intrusion by the state even as the latter increasingly includes more and more of the private within its sphere.

Our project of looking at the connections between the inclusions and exclusions that have shaped European societies is perhaps a typically *fin de siècle* effort. Perceiving the two processes as logically and empirically related, and connected through that stereotypically postmodern '/' slash may be an approach frozen in a particular time frame. Yet it has been conceived to show that, for sociology, the salience of our thinking about social change endures. The questions of inclusion and exclusion provide a means for overcoming sociology's traditionally restricted attention to national societies and to move towards a broader European and global focus. The European Sociological Association was founded as the processes of integration take on a renewed urgency and 'Europe' moves beyond merely meaning 'Western Europe'. The Association itself represents a movement towards intellectual inclusion which helps to articulate the national traditions in the new contours of a European sociology that is appropriate to the real-world integration of its objects while retaining the strangeness of the sociological perspective.

Notes

1 In the words of Walzer (1993: 55), the questions of 'who is in and who is out' are 'the first questions that any political community must answer about itself'.
2 To this could be added a fourth sector, that of the family (and other primary groups). Contrary to a popular view, families even in advanced societies are still an important institution of social inclusion and welfare, and are strengthened in this role by the public sector, as has been demonstrated, e.g., by studies of transfers between generations (Kohli 1999b, Arber and Attias-Donfut 2000).
3 The political utilization – some would say exploitation – of the welfare state in the process of German unification is a case in point, and foreshadows the demands that will be posed by the EU's extension to the East.

4 A recent search of Amazon.com turned up 15 books with social exclusion in the title published after 1997 – and this alone for the literature in English. As we have shown, social science attention to this concept is even higher in France, and has developed in the other welfare states of continental Europe as well, which is only spottily reflected in the English-speaking literature.

5 Most of the papers were commissioned as keynote lectures of the Third European Sociological Association Conference at the University of Essex in 1997, and then substantially revised for this publication. We wish to thank other speakers whose contributions were shared among the participants and provided additional intellectual stimulation in this project, including Margaret Archer, Daniel Bertaux, Margaret Maruani and Yasemin Soysal.

References

Arber, S. and Attias-Donfut, C. (eds) (2000) *The Myth of Generational Conflict: The Family and State in Ageing Societies*. London: Routledge.

Aron, R. (1983) *Les Étapes de la Pensée Sociologique*. Paris: Gallimard.

Boudon, R. (1993) 'European sociology: the identity lost', in *Sociology in Europe. In Search of Identity*, B. Nedelmann and P. Sztompka (eds). Berlin: de Gruyter.

Bourdieu, P. (1993) *La Misère du Monde*. Paris: Seuil.

Brubaker, R. (1996) *Nationalism Reframed: Nationhood and the National Question in the New Europe*. Cambridge: Cambridge University Press.

Byrne, D. (1999) *Social Exclusion*. Buckingham: Open University Press.

Castel, R. (1995) *Les métamorphoses de la question sociale*. Paris: Fayard.

Chamberlayne, P. and Rustin, M. (1999) *From Biography to Social Policy*. Final report of the SOSTRIS Project. London: University of East London.

Commission of the European Communities (1993) *Background Report: Social Exclusion – Poverty and Other Social Problems in the European Community*. Luxembourg: Office for Official Publications of the European Communities.

Crouch, C. (1999) *Social Change in Western Europe*. Oxford: Oxford University Press.

Dogan, M. (2000) 'Deficit of confidence within European democracies', in *The Making of the European Union: Contributions of the Social Sciences*, M. Haller (ed.). Berlin: Springer.

Erikson, R. and Goldthorpe, J. (1992) *The Constant Flux*. Oxford: Clarendon.

Esping-Andersen, G. (1985) *Politics Against Markets: The Social Democratic Road to Power*. Princeton, NJ: Princeton University Press.

Esping-Andersen, G. (ed.) (1996) *Welfare States in Transition: National Adaptations in Global Economies*. London: Sage.

Geyer, R. (1999) 'Can EU social policy save the social exclusion unit and vice versa?', *Politics* 19: 159–64.

Giddens, A. (1996) *In Defense of Sociology: Essays, Interpretations and Rejoinders*. Cambridge: Polity Press.

Goodin, R.E. (1996) 'Inclusion and exclusion', *Archives Européennes de Sociologie* 37: 343–71.

Haataja, A. (1998) *Unemployment, Employment and Social Exclusion*. Luxembourg Income Study, Working Paper 195. Luxembourg.

Huster, E.-U. (1997) 'Armut in Europa – ausgewählte Ergebnisse des Armutsobservatoriums der Europäischen Union', in *Einkommensverteilung und Armut. Deutschland auf dem Weg zur Vierfünftel-Gesellschaft?*, I. Becker and R. Hauser (eds). Frankfurt/M: Campus.

Jäntti, M. and Danziger, S. (1998) *Income Poverty in Advanced Countries.* Luxembourg Income Study, Working Paper 193. Luxembourg.

Kaelble, H. (1987) *Auf dem Weg zu einer europäischen Gesellschaft?* München: Beck.

Kohli, M. (1999a) 'Ausgrenzung im Lebenslauf', in *Soziale Ausgrenzungen: Gesichter des neuen Kapitalismus*, S. Herkommer (ed.). Hamburg: VSA.

Kohli, M. (1999b) 'Private and public transfers between generations: linking the family and the state', *European Societies* 1: 81–104.

Kohli, M. (2000) 'Arbeit im Lebenslauf: Alte und neue Paradoxien', in *Geschichte und Zukunft der Arbeit*, J. Kocka and C. Offe (eds). Frankfurt/M: Campus.

Kohli, M. and Novak, M. (2001) 'Introduction: will Europe work?', in *Will Europe Work?*, M. Kohli and M. Novak (eds). London: Routledge.

Koopmans, R. and Statham, P. (1998) *Challenging the Liberal Nation-State? Postnationalism, Multiculturalism, and the Collective Claims-Making of Migrants and Ethnic Minorities in Britain and Germany.* Discussion Paper FS III 98–105. Berlin: WZB.

Korpi, W. (2001) 'Gender, class and patterns of inequality in different types of welfare states', in *Will Europe Work?*, M. Kohli and M. Novak (eds). London: Routledge.

Kronauer, M. (1999) 'Die Innen-Außen-Spaltung der Gesellschaft. Eine Verteidigung des Exklusionsbegriffs gegen seinen mystifizierenden Gebrauch', in *Soziale Ausgrenzungen: Gesichter des neuen Kapitalismus*, S. Herkommer (ed.). Hamburg: VSA.

Kymlicka, W. (1995) *Multicultural Citizenship.* Oxford: Oxford University Press.

Leibfried, S. and Pierson, P. (eds) (1995) *European Social Policy: Between Fragmentation and Integration.* Washington, DC: The Brookings Institute.

Leisering, L. and Leibfried, S. (eds) (1999) *Time and Poverty in Western Welfare States.* Cambridge: Cambridge University Press.

Lister, R. (1997) *Citizenship: Feminist Perspectives.* London: Macmillan.

Littlewood, P. and Herkommer, S. (1999) 'Identifying social exclusion: some problems of meaning', in *Social Exclusion in Europe: Problems and Paradigms*, P. Littlewood, I. Glorieux, S. Herkommer and I. Jönsson (eds). Aldershot: Ashgate.

Luhmann, N. (1995) 'Jenseits der Barbarei', in *Gesellschaftsstruktur und Semantik: Studien zur Wissenssoziologie der modernen Gesellschaft*, Vol. 4. Frankfurt/M: Suhrkamp.

Marshall, T.H. (1950) *Citizenship and Social Class.* Cambridge: Cambridge University Press.

Münch, R. (1993) 'The contribution of German social theory to European sociology', in *Sociology in Europe: In Search of Identity*, B. Nedelmann and P. Sztompka (eds). Berlin: de Gruyter.

O'Dowd, L. (2001) 'State borders, border regions and the construction of European identity', in *Will Europe Work?*, M. Kohli and M. Novak (eds). London: Routledge.

Paugam, S. (ed.) (1996) *L'Exclusion, l'état des savoirs.* Paris: La Découverte.

Percy-Smith, J. (2000) 'Introduction: the contours of social exclusion', in *Policy Responses to Social Exclusion: Towards Inclusion*, J. Percy-Smith (ed.). Buckingham: Open University Press.

Phillips, A. (1991) *Engendering Democracy.* University Park, PA: Pennsylvania State University Press.

Saraceno, C. (2001) 'Constructing Europe, constructing European citizenship: contradictory trends', in *Will Europe Work?*, M. Kohli and M. Novak (eds). London: Routledge.

Scharpf, F.W. (1999) *Governing in Europe: Effective and Democratic?* Oxford: Oxford University Press.

Schelkle, W., Krauth, W.-H., Kohli, M. and Elwert, G. (eds) (2000) *Paradigms of Social Change: Modernization, Development, Transformation, Evolution.* Frankfurt/M: Campus.

Schütz, A. (1964) 'The Stranger', in *Collected Papers*, vol. 2. The Hague: Nijhoff.

Simmel, G. (1908) *Soziologie*. Berlin: Duncker & Humblot.

Soysal, Y.N. (1994) *Limits of Citizenship*. Chicago: University of Chicago Press.

Streeck, W. (2001) 'International competition, supranational integration, national solidarity: the emerging constitution of "social Europe"', in *Will Europe Work?*, M. Kohli and M. Novak (eds). London: Routledge.

Therborn, G. (1995) *European Modernity and Beyond*. London: Sage.

Therborn, G. (2000) 'Globalizations: Dimensions, Historical Waves, Regional Effects, Normative Governance', *International Sociology* 15: 151–79.

Vranken, J., Geldof, D. and van Menxel, G. (1996) *Armoede en Sociale Uitsluiting*. Leuven: Acco.

Walzer, M. (1993) 'Exclusion, injustice and the democratic state', *Dissent* 40, 2: 55–64.

Wilson, W.J. (1996) *When Work Disappears: The World of the New Urban Poor*. New York: Knopf.

Yérez del Castillo, I. (1994) 'A comparative approach to social exclusion: lessons from France and Belgium', *International Labour Review* 133: 613–33.

Part I

Framing inclusions and identities in Europe

Theoretical perspectives on citizenship and belonging

2 At the turn of the centuries

Georg Simmel then and now[1]

Birgitta Nedelmann

Simmel and the problem of inclusion/exclusion

Contemporary sociological research on problems of inclusion/exclusion can profit in many different ways from going back to the sociological classics, especially to Georg Simmel. The establishment of sociology as an autonomous academic discipline coincided with a historical phase in which a hot social and political battle was going on regarding the inclusion of the working class into the emerging democratic system, the extension of welfare provisions to deprived social groups, and about the participation of women in social institutions. Many of the sociological classics engaged themselves personally in this battle. Georg Simmel participated in different social movements and fought for workers' and women's rights, for the introduction of poverty relief, of penal reform, and of public hygiene (Köhnke 1996, Levine 1997: 187–9). Being labelled and treated as a Jew, he was specifically sensitive to the marginal role of strangers in the German *Kaiserreich* (Köhnke 1996: 122–49).

The following examples show the great differentiation with which Simmel treats the inclusion/exclusion theme in his sociological *oeuvre*: In his famous analysis of 'The Stranger', he develops the problem of inclusion/exclusion as a problem of individuals being both included *and* excluded from the hosting group. In his role as a guest, the stranger is included into the hosting group, but in his role as a stranger he is excluded from it because he introduces foreign characteristics into the hosting group (GSG[2] 11: 764–71, Levine 1979). Another example of approaching the problem of inclusion/exclusion is Simmel's work on 'Female Culture' (GSG 7: 64–83). Women, representing 'female culture', are excluded from creating and shaping the 'objective' culture, dominated, according to Simmel, by 'male culture'. What are the social costs, he asks, of women being excluded from a cultural world dominated by men? And which price will women have to pay if they were to participate in the official male culture? Another example of how Simmel treats the problem of inclusion/exclusion is his work on 'Secrecy and the Secret Society' (GSG 11: 383–455). It can be read as a sociological contribution to the problem of being included or excluded from highly valued knowledge. Secrecy is, on the one hand, a mechanism of social integration, since sharing a secret brings people closer together. On the other hand, secrecy is a mechanism of exclusion because it puts a barrier between secret holders and those who are excluded from sharing the secrecy. Secrecy, therefore, is a mechanism of both inclusion *and* exclusion. In his 'Excursus on Voting Down' (*Überstimmung*) (GSG 10: 218–28), Simmel formulates the problem of inclusion/exclusion in yet another sense when asking: Which decision-making procedure is best suited to solve the problem of integrating dissenting group members into the group majority? The problem of inclusion/exclusion is here presented as a problem of finding the appropriate formal procedure for linking deviating individuals to the decision made by the group majority.

These examples may already have shown that Simmel has elaborated the problem of inclusion/exclusion in many different ways. Is there a more general sociological problematic linking these different versions of the inclusion/exclusion theme together? I believe that there is such a general sociological problematique underlying Simmel's various ways of approaching the topic of inclusion/exclusion. Generally speaking, like so many other sociologists at that time, he was interested in the part/whole problem. How can the individual part be integrated into the social whole without having to give up its right to self-determination and autonomy? And how can the social whole maintain itself and claim autonomy, when being composed of individual parts? For Simmel, the individual and the whole represent two different principles, the principle of individuality and the principle of generality. The problem of part/whole is, consequently, also a problem of integrating two different social principles without either having to make sacrifices. The more specific Simmelian version of the part/whole problem is the question of how it is possible to find a *balanced relationship* between the individual parts (or the principle of individuality) and the supra-individual social unity (or the principle of generality). How does this relationship have to look like more precisely, if both individual parts and the social unity are to maintain their right to self-determination and autonomy? According to this Simmelian version, the inclusion/exclusion problem is first and foremost a *relational* problem between individuals and supra-individual social forms.

For Simmel, the regulation of the relationship between the social whole and its constitutive parts is not just a formal problem. Underlying this formal problem is a more substantive concern about the development of modern individuals, on the one hand, and modern culture and society, on the other. Under the conditions of an increasingly objectified and dehumanised culture, it becomes increasingly difficult for modern man[3] to protect his personal self and develop his individuality. Simmel was convinced that individuals and culture (and society) are drifting apart more and more, this having destructive consequences for both individuals and culture (and society). To solve the problem of finding a balanced relationship between individuals and culture under the conditions of an advanced money economy was, therefore, not only a theoretical problem, but also a practically substantive problem of utmost importance for Simmel.

What answers do we find in Simmel's sociological opus and what can we learn, more specifically, from this classic about the problem of inclusion/ exclusion? I will apply Simmel's own methodology and depart from a minor example, Simmel's essay on the 'Picture-Frame', and, then, proceed to making more general observations, including also other Simmelian works of relevance for the problem under discussion. The sociological importance of Simmel's 'Picture-Frame' cannot be understood when reading it in isolation from his general sociological opus. It is, therefore, necessary to give a brief introduction to the sociological work that Simmel produced at the turn of the last century. Placing the essay on the 'Picture-Frame' into the broader context of Simmel's sociological work, helps counteract the common view of Simmel as unsystematic, impressionistic and fragmentary (Levine 1997: 196–202).

Simmel's opus at the turn of the last century

The quantitative side

In purely quantitative terms, Simmel's opus is impressive indeed. During just fifteen years at the turn of the last century, between 1894 and 1908, Simmel published roughly one hundred articles (Köhnke 1996: 515–46). Some of these works are rather long (for example, his treatise on the 'Sociology of the Space' (GSG 7: 132–83) is about fifty pages long); others are very brief, like, for example, his essay on 'Leonardo da Vinci's Last Supper' (GSG 7: 304–9), or 'The Handle' (GSG 7: 345–50) which have only five pages each. According to contemporary academic standards, Simmel could be criticised because of his highly uneven productivity.

In those fifteen years, Simmel not only published articles and essays, but also several books. His famous sociological opus, the 'Philosophy of Money', appeared in 1900, and contains more than 700 pages (GSG 6). In 1904, his book on 'Kant' was published (GSG 9: 7–226); in the next year, 1905, his 'Problems of the Philosophy of History' (GSG 9: 227–419) appeared in a totally revised second edition; in 1907, he published 'Schopenhauer and Nietzsche' (GSG 10: 167–408), and in 1908, 'Sociology' (GSG 11), among Simmel's researchers also known as the 'Great Sociology' (863 pages), in contrast to his 'Tiny Sociology', the '*Grundfragen der Soziologie*', written in 1917 (GSG 16: 59–149). Making a very rough calculation about Simmel's total output in these fifteen years, it turns out that he produced around 3200 pages, that is, more than 200 pages per year. In pure quantitative terms, Simmel can easily match such contemporary 'workaholics', as Anthony Giddens, Niklas Luhmann or Alain Touraine, who manage to publish one book per year of the same size.

How could Simmel produce so much? And how could he be so productive without the help of such modern means of production as a personal computer or even a typewriter? (The latter was invented in 1873, but Simmel did not use it.) To answer this question we have to turn to the qualitative side of his production.

The qualitative side

After reading only some of the work Simmel wrote at the turn of the last century, the reader will discover that he was a master in copying himself. He perfectly mastered the art of recycling his own work. This recycling process usually started with a public lecture held in one of Berlin's intellectual circles or academic associations. This lecture would then be published in a daily newspaper, such as the *Berliner Tageblatt*, or in a weekly journal, like *Der Tag* or *Die Zeit*, or, in still another monthly or bi-monthly review. The last station in this recycling process was the publication of a book where the articles he had published previously reappeared either as entire chapters or as parts of chapters. Sometimes, he did not change a single word, at other times he made considerable changes.

Simmel's 'practice of placing sections of essays and thematic issues in a variety of different contexts within his own work' (Frisby and Featherstone 1997: 1) does not make the amount of his publications less impressive. On the contrary, it reveals another quality of his sociological opus which some of his critics have denied, namely, its internal coherence and systematic construction. It is only when rereading his articles and essays within the larger context of his monographical studies, that this systematic quality of his sociological work fully comes to the fore. Reading such essays as, for example, the 'Picture-Frame', the 'Handle' or the 'Travel to the Alps' in isolation from his sociological work at large, one may at best be impressed by his highly original insights, his sharp analytical observation and brilliant style. But when asking how these single pieces of work fit into his larger body of sociological thought, the reader is left at a loss. Those scholars who criticise Simmel for having left behind a number of unsystematic pieces of work have most likely not been able to read his essays in the context of his entire monographical work (see also Levine 1997: 196–202, Sica 1997: 294). Only today (1999), when twelve out of twenty-one planned volumes of the complete Simmel edition are available, do we have easy access to the greater parts of his opus.

Which themes did Simmel write on at the turn of the last century? Contributions to the sociology of culture and aesthetics are in the majority, followed by contributions to general sociology. To the latter category belong his analyses of competition, conflict, fidelity, shame, discretion, avarice and poverty – just to mention a few pieces he later integrated in his 'Great Sociology'. Ranking third are his works on outstanding personalities, such as Kant, Goethe, Nietzsche and Schopenhauer. These works are difficult to classify, because there is no label in contemporary sociology covering this type of work. Perhaps one could subsume them under the category of the 'sociology of biography'. Essays on the sociology and philosophy of religion rank in the fourth place. These contributions are especially difficult to read today. In these essays, Simmel does not present himself as the sharp observer and analyst we have become accustomed to, but as an opaque author preferring an old-fashioned and pompous vocabulary. Other titles such as 'Militarism and the Position of the Woman', 'Female Culture', and

'Woman and Fashion' confirm Simmel's deep concern for gender issues. They rank fifth in our list. Another field of research is close to what we today label as 'political sociology'. To this belong his analyses on 'Voting Down' (*Überstimmung*), 'Super- and Subordination', and 'The Inherited Official Position' (*Das Erbamt*).[4] His essays on the three Italian cities, Rome, Florence and Venice, can be read from different points of view, as contributions to the sociology of art, to general sociology or to the sociology of the city.

This brief overview shows that Simmel was interested in the most different phenomena of modern life. The broad scope of his intellectual interests has irritated many Simmel readers and given rise to the prejudice about his ecclecticism and incoherence (Levine 1997). But on closer examination, there is a general sociological 'problematique', integrating these different fields of research into a coherent body of sociological thought. It is exactly this Simmelian sociological problematique which is of relevance for the problem of inclusion/exclusion.

Having sketched the general context of Simmel's sociological work, we can now better understand his essay on the 'Picture-Frame'. What seems to be nothing else but a witty essay on a minor aesthetic problem is, in fact, a central contribution to general sociology, containing the key for tackling the problems of part/whole and of inclusion/exclusion.

The example of the 'Picture-Frame'

Simmel's essay on the 'Picture-Frame' appeared in the journal *Der Tag* in 1902 (GSG 7: 374–84). Its sub-title, 'An aesthetic attempt', does not encourage reading this short piece of work as a contribution to sociology. But the labels Simmel used for his own pieces of work are often misleading, because he lacked the precise terminology we sociologists are familiar with today.[5] I prefer classifying this essay as a central contribution to general sociology. Simmel's discussion of an aesthetic problem, in this case, the relation between the painting and the frame, functions as a metaphor for the discussion of a fundamental social problem. In so doing, Simmel demonstrates one of his preferred methodological procedures, i.e., the procedure of arguing by analogy (*Analogieverfahren*).[6] It is only at the end of this short essay that he discovers, as it were, that he has used the example of the frame–picture relationship in analogy to the individual–society relationship. The frame, says Simmel, has the function of mediating between a piece of art and its environment (the art consumer), by both separating *and* uniting, a 'task in which, in analogy to history, *the individual and society crush each other*'[7] (GSG 7: 108; my emphasis). What does Simmel mean? Let me, *first*, roughly explain Simmel's main thoughts on the problematic relationship between the frame and the picture.

For Simmel, a work of art, a painted picture, constitutes a unity in and for itself; it is '*l'art pour l'art*', or, as he says, an 'island in the middle of life' (GSG 7: 103). As such it separates itself from the external world and from the art consumer. The frame has to fulfil two functions; the first consists in relating the work of art to its environment, the second in preserving the inner world of the piece of art from being invaded and misused by the onlookers. This double function of external and internal mediation, of separating from the environment and of internal integration, has to be expressed aesthetically by the very shape of the frame. How does the frame have to look in detail, if it is to fulfil these functions?

Simmel answers this question by discussing in detail three cases of unsuccessful solutions to this aesthetic problem. The *first* case refers to frames which are shaped as autonomous pieces of art claiming an artistic value of their own. Artistically shaped frames fail to fulfil the function of mediation, because they isolate the environment from the aesthetic world of the painting and create a second, competing world of arts. This dysfunction can manifest itself in frames which are, for example, richly ornamented, or which have highly attractive colours, forms, or symbols (GSG 7: 105). Making claims on belonging to an autonomous world of art itself, the frame denies its subordinated function to serve as a mediator between the piece of art and the environment. In order to fulfil this function, the frame has instead to be shaped as craft (*Handwerk*), not art, representing style, the principle of generality, rather than art, the principle of individuality.

The *second* case of failed mediation refers to those cases in which the frame overstresses its characteristic as a work of craft. This can be expressed if the external parts of the frame are too much pronounced, for example, by pillars or pilastres giving support to ledges or pediments (GSG 7: 106). This heavy architectonic style of the frame also has the effect of excluding the art consumer from relating to the painting. Thus, it is isolated from the rest of the world. In this case it is, however, the dominance of the frame as a piece of craft, and not art, which has the effect of excluding the onlooker from art consumption. The frame, as an exaggerated object of art, overstresses the principle of individuality and thus distracts the attention from the picture, the real object of art; the frame, as an exaggerated object of craft, overstresses the principle of generality and suppresses art.

The *third* way of failed mediation refers to those cases in which the frame is shaped too weakly leaving behind the impression of being an extremely fragile construction. In these cases, the frame fails to make a clear distinction between the external world of life and the internal world of arts. This, for example, is the case when the painting partially continues on the frame, or, in which the frame is interrupted by empty spaces. The frame's lack of symbolic closure breaks down all frontiers between the internal world of art and the external world of art consumption. The painting can freely penetrate the sphere of the art consumers, and, vice versa, the onlookers can freely invade the inner sphere of arts. As a consequence, the character of the painting as a 'blessed island' (Simmel 1908/1991: 67), as a world in and of itself (GSG 7: 103), is destroyed.

The ideal type of a frame, *finally*, is only described very vaguely and poetically by Simmel. It has to be shaped in such a way, he says, that it enables 'a continuous flow of the glance' from the onlooker to the painting, as a singular, unique piece of art and back again to the art consumer.

Let me return to the remark Simmel makes at the end of this essay: the relation between the frame and the painting is analogous, he says, to the relation between the individual and the society. Whereas the frame, at least in principle, could take over the function of mediating between the picture and its environment, Simmel seems to believe that there is no such possibility of a successful social framing, that is, of an equilibrated relationship between the individual and the society: they 'crush' each other. What does Simmel mean more precisely with this expression? Unfortunately, he finishes his essay before having made an attempt at giving an answer to this question. He leaves the reader with a puzzle: what exactly corresponds to the three types of failed mediation between frame and picture in the world of social life? And why does Simmel seem to exclude the possibility of an equilibrated relationship between the individual and the society?

To think about such types of questions is, indeed, what Raymond Boudon (1993) calls a 'puzzle-solving activity' which is typical of the classics of sociology. In contrast to his contemporaries Weber and Durkheim, Simmel focused on *finding* rather than on solving puzzles. Very often, he left his readers alone in solving the puzzle he had submitted to them. In an attempt to solve the puzzle of the picture frame, the problem Simmel is interested in more generally has to be highlighted again. He wants to discover the social conditions under which the individual and the society/culture are in a balanced relationship. This general interest implies at least two questions: first, under which social conditions can the individual integrate the influences from the cultural environment into her or his personality and become a socially-recognised unique individual? This question refers to what Simmel has also called the process of internalisation of cultural products into the personality structure and the creation of subjective culture. Secondly, under which social conditions is culture itself able to integrate the inputs, that is, the desires, needs and wishes from the individuals and become what Simmel calls an objective culture? This second process could be referred to as the process of objectification, or externalisation. Formally speaking, he is concerned with the conditions under which a balanced, reciprocal influence between individual and culture can be created. Underlying this interest is his assumption that neither individuals, nor culture can realise themselves without mutually referring to each other. Subjective and objective culture are mutually dependent upon each other, and yet, being antagonistically related to each other, they tend to create their own autonomous worlds. According to Simmel's analysis, the conditions of modern life are not favourable to establishing a balanced relationship between individuals and culture. On the contrary, modern life distorts the interaction processes between individuals and culture and raises obstacles in the way of internalisation and externalisation.

Simmel refers to this problem over and over again when discussing the most different themes, such as aesthetic and religious questions, gender issues, power relations, and – alas – the problem of war! What at first glance seems to be a highly heterogeneous work is in fact a homogeneous body of thought integrated by this general *Leitmotiv* of how to create an equilibrium between individuals and culture (or society). Simmel became more and more convinced that it is highly difficult to solve this problem. At the beginning of 1914, when he finally held a chair in philosophy at the University of Straßburg, he welcomed the war as a means of overcoming this problem. The metaphor of the three types of failed mediation between the picture and its frame corresponds to three types of failed mediation between individual and culture in modern society. In an earlier publication (Nedelmann 1991), I have referred to these problems, *first*, as the problem of cultural domination or cultural hypertrophy; *second*, as the problem of exaggerated individualism; and, *third*, as the problem of blocked mediation or paralysation. Going beyond Simmel, I argue that these three types are dynamically interrelated to each other, one giving rise to the next following a dynamic model consisting of three successive stages. Let me, first, briefly explain these three types of cultural problems, and then show how they are related to each other.

Cultural domination, individual exaggeration and paralysation

Cultural domination

Simmel's well-known treatise on 'The Metropolis and Mental Life', written in 1903, is an excellent illustration of the first type of cultural problem in which objective culture dominates the individual culture (GSG 7: 116–31).[8] The 'superpowers' (*Übermächte*) of modern society dominate the individuals in every aspect of their lives. The phenomena Simmel referred to then are even more pressing and suppressing today: the continuous noise in the streets, the multiplicity of brief encounters with anonymous people, the uninterrupted confrontation with contrasting auditive and, especially, visual impressions (GSG 11: 727), and the permanent exposure to polluted air and various other oppressive scents.[9] If the metropolis at the turn of the last century has turned its inhabitants into – in Simmel's words – a mere 'speck of dust' (*Staubkorn*), a 'quantité negligeable' (GSG 7: 129), what has become of the city dwellers at the turn of this century? The two world wars have proved that modern human beings have been reduced even further from a 'quantité negligeable' into a 'quantité terminable', or, into 'terminal post-modern writing' (I will come back to this expression coined by the Weinsteins (1993)).

Simmel was not the only one to focus attention on the topic of suppression of modern man by modern society. It is a familiar topic discussed broadly by other sociologists at the turn of the nineteenth century. Ferdinand Tönnies complained about the lack of 'Gemeinschaft' in favour of 'Gesellschaft'; Max Weber invented the metaphor of the 'iron cage' to express his concern about the overwhelming power of bureaucratic institutions. Instead of falling back into an attitude of cultural pessimism or romantic nostalgia,[10] Simmel added another aspect to this general problem when asking: Which defense mechanisms, or strategies, can individuals invent in order to defend their personalities from being crushed by the superpowers of modern culture? How can they resist 'being levelled and consumed in a societal-technological mechanism' (Simmel 1903/1971: 324; my transl.)? The answer Simmel has given to these questions makes him stand out among his contemporaries.

Modern man, he says, has to develop both defensive and offensive strategies of lifestyle management in order to protect his individuality from being totally consumed by objective culture. Simmel scholars have paid more attention to the first, the defensive strategy, the elaboration of an attitude of 'blasé' or aloofness. It allows the individual to put a distance between his or her personal sphere and the stimuli received from the environment. The stylisation of this attitude of being aloof, or, as we would simply say today, 'cool', functions like a frame which we put between our inner, personal sphere and the oppressive cultural environment. It could, therefore, be called a defensive framing strategy. The second framing strategy mentioned by Simmel refers to offensive mechanisms of lifestyle management. In order to save the 'most personal element' of their selves, individuals have to elaborate an extreme version of their personalities. They even have to over-exaggerate their peculiarities in order to be brought into the awareness of others and – as Simmel adds – of themselves (Simmel 1903/1971: 338, GSG 7: 130). Only those individuals who consciously accentuate specific traits of their personalities are, according to Simmel, at all able to counterbalance the oppressive impact of objective culture. As a result, a particular type of competition between individuals exaggerating their personality traits and the developing objective culture sets in. The greater the dominance of culture, the greater the need for modern man to emphasise his personality. He must display a certain extravagance and 'capriciousness', Simmel says, in order to be recognised as something special and unique. Let me recall the origin of the term 'capriciousness': 'The inventive wits are termed in the Tuscan tongue capricious for the resemblance they bear to a goat, who takes no pleasure in the open and easy plains but loves to caper along in the hill tops' (The Oxford English Dictionary: 869). To caper along in the social hill tops becomes a social necessity for being recognised by others as a unique personality – and this is even more the case today than in Simmel's time. The stylisation of capriciousness has become a social requirement, or, to put it in other words, it is almost normative to behave deviantly; briefly, it is a case of *normative deviance*. Robert K. Merton's (1968: 195–203) insight into innovation as deviant behaviour comes to mind. The social norm to behave capriciously is a paradoxical expectation difficult to realise, because it socially demands to be 'guided by whim or fancy rather than by judgements or settled purpose', as capriciousness is further defined in the Oxford Dictionary.

Normative deviance is highly demanded in many different social areas of contemporary social life. In show business, for example, the fulfilment of this norm is a *conditio sine qua non* without which pop stars, and artists in general, cannot survive in public. Whenever it is professionally required to attract and keep public attention in the media, normative deviance in Simmel's and Merton's sense becomes a matter of professional survival. Politics is another social sphere in which acting against established rules, breaking with the conventional language, or violating the traditional styles of self-presentation are a necessary precondition for survival among other competitors. The speed with which new forms of deviance have to be invented is increased by other competing politicians imitating these innovations, once they have proved themselves successful in the political arena. A merry-go-round process of innovation and imitation is initiated, a process brilliantly analysed by Simmel with reference to fashion (GSG 10: 7–37, Simmel 1904/1971: 294–323).

We academics are no exception from joining this merry-go-round of innovation and imitation. Let me just mention the fashion of writing in a deconstructivist style which, for example, in the field of Simmel studies, has been introduced by Deena and Michael Weinstein (1993). It seems that the development of capricious forms of writing and theorising in social science has, just like in show business or politics, become a strategy of professional survival in a situation in which a *bona fide* sociologist has become a mass article in the highly competitive academic market.

Two questions immediately arise: is there a limit to normative deviance which, once surpassed, is dysfunctional for the development of individuality? Can defensive and offensive framing strategies be self-destructive and, instead of protecting and promoting the individual personality, distort and even destroy it? In another essay of Simmel, we can find an answer to these questions.

Exaggerated subjectivity

In his essay 'The Problem of Style' written in 1908 (GSG 8: 374–84),[11] Simmel heavily criticises the attitude of modern human beings to reject all kinds of culturally shaped forms, such as works of craft, social institutions, traditions, conventions, and legal prescriptions. They do so, Simmel complains, just because social institutions are perceived as representing the principle of 'the social' and 'the general' which are perceived as threatening human individuality. Simmel observes this negative attitude towards social forms in different social areas, but especially in the world of aesthetics. The way in which his contemporaries furnished their homes, how they dressed, and how they related to aesthetic objects in their environment are, according to Simmel, a manifestation of their general rejection of over-individual social forms. He concludes thus: if we treat objects we need and use in everyday life, such as chairs or glasses, as if they were works of art, we deprive these objects of their immediate use-value. The chair which is admired as a work of art no longer functions as a seat; the glass which is put behind locked doors can no longer be used to offer a drink. If objects of craft are perceived and treated as works of art, Simmel claims, then we misunderstand modern individualism. He goes even further when qualifying this misunderstanding as 'the most extreme caricature of misunderstanding modern individualism' (GSG 8: 379; my transl.).[12] Modern men, who are guided in their everyday life by such an image of exaggerated individualism, are compulsively driven by the search for idiosyncratic style. Such a '*mania for originality*' (Simmel

1976: 233) has as a consequence that we detest everything in our environment that raises the suspicion of having a *social* character. The categorical rejection of common rules of behaviour, of general principles of aesthetic perception and consumption destroys the very social basis of individualism. As we have already seen, Simmel believes that individuality and what he calls 'life' can only be realised and expressed in its opposite, that is, in social forms. 'Life is ineluctably condemned to become reality only in the guise of its opposite, i.e., as form' (Simmel 1976: 240). But if formlessness is declared as the main principle of individualisation, then culture too is, in the long run, deprived of 'life', that is, of the inputs necessary for developing vital cultural forms. As a consequence, not only culture becomes de-individualised and de-vitalised, but also individual- ity becomes more and more 'de-cultured'. Consequently, exaggerated individu- alism, developed as a reaction against the hypertrophy of objective culture, initiates a two-sided process of atrophy, mutually feeding upon each other: the atrophy of individual culture speeds up the atrophy of objective culture which, in its turn, further weakens individual culture.

The example of Margaret Thatcher's statement 'There is no society, there are only individuals' shows that Simmel's observation of exaggerated individual- ism has some actuality in society today. This declaration of the death of society is not only impressive in and of itself, but also because of the positive response it enjoys among sociologists. At present, theories of individualisation, especially those developed by Ulrich Beck (1997), Beck, Giddens and Lash (1996) are highly fashionable among not only German sociologists. In a Thatcherian manner, the followers of theories of individualisation not only declare the end of society, but also the end of other macrostructures, like social class or social institutions. This amounts to declaring the end of sociology itself. Accordingly, many sociologists prefer calling themselves 'social scientists'. A hundred years after Simmel had made his observation on 'the most extreme caricature of mis- understanding modern individualism', sociologists today have themselves become victims of 'the most extreme caricature of misunderstanding individual- ism' when celebrating the funeral not only of society, but also of sociology. Before commenting further on this sad event, let me introduce the third type of failed mediation between individuals and society.

Paralysation

The third problem arises as a consequence of the two former types of failed mediation and refers to the situation in which the relationship between indi- viduals and culture is blocked or paralysed. We can now also understand the three types of failed mediation as a process model, in which cultural domination (or hypertrophy) is the first stage, giving rise to the second stage, exaggerated individualism, which in turn gives rise to the third stage of totally blocked mediation. This last stage is characterised by both individuals and culture devel- oping worlds of their own between which there is no longer any relationship. Using the terminology of Niklas Luhmann, both individuals and culture have now become self-referential systems, exclusively guided by their own developmental criteria. If culture becomes a self-referential system, it is absorbed by differentiating itself in orientation to aesthetics as '*l'art pour l'art*'. Luhmann (1995) has described in detail this process in his book on *Die Kunst der Gesellschaft*. If individuals become a 'social system', they are transformed into what Weinstein and Weinstein have coined 'terminal post-modern writing' (Weinstein and Weinstein 1993: 215). If the end of individual action is individualisation itself and if individualisation is defined as '*l'art pour l'art*', then the means-end-relation of rational action, typical of modern man, is broken. The 'terminal post-modern writing' also means the end of rational man.

Paralysation or blocked mediation between individuals and society has also 'terminal' consequences for culture. Objective culture needs, according to Simmel, the inputs of individual interests and desires, otherwise it becomes devitalised and ossified. The more culture develops autonomously from individual life, the more it assumes the characteristics of a lifeless social system. According to Luhmann's understanding, such a process of increasing autonomy and internal differentiation is an indication of evolutionary upgrading. For Simmel, however, whose sociological problematic consists in finding a balanced relationship between individual and culture, this process of the increasing two-sided autonomy of individuals and culture is equal to evolutionary loss.

Simmel called this situation of mutual paralysation between individuals and culture, understood as two separate social systems, the 'tragedy of culture'. This concept has created a lot of misunderstanding. Simmel himself had a precise definition of what he meant by this concept:

> (W)hen the destructive forces directed against some being are called forth from the deepest levels of this very being; or when its destruction has been initiated in itself, and forms the logical development of the very structure by which a being has built its own positive form,

then, Simmel speaks of tragedy (Simmel 1968: 43). In other words, if we conceive of paralysation as necessarily resulting from exaggerated individualism, and exaggerated individualism in turn as the necessary outcome of cultural domination, then paralysation is, in the sense defined above, the 'tragic' result of failed mediation between individuals and culture. We can now better understand why Simmel finished his essay on the 'Picture-Frame' with the statement quoted above that individuals and culture (or society) crush each other. He believed that there is no social solution to the problem of social framing in advanced modern societies. In 1914, he turned into a war enthusiast believing in the war as an event which finally could stop the on-going merry-go-round of individual exaggeration, cultural domination and mutual paralysation.

Conclusion

Why should a sociological classic be consulted who, at the end of his life, welcomed the war as a solution to the 'tragedy of culture'? It is certainly neither
because Simmel took sides with war enthusiasts, nor because he became a
victim of the nostalgia for the 'new human being' that it is highly recommended
to delve anew into his sociology today. Quite the contrary, his late turn towards
militarism is a healthy warning against worshipping a classic author as an
impeccable hero. The puzzle, however, remains as to how the sociologist
Simmel, the brilliant observer and sharp analyst, could change into another
Simmel, propagating simple solutions and destructive decisions. Instead of
trying to solve this puzzle, I prefer returning to the earlier Simmel, the brilliant
observer and sociological analyst. By way of conclusion, four main points are
highlighted to show why his contribution is of relevance for specifying the
problem of inclusion/exclusion.

First, the Simmelian perspective helps reformulate the theme of
inclusion/exclusion in a *relational* and *dynamic* way. Formally speaking, the
problem is how to relate to each other two social units which are both mutually
dependent upon each other for their self-realisation and which respond, at the
same time, dualistically, or even antagonistically, to each other. More precisely,
it has to be asked: which individual parts have to be related to which supra-
individual social units? Which social part has to be included into which larger
entity? Furthermore, what is the end of regulating the relationship between
parts and whole? In abstract Simmelian terms, the end is to find an equilibrated
relationship between individuals and the supra-individual whole, giving neither
side the chance to dominate or suppress the other. Procedures of inclusion and
exclusion must not end up in zero sum games, but both sides must have equal
payoffs from relating to each other. To illustrate this idea, Simmel's example of
the 'Female Culture' may again be helpful: the inclusion of more women into
social institutions has to have as an outcome that both male culture and female
culture profit from it. Or, as Simmel explains in his 'Excursus on Voting Down',
the introduction of decision-making by majority rule has to strengthen both the
social group and the position of the dissenting minority.

Second, the example of the 'Picture-Frame' has taught us to define the
problem of inclusion/exclusion as a problem of *mediation* between the individual
parts and the supra-individual social unity. Simmel's detailed discussion of the
aesthetic problems of the frame, in relation to the work of art and the art consumer challenges the research on problems of inclusion and exclusion to
examine the question of how to institutionalise the mediation between individual parts and the social whole. Which is the most adequate social form for
relating individual parts with the social whole? The answer to this question is of
vital importance for achieving the goal of establishing a balanced relationship.
Whether women should be given the right to participate in social institutions
by procedures of quantitative quotas, or by 'natural selection' is highly decisive
for the chances to develop a balanced and socially productive synthesis between

female and male culture. Whether decisions are made by majority rule or by the principle of unanimity is of crucial importance for the likelihood of the social group to persist and the individual group member to feel integrated into the group. This question of how mediation should be institutionalised is of special importance for problems of inclusion and exclusion, since, through Simmel's perspective, it has to been seen as a *dynamic* interplay between individuals, on the one hand, and supra-individual social units, on the other. Both parts and whole are changing over time, each obeying its own rules of development. Therefore, the linking mechanisms must be institutionalised in such a way that they can react flexibly to the changes both sides are undergoing.

Third, the introduction of mediating mechanisms into the discussion of inclusion/exclusion has as a consequence to reformulate the originally dualistic version of the problem of inclusion/exclusion into a problem between three parties, the individual parts, the social unity and the mediator. According to this triadic reformulation of the inclusion/exclusion problem, the mediator has the function of shaping a balanced relationship between the individual parts and the social group. Simmel's meticulous aesthetic reflections about the three cases of failed mediation can now be read as a contribution to the discussion of how to create a balanced relationship between three parties; the third, the mediator, being neither too general and taking sides with the social group, nor too individualistic and supporting the individual part. In order to be able to function as a mediator and counterbalance both sides, the third party has neither to be too strong, nor too weak. This requirement of the third, mediating party, to be institutionalised independently and autonomously from the two other parties, reminds very much of the problem Durkheim (1893/1973: i–xxxvi) discussed in relation to professional groups. At the turn of the last century, not only Simmel and Durkeim, but also other sociological classics were deeply engaged in problems of how to institutionalise the third intermediating party within the context of the nation state. At the turn of this century, the problem of institutionalising intermediation has become even more important and complex than at the turn of the last century. As we know from Simmel, increasing differentiation of society goes hand-in-hand with increasing individualisation of its parts. Not only the nation state itself is included into this parallel process of differentiation and individualisation, but also the emerging supra-national polities (like the European Union, or the United Nations). Whereas the sociological classics could limit the problem of intermediation to the context of the nation state, representing the highest level of the social whole, we contemporary sociologists are exposed to problems of multi-level intermediation between highly differentiated single parts. We not only have to solve the problem of finding the right frame for one piece of art, but of finding, on a higher level of abstraction, new frames for a great variety of framed pictures. We are lost in a multi-level art museum in which highly different pieces of art are exposed to a highly differentiated public, among which some may be labelled as art historians and aestheticians, others as tourists and art consumers, and others again as curious bypassers. Without wanting to abuse this analogy, it helps sharpen the view of a problem, discussed especially in the European Union today: as what and in which role are the individual inhabitants of the European Union supposed to be integrated into the European Union? This question underlines the importance of the first point. Which are the individual parts to be related to the social whole and how is the social entity defined more precisely? If the character of the supra-individual unity is under-defined (as the European Union definitely is), then it is also difficult to define more precisely the single parts that have to be included into the whole. In such a situation, intermediation becomes an impossible task. The problem today consists in institutionalising intermediary mechanisms on multiple levels and of relating highly differentiated social parts with weakly defined national and supra-national unities. In contrast to Simmel, we not only have to think about the adequate shape of the frame for one picture, but about the shapes and forms of different frames for different pictures. In addition, and most importantly, we have to think about the shapes and forms of 'meta-frames', that is, about social mechanisms coordinating different intermediary mechanisms on a higher level of intermediation.

Finally, there is a fourth reason why the 'Picture-Frame' is of relevance for the definition of the problem of inclusion/exclusion today. It was Simmel's ideal to find a *balanced* relationship between the individual part and the supra-individual social unity. The pre-war Simmel teaches that there is no simple solution to this problem in terms of one winning and one losing side. The individual part and the social whole have to coexist on the basis of maintaining their own specificity and autonomy. This perspective helps specify the problem of inclusion/exclusion. Rather than formulating it as a problem of *either* inclusion *or* exclusion, it should be formulated as a problem of inclusion *and* exclusion. This formulation corrects the one-dimensional way of thought dominating all spheres of contemporary society, which is paralleled by a normative requirement, to react in terms of black *or* white, yes *or* no, pro *or* contra, male *or* female, good *or* bad. One of Simmel's most fundamental lessons has not yet been fully learned, namely, to recognise the co-presence of dualistic forces, not lending themselves to being resolved in favour of one side or the other. As the examples discussed above have shown, the dominance of one side necessarily creates the precondition for a self-destructive process at the end of which the initially dominating side will also become a loser. One-sided solutions of the inclusion/exclusion problem are necessarily self-destructive. From this point of view, Thatcher's statement is self-defeating: if there is no society, then there will be no individuals either in the long run. Individuals cannot realise themselves without society or culture, and vice versa. The German sociologist Richard Münch (1993) has applied this Simmelian thought to other fields of social reality. The dualism between organised labour and organised capital, he says, cannot be resolved by one side trying to dominate the other. They can only solve the economic problems by accepting their antagonistic counterpart and trying to live in an equilibrated relationship. He goes on to argue that this also holds true for the relationship between economy and ecology.

At the turn of this century we finally seem to be prepared to go 'The Third Way' (Giddens 1998), which Simmel already showed us at the turn of the last century. Social framing (and meta-framing), without crushing any of the parts and contradictory principles, was the puzzle Simmel had to solve in his time. It still remains one of the major puzzles we sociologists have to solve in the next millennium.

Notes

1 I wish to thank Sabetai Unguru (Tel Aviv) for insightful suggestions and style editing, and the editors of this book, Alison Woodward and Martin Kohli, for valuable comments.
2 GSG refers to the volumes of the *Georg Simmel Gesamtausgabe* edited by Otthein Rammstedt and his collaborators.
3 I use the term 'modern man' in a historically sensitive manner, specifically in the Simmelian way which includes both women and men; 'modern man' is, then, 'mankind' (which includes, of course, 'womankind').
4 I wish to thank David Frisby for this translation.
5 The editors of Volume 7 of the *Georg Simmel Gesamtausgabe* (in which this essay was published in 1995) classify this essay as a contribution to the philosophy of aesthetics (GSG 7: 356), a label also used by Simmel to characterise his work. Their classification is supported by the fact that Simmel had presented this essay as a lecture in front of the so-called 'Kulturleben-Club' in Berlin, a private association in which aesthetic problems were discussed at length. At that time, Simmel was working both on his 'Sociology' and on aesthetic problems.
6 Simmel's analogical procedure was heavily criticised by Max Weber (1994: 79) for the 'dubiousness of its basic principles'.
7 The German original: (eine) '*Aufgabe, an deren Analogie im Geschichtlichen das Individuum und die Gesellschaft sich gegenseitig zerreiben*'.
8 The translation of this important text by E.A. Shils (in Levine 1971: 324–39) has its merits, but is not always precise and very often even misleading. I fully agree with Alan Sica (1997: 294) who strongly recommends to replace earlier translations with new ones more reflective of the complete Simmel.
9 In his 'Excursus on the Sociology of the Senses' (GSG 11: 722–42) Simmel writes: 'The social question is not only an ethical question, but also a question of the nose (*Nasenfrage*)' (GSG 11: 734).
10 This is true at least until 1914, when he, like so many other Germans, fell prey to the general war enthusiasm.
11 English translation in *Theory, Culture & Society* 8: 63–71.
12 The English text is wrong when translating 'das karikierendste Mißverständnis des modernen Individualismus' as 'the most common misunderstanding of modern individualism' (Simmel 1908/1991: 67).

References

Beck, U. (1997) *Kinder der Freiheit*. Frankfurt a.M.: Suhrkamp.
Beck, U., Giddens, A. and Lash, S. (1996) *Reflexive Modernisierung*. Frankfurt a.M.: Suhrkamp.
Boudon, R. (1993) 'European sociology: the identity lost?', in *Sociology in Europe: In Search of Identity*, B. Nedelmann and P. Sztompka (eds). Berlin: De Gruyter, 27–44.
Durkheim, E. ([1893] 1973) 'Quelques remarques sur les groupements professionnels.

Préface de la seconde édition', in *De la Division du Travail Social*, E. Durkheim (ed.). Paris: PUF, i–xxxvi.

Frisby, D. and Featherstone, M. (1997) 'Introduction to the texts', in *Simmel on Culture*, D. Frisby and M. Featherstone (eds). London, Thousand Oakes and New Delhi, 1–31.

Giddens, A. (1998) *The Third Way. The Renewal of Social Democracy*. Cambridge: Polity Press.

Köhnke, K.Ch. (1996) *Der junge Simmel in Theoriebeziehungen und sozialen Bewegungen*. Frankfurt a.M.: Suhrkamp.

Levine, D.N. (ed.) (1971) *Georg Simmel on Individuality and Social Forms*. Chicago: The University of Chicago Press.

Levine, D.N. (1979) 'Simmel at a distance: on the history and systematics of the sociology of the stranger', in *Strangers in African Societies*, W.A. Shack and E.P. Skinner (eds). Berkeley, Los Angeles, London: University of California Press, 21–36.

Levine, D.N. (1997) 'Simmel reappraised: old images, new scholarship', in *Reclaiming the Sociological Classics*, Ch. Camic (ed.). London: Blackwell, 173–207.

Luhmann, N. (1995) *Die Kunst der Gesellschaft*. Frankfurt a.M.: Suhrkamp.

Merton, R.K. (1968) *Social Theory and Social Structure*. New York: The Free Press.

Münch, R. (1993) 'The contribution of German social theory to European sociology', in *Sociology in Europe: In Search of Identity*, B. Nedelmann and P. Sztompka (eds). Berlin and New York: De Gruyter, 45–66.

Nedelmann, B. (1991) 'Individualisation, exaggeration and paralysation: Simmel's three problems of culture', *Theory, Culture and Society*, 8, 3: 169–93.

The Oxford English Dictionary, Oxford: Clarendon Press, vol. II, 869.

Sica, A. (1997) 'Acclaiming the reclaimers: the trials of writing sociology's history', in *Reclaiming the Sociological Classics*, Ch. Camic (ed.). London: Blackwell, 282–98.

Simmel, G. ([1903] 1971) 'The metropolis and mental life', in *Georg Simmel on Individuality and Social Forms*, D.N. Levine (ed.). Chicago: The University of Chicago Press, 324–39.

Simmel, G. ([1904] 1971) 'Fashion', in *Georg Simmel on Individuality and Social Forms*, D.N. Levine (ed.). Chicago: The University of Chicago Press, 294–323.

Simmel, G. ([1908] 1991) 'The problem of style', *Theory, Culture and Society*, 8, 3: 63–71.

Simmel, G. (1968) 'On the concept and the tragedy of culture', in *Georg Simmel. The Conflict in Modern Culture and Other Essays*, K.P. Etzkorn (ed.). New York: Teachers College Press, 27–46.

Simmel, G. (1976) 'The conflict of modern culture', in *Georg Simmel. Sociologist and European*, P. Lawrence (ed.). Sunbury-on-Thames: Nelson, 223–42.

Simmel, G. (1993) 'Das Problem des Stils', in *Georg Simmel Gesamtausgabe*, Band 8. Frankfurt a.M.: Suhrkamp, 374–84.

Simmel, G. (1995) 'Der Bildrahmen. Ein ästhetischer Versuch', in *Georg Simmel Gesamtausgabe*, Band 7. Frankfurt a.M.: Suhrkamp, 101–8.

Simmel, G. (1995) 'Die Großstädte und das Geistesleben', in *Georg Simmel Gesamtausgabe*, Band 7. Frankfurt a.M.: Suhrkamp, 116–31.

Weber, M. (introduction by D.N. Levine) (1994) 'Georg Simmel as Sociologist' in *Georg Simmel. Critical Assessments*. Vol. 1, D. Frisby (ed.). London and New York: Routledge and Kegan, 76–81.

Weinstein, D. and Weinstein, M.A. (1993) *Postmodern(ized) Simmel*. London and New York: Routledge.

3   Recombinant citizenship

Rainer Bauböck

What does it mean to be a citizen in Europe? Imagine a Kurdish immigrant who has been naturalized in France keeping, as most do, his Turkish passport. Using his right of free movement as a EU citizen he has recently settled in Germany. He can now vote there in local and European Parliament elections. He may also participate in general elections in France and Turkey if he cares to travel there to cast his vote. He is a citizen of two nation states, of a municipality in another state and of a supra-national union, and may yet feel to be a foreigner whose strongest political affiliation is with a stateless Kurdish nation that cannot offer him citizenship.

In the wake of T.H. Marshall's famous lectures of 1949 (Marshall 1965), most accounts of citizenship since World War II have focused on the evolution of legal rights and duties. Some have emphasized the widening circles of inclusion that have turned former slaves, workers, women or minors into citizens. Many have cautioned that the equality of legal status and individual rights is not enough to overcome the effects of social exclusion. Yet, until a few years ago, the allocation of citizenship between various political communities did not come up as a theoretical question. A citizen was assumed to be a member of a nation state and of one nation state only[1] and each state had the sovereign right to control the gates of admission for new members. Today, no theory of citizenship can afford to ignore the bewildering complexities of multiple and ambiguous memberships illustrated in the case I have outlined above.

In Europe three interrelated developments undermine the correspondence between state borders and boundaries of citizenship. First, there is immigration from non-European origins. While control over territorial entry is increasingly shifted towards European levels, resident immigrants have gained access to rights that were formerly regarded as privileges of national citizens.[2] Second, there is European Union citizenship. Its supra-national conception of rights is still tied to legal nationality and cultural identities of the member-states, excluding thereby immigrants from third countries. Third, there are movements for national self-determination. The break-up of the Soviet Union, of Czechoslovakia and Yugoslavia has multiplied the units of citizenship and at the same time generated massive exclusion or expulsion of populations stranded on the wrong side of a new national border, while devolution in Spain, Belgium and the UK moves previously unitary states towards an asymmetric federalism[3] and multinational citizenship.

Citizenship in today's Europe is no longer a homogeneous status and set of rights that defines a singular affiliation to a polity. Memberships overlap and rights are increasingly differentiated. But that does not mean that citizenship has lost importance in a globalizing society or that its core principles can no longer be spelled out and applied. Citizenship is rather like recombinant DNA – it consists of a few easily identifiable elements that can be rearranged to generate a great variety of forms of political life. Europe has become a laboratory for cutting the different strands of citizenship and recombining them in novel, and sometimes disturbing, ways. The first part of this chapter is concerned with conceptual differentiation and looks at recombinations of citizenship in political theory; the second part examines differentiated structures of citizenship that emerge from transnational migration and ethno-national conflict and deviate from a traditional model of membership in sovereign, closed and homogeneous political communities. My conclusion is that only a pluralistic understanding of citizenship can adequately reflect the growing fluidity and multiplicity of political, social and cultural ties, which relate individuals to various political communities.

Thin and thick conceptions of citizenship

Let us start with a preliminary and somewhat makeshift definition of citizenship as a status of equal and full membership in a polity and briefly explore the key elements of this definition. First, it uses the term 'polity' rather than 'state' or 'society'. From an external perspective, the state can be seen as the basic unit of the international political system, while from an internal one it is an ensemble of institutions exercising political authority in a certain territory. A polity is the population permanently subjected to this authority when seen as a political community. In contrast with the notion of civil society the concept of polity implies a discourse of political legitimation and a formal structure of membership. Political authority must at least claim to be in the common interest of those who are subjected to it. And the polity is understood as an intergenerational community whose members share in benefits and burdens which derive from living under a common political authority.[4]

However, according to the definition, not any kind of membership in any kind of polity can be properly called citizenship. Citizenship requires equal and full membership and both qualifications combined presuppose a *democratic* political community, at least as a regulatory ideal.[5] First, citizens are *equal* as members of the polity however unequal they may be in other social spheres. And, second, citizenship is *full* membership when it is linked to the notion of popular sovereignty. Political authority is not merely exercised on behalf of the citizens, but they are understood to collectively rule themselves by mandating all such authority. Full membership implies therefore *comprehensive* powers as well as an *inclusive* definition of the set of persons who are members of the polity. Let me give two counterexamples: multiple votes for members of specific groups would make citizenship *unequal*, while a denial of the franchise for certain groups creates *partial* citizens. J.S. Mill's endorsement of multiple votes for educated élites would have created unequal political citizenship (Mill 1972: 306–14).[6] Minors, inmates of prisons or psychiatric hospitals and foreign residents are residual categories of partial citizens in contemporary western democracies.

These examples already show that the major benefit of citizenship lies in the rights that come along with membership. Rights are not an accidental side-effect, but a constitutive dimension of citizenship. The standards of equality and full membership can only be defined with regard to a comprehensive bundle of rights shared by all citizens. And these rights are not merely moral entitlements but are necessarily specified within a system of laws. As Jürgen Habermas has explained, the basic rights of liberal democratic citizenship are those that citizens must mutually grant each other if they wish to regulate their coexistence by means of positive law (Habermas 1992: 151–65).

If membership and rights are two dimensions of citizenship, a third one is to regard citizenship as a practice. Sustaining citizenship requires some activity on the part of citizens. Imagining oneself as a member of a political community will have to be supported by practices of 'good citizenship' ranging from narrowly political behaviour such as participating in elections to the ordinary virtues of civility in everyday life. While the institutions of liberal states do not necessarily depend on citizenship practices, the polity as a democratic community disintegrates when few citizens care to vote, when only tiny minorities engage in debates, associations or movements about issues of common interest, when laws regulating taxes or employment are routinely ignored, or when there is a general lack of trust in public encounters between anonymous individuals of different religious creeds, ethnic origins or phenotypes. Obviously, in a liberal democracy practising good citizenship is not an individual precondition for being a member and enjoying rights.[7] However, a certain level of habitual citizenship practices will be necessary in order to support the imagination of a shared political community and to empower individuals through the system of legal rights.

A comprehensive theory of citizenship has to address all three dimensions, but different conceptions emphasize and interpret them differently. One way to represent this conceptual field is to distinguish between thin conceptions, which regard citizenship as a strictly legal relation, and thick ones, which emphasize the aspect of community. Table 3.1 outlines how various thin and thick conceptions define citizenship along the three dimensions.

Membership

At the thinnest end of the spectrum membership boils down to the notion of 'nationality' as it is used in international law. In this sense, nationality has nothing to do with being a member of a nation understood as a political and cultural community, but simply signifies a legal status that links individuals to

Table 3.1 Conceptions and dimensions of citizenship

	Conceptions thin ← → thick		
	Legal positivism	*Civic republicanism*	*Nationalism*
Dimensions	*Libertarianism*		*Communitarianism*
Membership	legal status	political identity	cultural identity
Rights	negative liberties	rights as obligations	moral duties
Practices	passive citizenship	civic virtues	heroic virtues

states.[8] Formulated within a framework of legal positivism this concept also does not carry explicit normative connotations. The relation is understood to be an empty one that can be filled with various kinds of rights or obligations but does not conceptually presuppose any of those traditionally associated with citizenship.[9] What it does presuppose are sovereign states that effectively exercise political authority not only in a territory, but also over a population who are the addressees of their laws. The basic relation is therefore one of subjection of individuals to states and of mutual recognition between states. Citizenship in this narrowest sense links individuals to states rather than to political communities and it does not distinguish between authoritarian and democratic regimes.

At the other end of the spectrum citizenship is much more than merely one kind of membership in a specific type of association alongside others. It is a collective cultural identity that identifies, for outsiders, who the individual members of the polity are and, for themselves, how they ought to see each other. The thickest versions attribute a special importance to the polity as the *largest* collectivity that defines individual identities as well as the most *important* one to which all other identities are subordinated. This is characteristic for nationalist ideologies. There are, of course, many different varieties of nationalism. For ethnic nationalists the nation is first a cultural community that precedes the polity, for civic nationalists it is first a political community that assimilates all citizens into a shared culture. Although their starting points may differ, most nationalisms strive thus for congruence between political and cultural boundaries (Gellner 1983: 1).

Table 3.1 identifies civic republicanism as an intermediate conception. Republicanism is a broader and much older tradition than nationalism and reaches back via Rousseau to Machiavelli, the ancient Roman republic and, in certain interpretations, to Aristotle's theory of the polity (Aristotle 1981).[10] It differs from nationalism in its emphasis on the political rather than cultural nature of membership. Contemporary civic republicans often contrast citizenship with national identity. The former signifies a collective identity of free members in a self-governing polity sharing a common future, whereas the latter is regarded as an unreflective and ascriptive membership in a community of shared culture and origin (Viroli 1995). For civic republicans, citizenship must be *strong* (Barber 1984) rather than *thick*. It is a bond strong enough to unite the members of a polity who are thoroughly divided by their private interests. But this cloth is woven from universalistic principles and shows no particular ethnic patterns.

Rights and obligations

If we take the legal status of nationality as our starting point, the thickness of conceptions increases not only as we move towards the right column in Table 3.1 but also as we move down the rows and add the dimensions of rights and practices to our theory. Although the content of rights of citizenship may be seen as indeterminate in legal positivist approaches, it is hardly possible to deny that the very idea of the rule of law must address the citizen as a bearer of what the legal scholar Georg Jellinek called subjective public rights (1892). Hannah Arendt defended a corresponding view of citizenship as 'the right to have rights' (Arendt 1967: 296). She thought that being a citizen of a particular polity is a fundamental precondition even for the enjoyment of supposedly universal human rights. During the post-war period this 'paradox of human rights' has been resolved at the conceptual level, although certainly not yet in political practice, by including a right *to* citizenship in an expanding catalogue of human rights.[11]

The specific rights *of* citizenship can be usefully distinguished along the well-known triad of civil, political and social rights developed by T.H. Marshall and, half a century before, in quite similar terms by Jellinek. Yet if we want to link citizenship as a bundle of rights to its external aspect as a legal status of persons in international law, there is another relevant distinction which has found much less attention in the theory. Citizenship rights may be external in the sense of being enjoyed also by those who live outside their state of nationality, or internal because they depend on residing in the territory. On the one hand, citizens travelling or living permanently abroad enjoy a number of rights that retain their link with the state whose passport they carry.[12] On the other hand, it is also obvious that internal citizens enjoy a much more comprehensive set of rights than both citizens outside the territory and foreigners in the territory. Some of these internal rights have, over time, become tied to residence or employment rather than to the formal status of citizenship, so that foreign immigrants can now also enjoy them. Tomas Hammar has introduced the term 'denizenship' to characterize the legal position of long-term foreign residents, which since 1945 has gradually approached that of citizens in a number of Western democracies (Hammar 1990).[13] A thin conception of citizenship as a bundle of legal rights can therefore reach beyond the narrow framework of 'nationality'. The status of citizenship generates rights outside the sphere of territorial sovereignty, and rights have expanded beyond the formal status within this sphere.

Thin conceptions of citizenship differ from thick ones in regarding rights as prior to obligations. The fundamental reason for the priority of rights is that every political order is coercive (Larmore 1996: 137–8, 220). Individuals can only rationally consent to being subjected to an authority that may legitimately coerce them if this order not only respects their freedom and rights but is necessary to maintain them in the first place. The basic obligation of citizenship to obey the law is therefore conditional upon the rights provided by the same legal order. As T.H. Marshall pointed out, other moral duties 'to live the life of a good citizen, giving such services as one can to promote the welfare of the community' are rather vague 'because the community is so large that the obligation appears remote and unreal' (Marshall 1965: 129). This asymmetry characterizes not only the liberal legitimation of political authority but also the bundle of legal rights and obligations of citizenship in liberal democracies. There is 'a changing balance between rights and duties. Rights have been multiplied, and they are precise' (ibid.: 129). But the core legal obligations are few – paying taxes, compulsory education and military service – and they are not *equal* obligations for *all* citizens in the same way as basic rights are. In order to become universal, rights such as the franchise had first to be disconnected from the unequal obligations of taxpaying or conscription.

Thick conceptions of citizenship often accept this priority of rights as a correct diagnosis of contemporary liberal democracy, but deplore it from a normative perspective. Socialist, nationalist and communitarian theories fear that the liberal priority for rights promotes the bourgeois rather than the citizen, disconnects the individual from the causes of the nation or encourages the narrow interests of particular groups against the common good of the polity. Although the community is large and anonymous, and although the rights citizens enjoy no longer depend on their individual contributions, they should learn to think about the polity as if it were an extended family, a circle of friends or an association whose members are tied to each other by special obligations. Excessive individualism and group particularism are the major ills of liberal democracy, which can only be cured by inculcating in citizens a strong sense of obligation.

Civic republicanism appears to occupy again a middle ground with regard to the proper balance between rights and obligations. At the heart of the republican vision are rights that are *simultaneously* obligations for their bearers.[14] And while enjoying civil rights makes individuals members of a civil society, only those rights that go along with obligations make them members of a self-governing polity. Core rights that fall into this category are those of public education, political participation, military service in the defence of the republic and resistance against oppression and tyranny. These republican rights are at the same time moral duties and – apart from the last one in the list – states can legitimately turn them into legally enforceable obligations where citizens fail to perform them. All states do so with regard to education requirements, but they may also extend the scope of rights-as-obligations by drafting soldiers or by obligatory voting.

Practices and virtues

The communitarian and republican emphasis on obligations promotes the active citizen and leads quite naturally to the idea of citizenship as a practice rather than a mere legal status of bearers of rights. This brings us finally to the last row in Table 3.1. Of course, all rights of citizenship create ranges of action protected by the law. However, while thin liberal citizenship protects autonomous practices of citizens who pursue their own private goals, it does not necessarily generate practices of *citizenship*. The liberal regime of rights merely allows for active citizenship but cannot directly bring it about. If civil and political rights are formulated as negative liberties, this means that refraining from a protected action is just as legitimate as performing it. Citizens are free to form voluntary associations or to vote, but do not have to engage in these practices. Social rights are different because they involve positive benefits rather than non-interference.[15] However, here the emphasis is on the agency of providing institutions rather than of citizens, whose role is generally that of recipients rather than of agents. In a purely rights-based conception, citizenship may then remain a merely passive status. From some perspectives this is not to be deplored. In a Schumpeterian theory of democracy, it is safer to leave the business of governing to competent élites and to reduce the involvement of citizens to a periodic opportunity to deselect bad leaders (Schumpeter 1950). Likewise, for libertarians extending citizenship beyond negative liberties entails a dual danger of empowering the state to encroach on individual freedom (e.g. by levying taxes for redistributive social rights) and of empowering tyrannical majorities (e.g. through plebiscitarian forms of political participation).

For thicker conceptions, the egotistic individual who uses his or her liberties only in order to pursue private interests and the passive citizen who does not care to form and defend a political opinion or to cast a vote are not full members of the polity. In their view, the polity is not only sustained by a mode of legitimation which emphasizes mutual obligations, but also by practices in which citizens must engage so that the imagined political community becomes a real experience in their daily lives. In this regard the idea of citizenship as a practice goes beyond the moral discourse about political obligations.[16] A political community that lives up to the standards of communitarian or republican expectations is one where citizens do not have to be reminded of their obligations but identify their private interest with the common good and habitually engage in public practices of good citizenship. Civic virtues do not present themselves as legal obligations, i.e. commandments issued by an external authority. Their habitual character distinguishes them also from the imperative nature of moral duties that are personally experienced as the call of an internal conscience defending a higher moral standpoint detached from individual interests.

When nationalists write about the virtues of citizens they emphasize the readiness to kill or die in battle for the survival or the expansion of the community. However, the virtues of citizenship are only at rare occasions heroic ones which involve sacrificing one's property, social status or even one's life for the sake of the polity. These are called for when the community is threatened by enemies from outside or by authoritarian power from inside. In the former case conscription is anyway enforced as a legal obligation. The major and constant danger in liberal democracy is slackness in citizenship practices. Education is not enough to acquire the civic virtues that are required against this danger and their rhetorical invocation is not sufficient to sustain them. What is needed is constant practices that make good citizenship a widespread habit (van Gunsteren 1998). In a certain sense, these citizenship practices can be learned only 'on the job'. This leaves open the question which kinds of public policies and institutional reforms could foster civic virtues without unduly constraining the rights and liberties of citizenship.[17]

There are three different ways of looking at the controversies between thin libertarian and thick communitarian conceptions of citizenship. One is to regard them as irreconcilable opposites. We would then have to choose between either the left row or the right row of Table 3.1. The second option is to see them as endpoints of a continuum. Positions somewhere between the extremes, such as liberal republican ones, are then not necessarily messy compromises but could be coherent and intellectually appealing. I would, however, opt for a third and deliberately eclectic strategy that allows for various recombinations of the dimensions and conceptions. We choose one position as a starting point rather than as a complete conception and expand it gradually as we find it necessary to include the concerns addressed by apparently rival theories. In this way we could chart a path through the conceptual maze of citizenship. Unless we already have a clear target before our eyes we will need a sort of compass for this venture. The norms of equal and full membership, which I have suggested initially as defining principles of citizenship, could serve as such a guideline.

Starting from thick conceptions of citizenship carries not only the danger of producing a sterile contrast between idealized assumptions about political community, on the one hand, and 'degenerate' citizenship in actually existing liberal democracies, on the other hand. It will also blind us to some of the most important challenges for citizenship in contemporary societies, which have to do with the allocation of membership and rights. Thick conceptions generally take the dimensions of membership and rights for granted and see the central task in enriching them with obligations and practices. Their view of the polity is an internal one that presupposes clearly defined external boundaries, full inclusion and equal rights as given features of democratic nation states. However, as I have pointed out in the introduction, none of these achievements is really so obvious and unchallenged. Starting from a thin conception of membership as a legal status will allow us to draw a more complex and more realistic picture of contemporary citizenship conflicts than can usually be found in republican and communitarian accounts. The three conceptions I have identified should then not be seen as strict alternatives but rather as clusters of arguments[18] that are neither necessarily internally coherent nor mutually incompatible. The general norm of equal and full membership does not itself ground a preference for any of these conceptions. When we consider its implications in the different contexts of citizenship we will find ourselves drawn to various arguments that have been ideologically linked with certain conceptions but can be disconnected from these and recombined into a more attractive and comprehensive one. This may sound like an exercise in arbitrariness and eclecticism, but there is an underlying feature that distinguishes the approach I would be inclined to defend. While each of the three conceptions taken by itself is monistic, the account that will emerge from the procedure I have suggested is necessarily pluralistic. It is pluralistic in a double sense, not only in its willingness to combine traditionally opposed ideas about citizenship, but even more so by taking into account the impact of various group identities and interests on the citizens' relation to the political community.

Differentiated memberships

I will argue in this section, first, that principles guiding the allocation of citizens to states in the international state system pursue contradictory aims and produce unintended results. Second, I want to show that, far from being already sufficiently respected in existing policies of allocating citizenship, liberal democratic norms would demand quite radical reforms. Third, I suggest that citizenship theories have also tended to ignore the contestation of territorial boundaries between and within states by nationalist movements. My conclusion is that the outcome of applying these norms to the present state system is a structure of vertical and horizontal multiplicity of membership which requires a corresponding differentiation of citizenship rights.

The allocation of nationality

Legal theory generally considers states as a unity of three elements: territory, population and political authority. Political authority is then, on the one hand, grounded in *territorial* sovereignty, which turns every person present in this territory into an addressee of the laws, while the idea of *popular* sovereignty, on the other hand, refers to a set of persons who are defined as members of the polity rather than as residents in the territory. Before the introduction of universal adult franchise, the difference between both sets of populations was marked by gender, class and racist barriers. Although such markers of identity still serve in many ways to exclude groups from equal access and participation, legal equality has been largely achieved along these dimensions. This leaves the status of resident foreign citizens as the major remaining instance of formal exclusion. Their subjection to territorial sovereignty without representation in the making of laws is a deviation from the basic norms of democratic legitimation of political authority. At the same time, their continuing external citizenship in the polity of origin is a limitation on the territorial sovereignty of their state of residence. Migration produces a double incongruity between territorial and popular sovereignty. Internally, the polity does not include every permanent resident person and externally it extends into the territory of other states. Congruity would imply that the order of membership in polities matches the allocation of territories to states. In the contemporary world each point on the land mass of the globe belongs at any given point in time to one state and to one state only. A matching order of membership would have the same boundaries as state territories and be similarly complete and discrete so that there is neither statelessness nor multiple nationality.

The simplest way to resolve this contradiction would be a continuous reallocation of citizenship which automatically naturalizes every resident and denaturalizes every emigrant after a certain time.[19] The deviations generated by migration would then be only temporary and could thus be reconciled with maintaining a general norm of congruity. However, this solution clashes again with a second set of principles pertaining to liberal democratic rights and to the scope of state sovereignty. It violates, first, the idea that legitimate political authority can only be exercised over persons whose membership is voluntary. Because of the coercive nature and the pervasive impact of political decisions for the life of individuals, the criteria for voluntary membership in a polity differ from those of voluntary associations in civil society.[20] Membership is normally acquired without consent at birth and liberal states cannot exclude their members like a club. The two remaining tests for voluntary affiliation to a democratic polity are that no adult foreigner can be naturalized without his or her consent and that emigrants must be allowed to voluntarily renounce their citizenship of origin. Automatic naturalization or denaturalization would violate these requirements of consent.[21]

This solution would also contradict a principle enshrined in international law according to which it is for each state to determine under its own law who are its nationals.[22] Such a right of 'self-determination' in the allocation of citizenship has been a traditional core aspect of sovereignty jealously guarded by states against attempts to impose effective constraints in international law or to move towards international harmonization of the rules for loss and acquisition of citizenship.[23] The paradoxes of this situation are highlighted in the European context, where access to the common status of EU citizenship is regulated by the 15 different nationality laws of the member states. Although there is some European *convergence* in this area that results from shared democratic standards and similar conditions concerning permanent immigration (Weil 1999),[24] so far the institutions of the EU have not dared to *harmonize* the nationality laws of their member states.

Liberal democracies differ in their rules for naturalization and, more importantly, also in their rules for the transmission of citizenship to new generations. Efforts to adopt binding rules for avoiding the irregularities of statelessness and multiple nationality have so far been rather unsuccessful.[25] The problem is deeper than just a lack of coordination. Most states whose governments still regard dual citizenship as undesirable systematically contribute to its proliferation. Those which pass on their citizenship by *ius sanguinis* thereby produce dual citizenship for the offspring of mixed marriages as well as for all children of their emigrants in *ius soli* states. And countries which adopt *ius soli* for births in their territory, such as the US or Canada, at the same time use a principle of descent for attributing their citizenship to children born to their emigrants living elsewhere.

The inclusion of migrants

Our initial definition of citizenship as full and equal membership in a liberal democratic polity suggests alternative principles for the allocation of nationality. The first step in such an argument is to interpret full membership as referring not only to a comprehensive range of rights, but also to a comprehensive inclusion of persons. The question is then how to determine the range of persons to be included. As our discussion has just shown, republican and nationalist ambitions to create non-overlapping sets of membership are self-defeating. If all polities have the sovereign power to determine their own boundaries they cannot be prevented from naturalizing another state's citizens and cannot be forced to release or denaturalize their emigrants when these acquire another nationality. And if membership is determined by descent or cultural belonging, migration will inevitably generate mixed cases. The alternative is to apply the principles for the allocation of *rights* also to the admission to, and exit from, the legal *status*. A right *to* citizenship should then be inclusive and optional in the same way as the rights *of* citizenship. Such an individual right to citizenship would have several components: a first element is strong protection against statelessness resulting from denaturalization, from cases where neither *ius soli* nor *ius sanguinis* apply at birth[26] and from exclusionary initial definitions of citizenship in newly-formed states.[27] A second element is an individual right to the citizenship of the country where one has been born or has been resident for several years.[28] A third feature would allow individuals to retain their external citizenship after emigration but also to renounce it if they so wish upon acquiring the new citizenship of their state of residence.[29]

These interpretations of full inclusion do not balance the concerns of democratic legitimacy and state sovereignty in a symmetrical way but clearly side with the former against the latter. Including the resident population in the polity is more important than the dubious state privilege of controlling admission to its membership.[30] And the democratic principle with regard to the determination of membership is not to let a majority decide who ought to be accepted as a citizen, but to admit all those who are already subjected to political decisions by virtue of their permanent residence in the territory. Furthermore, the rights of emigrants to maintain their ties to societies of origin are more important than concerns about diminished territorial sovereignty or about conflicting loyalties among dual citizens. Yet the minimal criteria of voluntary membership have to be respected, too, and this implies an individual option not to adopt the citizenship of one's state of residence. Migrants may have many different reasons not to naturalize. Some fear the loss of external citizenship rights in their countries of origin or react to ethnic discrimination by turning their nationality into a symbol of collective identity and pride. Privileged migrants (such as EU citizens in other member states of the Union) mostly feel that naturalization would only marginally improve their position. As a result, citizenship as a legal status cannot be made fully inclusive in liberal democracies exposed to transnational migration. This is, however, no serious limitation because the range of inclusion ought to refer primarily to citizenship rights rather than to nationality as a status. The answer to the deficit is to extend rights of citizenship to permanent-resident foreigners. Suppose these 'denizens' enjoy all basic liberties and social rights of citizens as well as the local vote and other avenues of political representation. Under such conditions the national franchise and access to high public offices could remain tied to the formal status without a serious problem for democratic legitimacy. Foreign residents could choose to obtain these core rights of political citizenship by naturalizing. Moreover, immigrants would then no longer naturalize in order to escape legal discrimination to which they are exposed as aliens. Removing this instrumental incentive may lower application rates but will also create conditions under which naturalization can be motivated by a wish to fully belong to the polity and by a commitment to participate in its political affairs, i.e. the sort of reasons communitarian and republican conceptions of thick citizenship are keen to promote.[31]

While this suggests how a conception that starts from legal membership and liberal rights can take into account concerns about citizenship obligations and practices, it is obvious that these should not serve as a pretext for exclusion. In strong republican versions of citizenship, the very act of emigrating (unless it is motivated by political oppression) has been regarded as a disloyalty by which citizens put themselves outside the political community. Nationalist conceptions have insisted on an indissoluble bond of allegiance, which can neither be voluntarily renounced after emigration nor voluntarily acquired after immigration. In contrast with both these approaches, a liberal one has to make the rules of citizenship compatible with migratory practices. In this view, migration is not an obstacle, but a test case for the voluntary character of membership in a liberal polity. It puts individuals in a position where they confront a positive choice of affiliation that most native born citizens never have to face. Providing the adequate options for this essential choice while securing a maximally inclusive polity are the two goals which together require a transnational differentiation of citizenship.

Prima facie, the outcome of such full inclusion of migrants seems to violate the other core norm of equality. Instead of one single status that is the same for all members we get a variety of relations of individuals to the polity: external and internal citizens, transient migrants and denizens,[32] citizens with one and with more than one nationality would differ in a number of ways in terms of their rights and their membership status. It could seem that this differentiation reintroduces a structure of inequality which had been overcome when class and gender distinctions between passive and active citizenship were abolished. Yet this worry confuses equality with homogeneity.[33] As Ronald Dworkin (1977),

Charles Larmore (1996) and other theorists have pointed out, the basic norm for liberal democracy is equal respect, not equal treatment. Identity of legal status is one instance of equal treatment and can be overridden by concerns of equal respect for individuals who are differently positioned. Under conditions of transnational mobility, equal respect for natives and migrants means recognizing the specific bonds of the latter to societies of origin as well as destination. And this can only be done by differentiating both formal membership and rights.

Since World War II, liberal democracies have, to some extent, followed this path. However, apart from rare exceptions they have not explicitly embraced the underlying normative principles. Contrary to the by-now irreversible *formal* inclusion of groups previously excluded on the basis of class, gender, religion or race, the inclusion of migrants remains precarious. Western democracies have clung to a conception of sovereignty that allows for tightening the admission to citizenship as well as for depriving resident foreigners of rights already granted to them. In the 1990s we have witnessed a wave of such exclusionary policies even in traditional societies of immigration, such as the US, Australia or France.[34]

The allocation of territory

A second major difficulty for mainstream theories of citizenship, which take the membership dimension for granted, emerges from ethnic and national diversity within democratic polities. The most radical challenge is raised by nationalist movements for secession or unification, like those in Québec or in Northern Ireland. Liberal theorists have advocated two contrary principles of how to deal with such claims for revising the territorial borders of existing states. One school defends the view that secession is only justified if a state explicitly discriminates against an ethnic group and thus seriously fails to treat all its citizens equally,[35] while the other camp suggests that democratic legitimacy requires not only an individual right to emigrate, but also the right of collective exit by secession for any regional majority.[36] These two opposed liberal theories of legitimate secession derived from injustice or from choice confront a nationalist approach, which attributes a right to form an independent state to entities with a claim to nationhood and regards secession as an ultimate but legitimate way of transforming multinational states into nation states.[37]

This is a complex debate which I cannot even attempt to summarize here.[38] The parallel with the challenge of migration is that there are situations in which groups of individuals who live within the territory of a state conceive of themselves as members of a distinct political community different from the polity of their state of residence, and often are also regarded by national majorities as less than full members. The difference is that migration involves the question to which extent individuals can choose and combine different forms of membership and bundles of citizenship rights offered by existing states, while secession raises the question of whether groups can choose the shape of the state to which they want to belong. I believe that a choice-based approach to secession is not acceptable because it would fatally undermine the stability of political association which is a precondition for the protective as well as the liberating effects of democratic citizenship.[39] The nationalist interpretation of self-determination has much the same effect by creating an incentive for breaking up multinational states. Given the large and potentially ever-increasing number of would-be nations, a principle of self-determination that is no longer constrained by present concerns for the territorial integrity of existing states is a recipe for the proliferation of violent conflict. Moreover, the argument first advanced by John Stuart Mill and recently restated by David Miller that 'free institutions are next to impossible in a country made up of different nationalities' (Mill 1972: 392, Miller 1995: 98) has lost much of its plausibility in view of powerful tendencies towards growing ethnic, religious and national diversity even within relatively homogeneous liberal democracies.

However, the position that existing borders should never be challenged as long as all citizens enjoy full and equal individual membership is also hard to accept. It rests on a republican dogma of unique and homogeneous membership that does not allow for federal arrangements in which regional units with a distinct cultural character are perceived as autonomous political communities within the larger polity.[40] Actual political conflicts about secession nearly always emerge from such a federation between previously or potentially autonomous communities. And the grievances upon which secessionists build their case are not necessarily about individual discrimination, but often about a violation of federal arrangements that grant minorities self-government in their territories and special representation in the institutions of the larger state. This explains why secessionist conflicts have not only emerged in oppressive regimes but also in liberal democracies. The proper answer to these challenges is not to transform all such multinational federations into homogeneous nation states. This could only be achieved by oppressive means. The only alternative for liberal democracies is to negotiate fair terms of federation that allow minorities partial self-government but at the same time involve them in the collective decisions of the larger polity and thereby also commit them towards a common future of that state.[41] Such a federalist approach allows therefore, once more, to develop the dimensions of obligations and practices of citizenship without defining the larger polity as their exclusive focus. Minority members may well develop dual loyalties which need not contradict each other as long as the terms of federation are fair.[42]

This response implicitly relies on the premise that a collective desire for self-government which has been asserted over several generations should be taken as a sufficient indicator for the existence of a political community, but not as a sufficient reason to claim independent statehood. While a morally plausible challenge to existing borders has to provide evidence of severe collective grievances, the liberal paradigm of choice ought to prevail in recognizing the self-definition of groups as political communities. For national minorities, just as for migrants, full inclusion and equal membership cannot be achieved short of taking into account their special ties to different political communities. In the case of minorities, a basic reason for this is that the public culture of every liberal democracy is deeply immersed in particular traditions. This is most obviously true for linguistic identities. Unless minorities enjoy special representation and partial autonomy they will be disadvantaged in a public sphere dominated by cultural majorities (Kymlicka 1989, Chapter 9). For a theory of citizenship, the consequence is that the misguided ideal of homogeneity ought to be abandoned in favour of acknowledging two kinds of multiplicity of membership: horizontal multiplicity that emerges from migration, and vertical multiplicity that results from recognizing the inclusion of distinct political communities in the wider polity.

Conclusions

This line of thought can be continued in two different directions: one by extending the idea of federation from the sub-national level to supra-national and even global levels, and the other one by supplementing the theory of national minority rights with those of ethnic, cultural and religious groups who cannot reasonably claim territorial autonomy. The foremost example for how supra-national federation can lead to a new kind of citizenship is, of course, the European Union. In this case a federation driven by a desire for lasting peace and common interests in economic integration has developed into a project of becoming a supra-national polity without aspiring for the full sovereignty of a traditional federal state. Union citizenship was formally introduced in the Maastricht Treaty in order to symbolically claim democratic legitimacy for this project. Yet, as I have argued above, it is still a highly ambiguous construction both in terms of the allocation of membership and because of the meagre bundle of rights associated with being a citizen of the Union.[43]

The other extension of the theory would take up the debate about multiculturalism.[44] This controversy illustrates how a former focus on the diversity of interests in the economy and civil society has been gradually replaced by a new emphasis on the diversity of collective identities, with a growing fear that these undermine the cohesive force of common citizenship in the polity. One way to link this debate to citizenship theory is to ask whether cultural rights should be added as a separate dimension to the Marshallian triad of civil, political and economic ones. Another key theme is whether and how group-differentiated and collective rights are compatible with a framework of equal individual citizenship.[45]

The following diagram illustrates the three structures of differentiated membership that result from multinational federalism, transnational migration and multicultural citizenship. Federalism creates a vertically nested multi-level membership so that each citizen is a member of both a self-governing subunit and the wider federation. Transnational migration creates horizontally overlapping multiple membership, most visibly in the case of formal dual citizenship, but also by extending citizenship rights to permanent resident foreigners and to

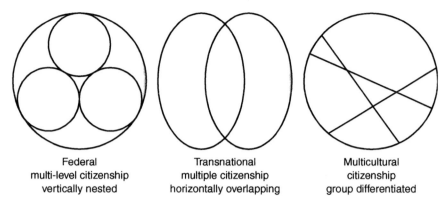

| Federal | Transnational | Multicultural |

Federal
multi-level citizenship
vertically nested

Transnational
multiple citizenship
horizontally overlapping

Multicultural
citizenship
group differentiated

Figure 3.1 Three structures of differentiated citizenship.

emigrants outside the territory. Multicultural citizenship, finally, introduces group differentiated rights into a shared framework of equal citizenship by recognizing particular collective identities related to gender, sexual orientation, religion, racial discrimination or ethnic background. Such rights respond to demands for protection from discrimination, for special exemptions from general obligations of citizenship, or for public resources and recognition.[46]

Both supra-national federation and cultural diversity are difficult questions for citizenship theory, which I cannot try to answer in this brief sketch. Yet even raising them as problems illustrates the inadequacy of approaches that rely on an idealized image of homogeneous polities. In contemporary liberal democracies, diversity is no longer confined to the realm of civil society, but infects the polity itself. A shared political identity that supports good practices of citizenship cannot emerge from ignoring those particular social and cultural identities in civil society that impact on the individual's relation to the polity. Citizenship provides a link between social integration and political legitimacy that necessarily reflects this diversity in its rules for determining membership and in its specification of rights and obligations. I have tried to outline a perspective that is sensitive to this political spill-over effect of social change. If I ought to suggest a label for it I would call it 'liberal pluralism'. It differs not only from republican, communitarian and nationalist conceptions, which build upon a thick conception of citizenship that is no longer adequate for complex modern societies, but also from traditional liberal conceptions, which have paid little attention to the contested boundaries of political community in Western democracies. Yet liberal pluralistic citizenship is not a completely novel and alternative perspective. It uses the established dimensions and conceptions of citizenship, rearranging and recombining them in response to persistent or new forms of exclusion.

Citizenship always has an exclusionary side.[47] It needs territorial borders as well as boundaries of membership. But large-scale migration and multiple collective identities transform some external boundaries into internal ones. European societies are increasingly exposed to both kinds of changes and their conception of citizenship ought to respond to this fact.

Notes

1 See Brubaker (1989: 4).
2 See Hammar (1990), Layton-Henry (1990), Bauböck (1994), Soysal (1994), Jacobson (1996).
3 The term was coined by Charles Tarlton who defined symmetric federalism as 'the extent to which component states share in the conditions and thereby the concerns more or less common to the federal system as a whole' (Tarlton 1965: 861).
4 See Bauböck (1998) for a more extensive discussion of the difference between polity, society and cultural community.
5 Democracy serves as a regulatory ideal for citizenship in three different ways: first, in non-democratic regimes where individuals are citizens merely in the narrow sense of legal nationality but otherwise subjects exposed to arbitrary exercises of power – in such regimes individuals may nevertheless engage in citizenship practices of resistance for which democracy serves as an ideal; second, in transitions to democracy when the political institutions that sustain citizenship rights are being built; and, third, in established liberal democracies as a corrective against the monopolization of politics by a professional elite.
6 It is interesting to note that the norm of equality applies only to the individual right to vote, not to the aggregate effects of representation which are often highly unequal in federal systems. For example, a Senator from California represents about 60 times as many voters as one from Wyoming. See Stepan (1999: 26) for an index of inequality of representation in the territorial chambers of twelve federal states.
7 See Lister (1997: 41).
8 The same term 'nationality' can refer to a thin legal or to a thick cultural conception of membership, which is a source of considerable confusion in the literature.
9 See, for example, de Groot (1989: 13).
10 See Viroli (1995: 117) for an attempt to draw a line between the ethnic particularism of Athenian democracy and the more universalistic thrust of Roman republicanism.
11 See Universal Declaration of Human Rights, Art. 15, International Covenant on Civil and Political Rights, Art. 24.
12 The most important among these is the right to return to this state without being subjected to immigration restrictions. The other fundamental external right is that to diplomatic protection. However, many states go far beyond this minimum by also granting their citizens an absentee ballot or the right to pass on their citizenship to their children born abroad. External citizenship also involves rights under international law towards the state of residence. Foreign citizens are, in some aspects, even privileged compared to internal citizens. The property and liberties of the former are to a lesser extent exposed to the jurisdiction of their state of residence, and diplomatic protection itself is a significant exemption from the general rule of territorial sovereignty (Goodin 1988).
13 Soysal (Plenary lecture at European Sociological Association Conference in Essex 1997) interprets this as 'a recasting of (national) citizenship rights as human (or personhood) rights'. In my view, this development signifies neither a limit (Soysal 1994) nor a decline (Jacobson 1996) of citizenship, but rather a widening range of inclusion that still refers to particular ties of residence or origin.
14 This contrasts with the liberal emphasis on rights like freedom of association and the protection of property, which impose *correlative* obligations of non-interference on other citizens and on the state.

15 The distinction between negative and positive rights is often misleading or over-drawn (Sen 1984). Protecting civil rights requires not merely non-interference by the state, but also the protection against interference by others and therefore a police force; the franchise cannot be exercised without the public provision of voter regis-ters, ballots and voting booths.

16 The emphasis on virtuous practices is also characteristic for an Aristotelian tradition in moral philosophy which contrasts with the duty-based approaches of deontologi-cal as well as utilitarian theories (see Larmore 1996, Chapter 1).

17 'While citizenship theorists bemoan the excessive focus given to rights, they seem reluctant to propose any policies that could be seen as restricting those rights' (Kym-licka and Norman 1994: 368–9).

18 I have to thank Andreas Føllesdal for suggesting this interpretation to me.

19 Alternatively, one might suggest a universal rule of *ius soli* for the transmission of citi-zenship between generations. However, this solution fails for two reasons. First, the problems of incongruity cannot be regarded as merely temporary if they put a whole generation of migrants in an irregular position and, second, those who obtain a citi-zenship by *ius soli* will end up in the same irregular status once they leave their country of birth.

20 See Bauböck (1994: 160–77) for a discussion of the difference between voluntary membership in a polity and other types of association.

21 These constraints are of rather recent origin. Nationality laws in nineteenth-century Europe often gave states wide powers to denaturalize their citizens or to refuse volun-tary expatriation. Some states also naturalized foreigners without their consent. The author of a recent book argues that – provided that multiple nationality is tolerated – automatic naturalization could be reintroduced as a way of guaranteeing the inclu-sion of foreign residents (Rubio-Marín 2000).

22 The Hague Convention on Certain Questions Relating to the Conflict of National-ity Laws of 1930, Art. 1.

23 In its Nottebohm decision of 1955, the International Court of Justice constrained an arbitrary handing out of citizenship by requiring some effective link between citizens and states (see Bar-Yaakov 1961).

24 Although all continental European laws are primarily based on *ius sanguinis*, most immigration countries provide now for facilitated, optional or automatic naturalization for those born in their territory or with parents themselves born in the territory. Many laws have made it easier for naturalization candidates to retain their previous national-ity. Finally, waiting periods and other requirements for discretionary naturalization tend to be reduced. There are, however, still significant exceptions to each of these trends. The recent reform of German nationality has joined the first and third trends, while sounding a retreat on the second one. Among EU members, Austria, Luxemburg and Greece have remained exceptionally restrictive in their nationality laws.

25 The 1963 Council of Europe Convention on the Reduction of Cases of Multiple Nationality has been recently replaced by a 1997 European Convention on Nation-ality that is much more permissive in this regard. This new convention also addresses the problem of statelessness, which has reemerged on a massive scale as a result of the break-up of the Soviet Union and Yugoslavia.

26 E.g. children found in the territory after birth whose parents' citizenship cannot be determined.

27 After gaining independence Estonia and Latvia adopted nationality laws that imposed long waiting periods and harsh admission requirements on their Russian minorities. See Brubaker (1992).

28 For a defence of this right, see Carens (1989).

29 These principles leave considerable space for variations in implementation. They do not require, for example, automatic *ius soli* for the first generation of immigrant origin born in the territory.

30 This does not imply that states are equally constrained in controlling admission to their territories. See Bauböck (1994: Chapter 13), Bader (1997).
31 See Bauböck (1994: 102–15).
32 Not all kinds of human mobility generate claims to an extensive range of citizenship rights in the country of present abode. While tourists and travelling professionals or business people do need access to basic civil rights, they will remain legitimately excluded from the political franchise and many social rights. It is the immigrants' prolonged residence, which turns them into members of society and exposes them to the long-term effects of political decisions, that gives a claim to more extensive citizenship.
33 This false dichotomy has been criticized in feminist theory as well as in theories of multiculturalism. For recent statements see Lister (1997: 91–100) or Parekh (1998).
34 The 1996 Welfare Reform Act in the US deprived resident aliens of benefits in most federal cash assistance programmes; in 1996 the Australian government increased waiting periods for welfare benefits to two years for new immigrants; in 1993 France abolished the automatic acquisition of nationality at majority by persons born in France of immigrant parents. The US reform has been partially reversed and the French reform has been fully reversed since.
35 Buchanan (1991), Habermas (1996: 163–71), Chwaszcza (1998).
36 Beran (1984), Gauthier (1994), Wellman (1995), Pogge (1997).
37 Raz and Margalit (1990), Miller (1995, Chapter 4). For more recent contributions to the secession debate see Lehning (1998) and Moore (1998).
38 For a more extensive discussion see Bauböck (1999).
39 This caveat substantiates my earlier objections against a contractual conception of the polity that regards it as a purely voluntary association.
40 In the US-American tradition, republicanism embraces regional federalism because it allows for smaller-scale self-government and as part of the system of checks and balances. But it vehemently opposes the idea of multinational federation, which articulates the distinct national identities of various parts of the federation. In Europe, Germany and Austria are regional federal states, whereas Belgium, Switzerland and Spain approach a multinational model.
41 For a more extensive statement of this argument see Bauböck (2000).
42 The Italian-Austrian settlement of the ethnic conflict in South Tyrol, the transformation of post-francist Spain into an *estado de las autonomías* and the recent devolution in Scotland and Wales can be mentioned as by-and-large successful European examples.
43 On the latter point see Shaw (1997).
44 The idea of differentiated citizenship was first introduced by Iris Young in a defence of special representation for culturally or economically oppressed groups (Young 1989). Kymlicka and Norman (1994) have applied it to the accommodation of cultural and national identities. More recently Lister (1997) has argued for 'differentiated universalism' as a general approach to citizenship.
45 See the excellent collection edited by Kymlicka and Shapiro (1997).
46 See Levy (1997) for a general typology of cultural rights.
47 See Bader (1997).

References

Arendt, H. (1967) *The Origins of Totalitarianism* (revised edition). London: George Allen & Unwin.
Aristotle (1981) *The Politics*. London: Penguin Books.
Bader, V. (ed.) (1997) 'Fairly open borders', in *Citizenship and Exclusion*, V. Bader (ed.). London: Macmillan Press.

Bar-Yaakov, N. (1961) *Dual Nationality*, Stevens & Sons Ltd., The Library of World Affairs, London.

Barber, B. (1984) *Strong Democracy: Participatory Politics for a New Age*. Berkeley, CA: University of California Press.

Bauböck, R. (1994) *Transnational Citizenship. Membership and Rights in International Migration*. Aldershot, UK: Edward Elgar.

Bauböck, R. (1998) 'Sharing history and future? Time horizons of democratic membership in an age of migration', *Constellations*, 4, 3: 320–45.

Bauböck, R. (1999) 'Why secession is not like divorce', in *Nationalism and Internationalism in the Post-Cold War Era*, K. Goldmann, U. Hannerz and C. Westin (eds). London: UCL Press.

Bauböck, R. (2000) 'Why stay together? A pluralist approach to secession and federation', in *Citizenship in Diverse Societies. Theory and Practice*, W. Kymlicka and W. Norman (eds). Oxford: Oxford University Press.

Beran, H. (1984) 'A liberal theory of secession', *Political Studies* 32: 21–31.

Brubaker, R.W. (1989) 'Introduction', in *Immigration and the Politics of Citizenship in Europe and North America*, W.R. Brubaker (ed.). Lanham, MD: University Press of America.

Brubaker, R.W. (1992) Citizenship struggles in Soviet successor states, *International Migration Review* xxvi, 2, summer: 269–90.

Buchanan, A. (1991) *Secession. The Morality of Political Divorce from Fort Sumter to Lithuania and Quebec*. Boulder, CO: Westview Press.

Carens, J.H. (1989) 'Membership and morality', in *Immigration and the Politics of Citizenship in Europe and North America*, R.W. Brubaker (ed.). Lanham and London: University Press of America.

Chwaszcza, C. (1998) 'Selbstbestimmung, Sezession und Souveräntität. Überlegungen zur normativen Bedeutung politischer Grenzen', in *Philosophie der Internationalen Beziehungen*, W. Kersting und C. Chwaszcza (eds). Frankfurt: Suhrkamp.

de Groot, G.-R. (1989) *Staatsangehörigkeitsrecht im Wandel. Eine rechtsvergleichende Studie über Erwerbs- und Verlustgründe der Staatsangehörigkeit*. Köln: Carl Heymans Verlag.

Dworkin, R. (1977) *Taking Rights Seriously*. Cambridge, MA: Harvard University Press.

Gauthier, D. (1994) 'Breaking up: an essay on secession', *Canadian Journal of Philosophy* 24: 357–72.

Gellner, E. (1983) *Nations and Nationalism*. Oxford: Blackwell.

Goodin, R. (1988) 'What is so special about out fellow countrymen?' *Ethics* 98, July: 663–86.

Habermas, J. (1992) *Faktizität und Geltung*. Frankfurt am Main: Suhrkamp.

Habermas, J. (1996) *Die Einbeziehung des Anderen. Studien zur politischen Theorie*. Frankfurt: Suhrkamp.

Hammar, T. (1990) *Democracy and the Nation State. Aliens, Denizens and Citizens in a World of International Migration*. Aldershot: Avebury.

Jacobson, D. (1996) *Rights Across Borders. Immigration and the Decline of Citizenship*. Baltimore: Johns Hopkins University Press.

Jellinek, G. (1892) *System der subjektiven öffentlichen Rechte*. Freiburg: Mohr.

Kymlicka, W. (1989) *Liberalism, Community, and Culture*. Oxford: Clarendon Press.

Kymlicka, W. and Norman, W. (1994) 'The return of the citizen: a survey of recent work on citizenship theory', *Ethics* 104, January: 352–81.

Kymlicka, W. and Shapiro, I. (eds) (1997) *Ethnicity and Group Rights*, NOMOS XXXIX, New York: New York University Press.

Larmore, C. (1996) *The Morals of Modernity*. Cambridge: Cambridge University Press.

Layton-Henry, Z. (ed.) (1990) *The political rights of migrant workers in Western Europe*. London: Sage.

Lehning, P. (1998) *Theories of Secession*. London: Routledge.

Levy, J.T. (1997) 'Classifying cultural rights', in *Ethnicity and Group Rights*, NOMOS XXXIX. W. Kymlicka and I. Shapiro (eds). New York: New York University Press.

Lister, R. (1997) *Citizenship. Feminist Perspectives*. London: Macmillan.

Marshall, T.H. (1965) 'Citizenship and social class', in *Class, Citizenship, and Social Development. Essays by T.H. Marshall*. New York: Anchor Books.

Mill, J.S. (1972) 'Considerations on representative government', in *Utilitarianism, On Liberty and Considerations on Representative Government*. London: Everyman's Library.

Miller, D. (1995) *On Nationality*. Oxford: Oxford University Press.

Moore, M. (ed.) (1998) *National Self-Determination and Secession*. Oxford: Oxford University Press.

Parekh, B. (1998) 'Equality in a multicultural society', *Citizenship Studies* 2, 3: 397–411.

Pogge, T. (1997) 'Group rights and ethnicity', in *Ethnicity and Group Rights*, NOMOS XXXIX. W. Kymlicka and I. Shapiro (eds). New York: New York University Press.

Raz, J. and Margalit, A. (1990) 'National self-determination', *The Journal of Philosophy* 87, 9.

Rubio-Marín, R. (2000) *Immigration as a Democratic Challenge*. Cambridge, UK: Cambridge University Press.

Schumpeter, J.A. (1950) *Capitalism, Socialism and Democracy*, third edition. New York: Harper Torchbooks.

Sen, A. (1984) 'Rights and capabilities', in *Resources, Values and Development*. Oxford: Basil Blackwell.

Shaw, J. (1997) 'Citizenship of the union: Towards post-national membership?', *Jean Monnet Working Paper* 6/97: www.law.harvard.edu/Programs/JeanMonnet

Soysal, Y.N. (1994) *Limits of Citizenship. Migrants and Postnational Membership in Europe*. Chicago: University of Chicago Press.

Spinner, J. (1994) *The Boundaries of Citizenship. Race, Ethnicity, and Nationality in the Liberal State*. Baltimore: The Johns Hopkins University Press.

Stepan, A. (1999) 'Federalism and democracy: beyond the U.S. model', *Journal of Democracy* 10, 4: 19–34.

Tarlton, C.D. (1965) 'Symmetry and asymmetry as elements of federalism: a theoretical speculation', *The Journal of Politics* 27: 861–74.

van Gunsteren, H. (1998) *A Theory of Citizenship. Organizing Plurality in Contemporary Democracies*. Boulder, CO: Westview Press.

Viroli, M. (1995) *For Love of Country. An Essay on Patriotism and Nationalism*. Oxford: Clarendon Press.

Weil, P. (1999) *Access to Citizenship*, report prepared for the Comparative Citizenship Project of the Carnegie Endowment for International Peace, June 1999.

Wellman, C.H. (1995) 'A defense of secession and political self-determination', *Philosophy and Public Affairs* 24, 2: 142–71.

Young, I.M. (1989) 'Polity and group difference: a critique of the ideal of universal citizenship', *Ethics* 99: 250–74.

4 The narration of difference

'Cultural stuff', ethnic projects and identities[1]

Nira Yuval-Davis

Cultures and identities occupy central positions in contemporary analytical and political projects. Carl-Ulrik Schierup has argued that

> a general 'culturization' of the political language has taken place. Here, strategies of dominance as well as those of rebellion become increasingly phrased in the culturized terms of ethnic particularity.
>
> (1995: 319)

Stuart Hall points out that 'there has been a veritable discursive explosion in recent years around the concept of "identity"' (1996: 1). This chapter discusses the interrelationship between cultures and identities and the ways they relate to notions of ethnicity, fundamentalism, hybridity and cultural rights. Some of the implications of these for contemporary constructions of 'multi-layered citizenship' will also be discussed. The chapter concludes with a brief introduction of 'transversal politics' as a possible political project which can begin to tackle some of the issues raised here.

The notion of culture

Even more than many other central concepts in the social sciences, the definition and meaning of the term 'culture' has been contested. Raymond Williams, the 'father' of 'Cultural Studies', has suggested three meanings for the term (1983: 90) – that of a general process of intellectual, spiritual and aesthetic development (culture as 'civilization'); one of 'the works and practices of intellectual and artistic activity' ('high culture') and one which is 'a particular way of life, whether of people, a period or a group'. It is this last one which, as Anthony Giddens points out (1989: 31), sociologists tend to use. According to him, this way of life is composed from 'the values the members of a given group hold, the norms they follow and the material goods they create' (Giddens op. cit.: 31).

The development of the concept of culture in the social sciences has been determined for a long time by the cyclical debate between those who hold universalist and relativist paradigms of culture (Friedman 1994). According to the first perspective there is one generic human culture in which different people and groupings have particular rank, according to their 'stage of development' which is often described in evolutionary terms. This is rejected by those who hold the relativist perspective according to which different civilizations have different cultures which need to be understood and/or judged on their own terms.

In spite of the difference between these two perspectives and the perpetual debate between them, they both share, as Chatterjee (1986) has pointed out, an essentialist view of 'culture' as having specific, fixed 'cultural stuff' of symbols, ways of behaviour and artifacts which coherently and unproblematically constitute cultures of specific national and ethnic collectivities. Internal differentiations and differences in positionings cannot be accounted for in either of these two approaches.

A much more useful way of theorizing culture has been developed during the last few years, using discourse analyses inspired by both Gramsci and Foucault, in which cultures have been transformed from static reified homogenous phenomena common to all members of national and ethnic collectivities, into dynamic social processes operating in contested terrains in which different voices become more or less hegemonic in their offered interpretations of the world (Bottomley 1992, Bhabha 1994, Friedman 1994). Cultural discourses often resemble more a battleground of meaning rather than a shared point of departure. Cultural homogeneity in this view would be a result of hegemonization, and it would always be limited and more noticeable in the centre rather than in the social margins, being affected by the social positioning of its carriers. As Gill Bottomley claims, '"Culture", in the sense of ideas, beliefs and practices that delineate particular ways of being in the world, also generate conscious and unconscious forms of resistance – to homogenization, to devaluation, to marginalising by those who fear difference' (1993: 12).

This raises questions about continuity and persistence of cultures as well as about the relationships between different cultures. Smith (1986) and Armstrong (1982) both argue that cultural myths and symbols have an enduring ability which is reproduced generation after generation, notwithstanding changing historical and material conditions. However, this seeming endurability can be very misleading. Firstly, because our view of it stems from a very particular temporal perspective – we can see all the cultural stuff that has endured all these historical changes and survived. We cannot be fully aware, however, how much cultural stuff has *not* survived historical change, archaeological and historical research notwithstanding. Moreover, even with cultural stuff that has survived historical changes, their meanings can and do undergo radical changes and often they become just symbolic markers of identity (Gans 1979, Armstrong 1982). Similarly, while some portray the world in terms of clashes between separate and opposing civilizations (Hartman 1995), others are much more aware of the synthetic nature of all contemporary cultures, their appropriations of symbolic artifacts and meanings from other civilizations and their own internal heterogeneity (Bhabha op. cit.).

Although, analytically, the discourse of culture and religion is distinct from that of power relations (Assad 1993), concretely and historically it is always embedded in them. This is true not only in relation to hierarchies of power within the cultural institutions and their relations to more general structures of class and power within the society. It is also relevant in relation to the cultural imagination and its hierarchies of desirability as well as to the constructions of inclusions and exclusions (King 1995).

Cultures operate within both social and spatial contexts (Dwyer, in Gunew and Yeatman 1993) which cannot be understood separately from the time dimension (Massey 1994). Different positionings, both socially and geographically, would affect the ways cultures are articulated and used, both inside and outside collectivities. Gerd Bauman (1994) has pointed out that, while dominant discourse assumes the congruence of culture and community, demotic (of the people) discourse tends to deny this. A clear example of such a 'demotic' discourse has been the slogan of Southall Black Sisters and Women Against Fundamentalism when they chanted in anti-domestic violence demonstrations in Southall and in countering the Islamist anti-Rushdie demonstration – 'Women's tradition – resistance, not submission!'

Rather than a fixed and homogenous body of tradition and custom, 'cultural stuff', therefore, needs to be described as a rich resource, usually full of internal contradictions, which is used selectively by different social agents in various social projects within specific power relations and political discourse in and outside the collectivity. Gender, class, membership in a collectivity, stage in the life cycle, ability – all affect the access and availability of these resources and the specific positionings from which they are being used.

Identity narratives and ethnic projects

It is important, therefore, to differentiate and avoid the conflation of cultural discourse, identity narratives and ethnic processes (Anthias and Yuval-Davis 1992, Yuval-Davis 1994). Identities – individual and collective – are specific forms of cultural narratives which constitute commonalities and differences between self and others, interpreting their social positioning in more or less stable ways. These often relate to myths (which may or may not be historically valid) of common origin, and to myths of common destiny. Martin points out the close relationships between identity narratives and political processes:

> the identity narrative channels political emotions so that they can fuel efforts to modify the balance of power; it transforms the perception of the past and the present; it changes the organization of human groups and creates new ones; it alters cultures by emphasizing certain traits and skewing its meanings and logic. The identity narrative brings forth a new interpretation of the world in order to modify it.
>
> (Martin 1995: 13)

Identity narratives often constitute major tools of ethnic projects. Ethnicity relates to the politics of collectivity boundaries, and by using identity narratives, dividing the world into 'us' and 'them'. Ethnic projects are continuously engaged in processes of struggle and negotiation aimed, from specific positionings within the collectivities, at promoting the collectivity or perpetuating its advantages, via access to state and civil society powers (Yuval-Davis 1994).

Ethnicity, according to this definition is, therefore, primarily a political process which constructs the collectivity and 'its interest', not only as a result of the general positioning of the collectivity in relation to others in the society, but also as a result of the specific relations of those engaged in 'ethnic politics' with others within that collectivity. Gender, class, political, religious and other differences play central roles in the construction of specific ethnic politics and different ethnic projects of the same collectivity can be engaged in intense competitive struggles for hegemonic positions. Some of these projects can involve different constructions of the actual boundaries of the collectivity (as, for example, has been the case in the debate about the boundaries of the 'Black' community in Britain (Modood 1988, 1994, Brah 1991). Ethnicity is not specific to oppressed and minority groupings. On the contrary, one of the measures of the success of hegemonic ethnicities is the extent to which they succeed in 'naturalizing' their social and cultural constructions.

Ethnic projects mobilize all available relevant resources for their promotion. Some of these resources are political, others are economic and yet others are cultural – relating to customs, language, religion and other cultural artifacts and memories. Class, gender, political and personal differences mean that people positioned differently within the collectivity could, while pursuing specific ethnic projects, sometimes use the same cultural resources for promoting opposite political goals (e.g. using various Koran surras to justify pro- and anti- legal abortion politics, as was the case in Egypt or using rock music to mobilize people pro- and anti- the Extreme Right in Britain). In other times, different cultural resources are used to legitimize competing ethnic projects of the collectivity – e.g. when Bundists used Yiddish as 'the' Jewish language – in an ethnic–national project whose identity boundaries were East European Jewry, and Zionists (re-)invented modern Hebrew (till then used basically for religious purposes) in order to include in their project Jews all over the world. Similarly, the same people can be constructed in different ethnic–racist political projects in Britain to be 'Paki', 'Black Asians', and 'Muslim fundamentalists'.

Given the above, it is clear why ethnicity cannot be reduced to culture, and why 'culture' cannot be seen as a fixed, essentialist category. The differential social positionings from which identity narratives and cultural constructions are formulated and stated is of crucial social and political importance in relation to the ways relationships are viewed with those outside the collectivity, the ways boundaries are constructed to decide who is 'in' and who is 'out' of the collectivity and on power relations within the collectivity.

It is from such a perspective that fundamentalist religious and ethnic movements need to be appraised. Fundamentalism is probably the most important social movement of our times (*Contention* 1995). Fundamentalist movements all over the world, with all their heterogeneity, are basically political movements which have a religious or ethnic imperative and seek in various ways in widely differing circumstances to harness modern state and media powers to the service of their gospel. This gospel, which can be based on certain sacred texts or evangelical experiential moments linked to a charismatic leader, is presented as the only valid form of the religion, the ethnic culture, the truth (Sahgal and Yuval-Davis 1992). Religious fundamentalist movements, therefore, need to be differentiated from liberation theologies which, while deeply religious and political, co-operate with, rather than subjugate, non-religious political struggles.

Fundamentalism can align itself with different political trends in different countries and manifest itself in many forms. It can appear as a form of orthodoxy – a maintenance of 'traditional values', or as a revivalist radical phenomena, dismissing impure and corrupt forms of religion, to 'return to original sources'. Jewish fundamentalism in Israel, for example, has appeared in basically two forms, for which the state has very different meanings. On the one hand, as a form of right-wing Zionism, in which the establishment of the Israeli state is in itself a positive religious act, and, on the other hand, as a non- if not anti-zionist movement, which sees in the Israeli state, a convenient source for gaining economic and political power to promote its own versions of Judaism. In Islam, fundamentalism has appeared as a return to the Quranic text (fundamentalism of the madrassa), and as a return to the religious law, the sharia (fundamentalism of the ulama). In the USA, the protestant fundamentalist movements include both fundamentalists in the original sense – those who want to go back to the biblical texts, and those 'born again Christians' who rely much more on emotional religious experiences (see Maitland, in Sahgal and Yuval-Davis 1992).

The recent rise of fundamentalism is linked to the crisis of modernity – of social orders based on the belief in the principles of enlightenment, rationalism and progress. Both capitalism and communism have proved unable to deliver people's material, emotional and spiritual needs. A general sense of despair and disorientation has opened people to transcendental religions as a source of solace. It provides a compass and an anchor which gives people a sense of stability and security, as well as a coherent identity. It shifts the centre of the structuration of meaning from the individual to religious leaders and institutions.

The reification and essentialization of identities which is linked to fundamentalist politics have also been presented as a defensive reaction to the processes of globalization. Both Stuart Hall (1996) and Verena Stolcke (1995) talk about cultural fundamentalism (although, considering its strong emphasis on immutable collectivity boundaries, it might be preferable to call it ethnic fundamentalism). Given the rise of global capitalism and the growing sense of disempowerment in a political world system in which political autonomy and sovereignty seem to mean less and less, more and more people feel the need for what Hall calls a symbolic retreat to the past in order to face the future. The myth of common origin and a fixed immutable, ahistorical and homogenous construction of the collectivity's culture is used in a similar way to that of religious fundamentalism. Indeed, religion often plays a central role of cultural signifier in these cultural fundamentalist constructions.

As Verena Stolcke points out, the apparent contradiction in the modern liberal ethos, between an invocation of a shared humanity which involves an idea of generality so that no human being seems to be excluded, and a cultural particularism translated into national terms, is overcome ideologically. A cultural 'other', the immigrant or a member of other communities who do not share the same myth of common origin, is constructed as an alien and as such as a potential 'enemy' who threatens 'our' national-cum-cultural integrity and uniqueness. In yet a further ideological twist, national identity and belonging interpreted as cultural particularity become, thus, an unsurmountable barrier to do what, as humans, in principle comes naturally, namely, to communicate. Total separation, preferably spatial, is considered to be vital for the common human welfare. As Aleksandra Alund (1995) argues, the human being is 'the bordering creature who has no borders'. There is a subtle dialectical relationship between humankind's need to culturally demarcate its unique being and the ability to socially transgress borders between human beings.

However, emanating from our discussion above and as Stuart Hall observes (1992, 1996), cultural identities are often fluid and cross-cutting. Even more importantly, perhaps, they are not only multiple, but they are multi-layered. In this I mean not only the fact that boundaries of certain identities are by definition wider and inclusive of other more specific identities – local, regional, national, racial, etc. but also that some identities which have no prefixed cohesion or assumption of common origin or even common destiny may co-exist within individual or communal subjective narratives. Those hyphenated identities have been theorized as hybrid identities (Anzaldua 1987, Bhabha 1990, 1994) located within the symbolic border (or, rather boundary) zone.

Hybrids have been celebrated in post-modernist literature as the symbol of the time, and are seen as both evoking and erasing the 'totalizing boundaries' of their adoptive nations. Located within the context of globalization, hybrids, nomads and other 'travelling identities' are being celebrated by writers like James Clifford (1992) and Rosi Braidotti (1993). Talal Assad (1993: 9–10), for instance, contrasts James Clifford's (1992) celebration of 'the widening scope of human agency that geographical and psychological mobility now afford' with the deep pessimism of Hanna Arendt (1975 [1951]), herself a refugee from the Nazis, who spoke of 'the uprootedness and superfluousness which has been the curse of modern masses'. The difference, of course, is embedded in the construction of the notion of free agency versus what Amrita Chhachhi calls 'forced identities' (1991). Whoever saw the terrible sights of the Rwandan refugees taken back to Rwanda from Zaire would question the global validity of the celebration of the nomad.

The problems with the notion of 'the politics of border' (Brah 1996, Welchman 1996) and its associated constructions of the nomad, the hybrid and 'travelling cultures' are twofold. Firstly, the image of crossing boundaries, travelling and miscegenation relies upon a fixed notion of location and culture which brings back essentialism through the back door. Secondly, by concentrating on the imagery, the signifier, the agency, all too often questions of political economy disappear. As a result, there is not enough attention to the differential power relations between the different cultures and locations which are supposedly hybridized or travelled.

My argument here is that the conflation of territorial borders and identity boundaries can have important political consequences. The example I want to bring to this relates to the politics of diaspora.

Diaspora politics and citizenship

It is important to differentiate between what Avtar Brah calls the 'homing desire' and the 'desire for homeland' (1996: 180), as well as between 'diasporic communities' (Lemelle and Kelley 1994, Brah 1996, Lavie and Swedenburg 1996) and political exiles. Political exiles are usually individuals or families who have been part of political struggles in the homeland and their identity and collectivity membership continues to be directed singularly, or at least primarily, towards there, aiming to 'go back' the moment the political situation changes. For diasporic communities, on the other hand, participation in the national struggles in the homeland, including sending ammunition to Ireland or 'gold bricks' to build the Hindu temple in place of the Muslim mosque in Ayodhya which was burned in December 1992, can be done primarily within an ethnic rather than a nationalist discourse, as a symbolic act of affirmation of their collectivity identity. Their destiny is primarily bound with the country where they live and their children grow in, rather than in their country of origin. Nevertheless, such acts of symbolic identification can have very radical political and other effects in the 'homeland', a fact which might often be only of marginal interest to the people of the diaspora. I came across this very clearly when I was speaking in the early 1970s in the USA on the effects American Jewry's support had on the continued occupation by Israel of the territories after the 1967 war, and the resulting violations of human rights by Israel. I was speaking before a synagogue audience known for its liberal politics concerning Vietnam and civil rights in the USA, trying to dissuade them from continuing to send money to Israel as a means of putting pressure on Israel to end the occupation. 'You don't understand,' explained a woman from the audience. 'I'm not interested in what Israel is doing – for me the most important thing is that I support Israel because Israel is part of me.' The sentiments are not always so extremely clear cut, but this is definitely one illuminating example of the danger of underemphasizing the difference between mythical desires for home and actual political realities as well as the conflation of identification and participation.

By participation I mean citizenship, following Marshall's definition of citizenship as 'full membership in the community' (1950). I do not have time and space here to develop the framework of analysis of multi-layered citizenship which I have done elsewhere (Yuval-Davis 1997a, 1999, Yuval-Davis and Werbner 1999). The aspect of citizenship which I do want to discuss here briefly is that which relates specifically to issues of cultures and identities.

Individual and collective rights are no longer determined exclusively by the state, while identities are still perceived as particularized and territorially bound. As Yasemin Soysal (1994) argues, this state of affairs has come about in the post World War II era, as a result of several factors, such as the internationalization of labour markets and massive decolonizations. The latter brought about new forms of migratory flows. Even more importantly, however, they have established new states which asserted their rights in universalistic parameters and participated in international agencies, such as the UN and UNESCO, in the development of international human rights discourse as well as legislation. This international human rights discourse was largely strengthened by the development of new social movements in the North as well as in the South which protested against both discrimination and disadvantage of various marginal sectors and collectivities in society, such as women, Blacks, Fourth World People, disabled people, etc. At the same time, the executors of these international codes of rights and the members of international bodies are still the states, and no international agency has the right to 'interfere in the internal affairs' of other states.

As Soysal (1994) and Cohen (1999) have argued, there has been a process of decoupling of the membership/identity component of citizenship from that of civil and legal rights. The former is attached to specific polities, both of 'nation state' and of others – sub, and transnational (Bauböck, this volume), while the latter are being constructed as 'human rights' and are attached to international law and supra-state institutions and agencies. Jean Cohen commented that the dimensions of citizenship which relate to participation in political communities relate to the Greek Polis tradition of citizenship and are necessarily exclusive, while the second dimension, which constructs citizenship as a legal status bearing rights conforms more to the Roman notion of citizenship and is much more inclusive in character.

However, the issue is not just the decoupling of these two elements of contemporary citizenships, but the fact that also in terms of identity and membership most people relate to more than just on political community – whether it is local, ethnic, national or transnational (see also Bauböck in this volume). The most problematic aspects of citizenship rights for racial and ethnic minorities relate to their social rights and to the notion of multiculturalism (see, for example, Parekh 1990, Jayasuriya 1990, Yuval-Davis 1992 and 1997a, b). For some (like Harris 1987 and Lister 1990), the problem remains within the realm of individual, though different, citizens. As Harris claims:

> The goal is to provide everyone with the wherewithal to enjoy and participate in the benefits of pluralism ... there are common elements underlying cultural variations which can effectively define minimum standards.
>
> (Harris 1987: 49)

The homogenous community of Marshall is being transformed into a pluralist one by the reinterpretation of his emphasis on equality of status into mutual respect (Lister 1990: 48). However, such a model does not take into account potential conflicts of interest among the different groupings of citizens, nor does it consider the collective, rather than the individual, character of the special provisions given to members of ethnic minorities (Jayasuriya 1990: 23).

The question of a collective provision of needs relates to policies of positive action aimed at group rather than individual rights. Multiculturalist policies construct the population, or rather, effectively, the poor and working classes within the population, in terms of ethnic and racial collectivities. Those collectivities are attributed with collective needs, based on their different cultures as well as on their structural disadvantages. Resistance to these policies has been expressed by claims that constructing employment and welfare policies in terms of group rights can conflict with individual rights and are therefore discriminatory. However, at least in countries which officially adopted multiculturalist policies, such as Canada, Britain and the USA, it has been widely accepted, at least until recently, that in order to overcome the practical effects of racism rather than just its ideology, collective provisions and positive action, based on group member-ship, are the only effective measures to be taken (see Burney 1988, Young 1989, Cain and Yuval-Davis 1990). Similar policies have been constructed in other pluralist states, such as India and South Africa.

The question becomes especially problematic when the provision relates not to differential treatment in terms of access to employment or welfare, but to what has been defined as the different cultural needs of different ethnicities. These can vary from the provision of interpreters to the provision of funds to religious organizations. In the most extreme cases, as in the debates around Aboriginals on the one hand and Muslim minorities around the Rushdie Affair on the other hand, there have been calls to enable the minorities to operate according to their own customary and religious legal systems. While the counter arguments have ranged from the fact that this would imply a *de facto* apartheid system to argu-ments about social unity and political hegemony, those who support these claims have seen it as a natural extrapolation of the minorities' social and political rights. This raises the question of how one defines the boundaries of citizens' rights.

Will Kymlicka (1995) suggests a differentiation between 'two kinds of group rights': one which involves the claim of a group against its own members and one which involves the group's claim against the larger society (or the state). Kymlicka opposes the use of state powers in the support of claims of the first kind, because he suspects that very often individuals within the group would be oppressed in the name of culture and tradition. On the other hand, in the second case, the issue often involves protection of a disadvantaged group by others – in such a case, state intervention should be welcome. While Kymlika's general line of argument can be supported, he reifies and naturalizes the groups' boundaries and does not differentiate between people with specific power positionings within the groups (which are not homogenous and can have differ-ing and conflicting interests) and 'the group'.

Iris Young (1989) has suggested that representative democracy should treat people not as individuals but as members of groups, some of them more oppressed than others. She argues that a discourse of universal citizenship which would ignore these differences would just enhance the domination of groups which are already dominant, and would silence the marginal and oppressed groups. She suggests, therefore, that special mechanisms have to be established to represent these groups as groups. Although Iris Young's insistence that difference and differential power relations should be recognized in the practice of citizenship is very important, her approach is problematic in several ways. As elaborated elsewhere (Cain and Yuval-Davis 1990, Anthias and Yuval-Davis

1992, Phillips 1993) such an approach can easily fall into the pitfalls of identity politics, in which the groups are constructed as homogenous and with fixed boundaries. The interests of people who are positioned in specific power positions within the groups is going to be constructed as necessarily representing the interests of the whole group, and the advancement of the powers of the specific group *vis-à-vis* others would become the primary aim of political activities which concern and relate to the citizenship body as a whole.

Instead of a given unitary standard, there has to be a process of constructing it for each specific political project. Black feminists like Patricia Hill-Collins (1990) and Italian feminists such as Raphaela Lambertini and Elizabetta Dominini (see Yuval-Davis 1994, 1997a and 1999) have focused on the transversal politics of coalition building, in which the specific positioning of political actors are recognized and considered. As I have elaborated elsewhere, this approach is based on the epistemological recognition that each positioning produces specific situated knowledge which cannot be but an unfinished knowledge, and therefore dialogue among those differentially positioned should take place in order to reach a common perspective as a basis for a common action or policy. Transversal dialogue should be based on the principles of rooting and shifting – i.e., being centred in one's own experiences while being empathetic to the differential positionings of the partners in the dialogue, thus enabling the participants to arrive at a different perspective from that of hegemonic tunnel vision. The boundaries of the dialogue would be determined by the message rather than its messengers. The result of the dialogue might still be differential projects for people and groupings positioned differently, but their solidarity would be based on a common knowledge sustained by a compatible value system, which is what defines the boundaries of the dialogue.

To conclude – cultures and identities need to be analysed within the specific historical context and power relations both within and between collectivities. Transversal epistemology and politics which have developed during the last few years point the way to transformatory political projects which transcend the terrain of the political debate beyond the ethnocentric assimilatory universalism of the Old Left on the one hand and the particularistic relativism of identity politics on the other hand, without going afloat with the apolitical free-floating signifiers of some of the deconstructionist post-modernist intellectuals.

Note

1 An earlier version of this chapter appeared as part of Chapter 3 in my book *Gender & Nation*, London: Sage, 1997.

References

Alund, A. (1995) 'Alterity in modernity', *Acta Sociologica* 38: 311–22.
Anthias, F. and Yuval-Davis, N. (1984) 'Contextualizing feminism: ethnic, gender and class divisions', *Feminist Review* 15: 62–75.
Anthias, F. and Yuval-Davis, N. (1992) *Racialized Boundaries*. London: Routledge.
Anzaldua, G. (1987) *Borderlines/La Frontera*. San Francisco: Spinsters/Aunt Lute Books.

Arendt, H. (1975 [1951]) *The Origins of Totalitarianism*. New York: Harcourt Brace Janovitch.

Armstrong, J. (1982) *Nations Before Nationalism*. Chapel Hill: University of North Carolina Press.

Assad, T. (1993) *Genealogies of Religion*. Baltimore: John Hopkins University Press.

Bauman, G. (1994) 'Dominant and demotic discourses of "culture".' Paper presented in the conference *Culture Communication and Discourse: Negotiating Difference in Multiethnic Alliances*. University of Manchester, December.

Bhabha, H. (ed.) (1990) *Nation and Narration*. London: Routledge.

Bhabha, H. (1994) *The Location of Culture*. London: Routledge.

Bottomley, G. (1992) *From Another Place: Migration and the Politics of Culture*. Cambridge: Cambridge University Press.

Bottomley, G. (1993) 'Post-multiculturalism? The theory and practice of heterogeneity.' Paper presented at the conference *Post-colonial Formations*. Griffith University, June.

Braidotti, R. (1993) 'Nomads in transformed Europe: figurations for alternative consciousness', in *Cultural Diversity in the Arts*, R. Lavrijsen (ed.). Amsterdam: Royal Tropical Institute.

Brah, A. (1991) 'Difference, diversity, differentiation', in *International Review of Sociology*, New Series no. 2, April: 53–72.

Burney, E. (1988) *Steps to Social Equality: Positive Action in a Negative Climate*. London: Runneymead Trust.

Cain, H. and Yuval-Davis, N. (1990) '"The Equal Opportunities Community" and the Anti-Racist Struggle' *Critical Social Policy*, Autumn 29: 5–26.

Chatterjee, P. (1986) *Nationalist Thought and the Colonial World: a Derivative Discourse*. London: Zed Books.

Chhachhi, A. (1991) 'Forced identities: the state, communalism, fundamentalism & women in India', in *Women, Islam & the State*, D. Kandiyoti (ed.). London: Macmillan.

Clifford, J. (1992) 'Travelling cultures', in *Cultural Studies*, L. Grossberg, T. Nelson and P. Treichler (eds). New York: Routledge.

Cohen, J.L. (1999) 'Changing paridigms of citizenship and the exclusiveness of the Demos', *International Sociology* 14: 245–68.

Contention (1995) special issue on *Comparative Fundamentalisms*, no. 2, winter.

Cox, R.W. (1995) 'Civilizations: encounters and transformations', *Studies in Political Economy* 7: 7–32.

Friedman, J. (1994) *Cultural Identity and Global Process*. London: Sage.

Gans, H.J. (1979) 'Symbolic ethnicity: the future of ethnic groups and cultures in America', *Ethnic and Racial Studies* 2, 2–20.

Giddens, A. (1989) *Sociology*. Cambridge: Polity Press.

Gunew, S. and Yeatman, A. (eds) (1993) *Feminism and the politics of difference*. Boulder: Westview Press.

Hall, S. (1992) 'New ethnicities' in *'Race', Culture and Difference*, J. Donald and A. Rattansi (eds). London: Sage.

Hall, S. (1996) 'Who needs "identity?"' Introduction to S. Hall and P. du Gay (eds). *Questions of Cultural Identity*. London: Sage.

Harris, D. (1987) *Justifying State Welfare: The New Right v. The Old Left*. Oxford: Basil Blackwell.

Hartman, H. (1995) 'Clash of cultures, when and where: Critical comments on a new theory of conflict – and its translation into German', *International Sociology* 10, 2: 115–25.

Hill-Collins, P. (1990) *Black Feminist Thought*. Boston: Unwin Hyman.

Jayasuriya, L. (1990) 'Multiculturalism, citizenship and welfare: new directions for the 1990s.' Paper presented at the *50th Anniversary Lecture Series*, Dept. of Social Work and Social Policy, University of Sydney.

King, U. (ed.) (1995) *Religion & Gender*. Oxford: Blackwell.

Kymlicka, W. (1995) *Multicultural Citizenship: A Liberal Theory of Minority Rights*. Oxford: Clarendon Press.

Lavie, Smadar and Swedenburg, T. (eds) (1996) *Displacement, Diaspora and Geographies of Location*. Durham NC: Duke University Press.

Lemelle S. and Kelly R. (eds) (1994) *Imagining Home: Class, Culture and Nationalism in the African Diaspora*. London: Verso.

Lister, R. (1990) *The Exclusive Society: Citizenship and the Poor*. London: Child Poverty Action Group.

Marshall, T.H. (1950) *Citizenship and Social Class*. Cambridge: Cambridge University Press.

Martin, D.-C. (1995) 'The choices of identity', in *Social Identities* 1, 1: 5–16.

Massey, D. (1994) *Space, Place and Gender*. Cambridge: Polity Press.

Modood (1988) '"Black", racial equality and Asian identity', *New Community* 24, 3: 397–404.

Modood (1994) 'Political blackness and British Asians', *Sociology* 28: 859–76.

Parekh, B. (1990) 'The Rushdie affair and the British press: some salutary lessons', in *Free Speech*, a report of a seminar by the CRE, London.

Phillips, A. (1993) *Democracy and Difference*. Cambridge: Polity Press.

Rah, A. (1996) *Cartographies of Diaspora: Contested Identities*. London: Routledge.

Sahgal, G. and Yuval-Davis, N. (eds) (1992) *Refusing Holy Orders: Women and Fundamentalism in Britain*. London: Virago Press.

Schierup, C.-U. (1995) 'Multiculturalism and universalism in the USA and EU Europe. Paper for the workshop 'Nationalism and Ethnicity', Bern, March.

Smith, A. (1986) *The Ethnic Origin of Nations*. Oxford: Basil Blackwell.

Soysal, Y. (1994) *Limits of Citizenship: Migrants and Postnational Membership in Europe*. Chicago: University of Chicago Press.

Stolcke, V. (1995) 'Talking culture: new boundaries, new rhetorics of exclusion in Europe', *Current Anthropology* 16, 1: 1–23.

Welchman, J.C. (ed.) (1996) *Rethinking Borders*. Basingstoke: Macmillan.

Williams, R. (1983) *Keywords*. London: Fontana.

Young, I.M. (1989) 'Polity and group difference: a critique of the ideal of universal citizenship', *Ethics*, 99.

Yuval-Davis, N. (1992) 'The citizenship debate: women, the state and ethnic processes', *Feminist Review*, Autumn, 39: 58–68.

Yuval-Davis, N. (1994) 'Women, ethnicity and empowerment', in *Shifting Identities, Shifting Racisms, A Feminism and Psychology Reader*, K. Bhavnani and A. Phonix (eds).

Yuval-Davis, N. (1997a) *Gender and Nation*. London: Sage.

Yuval-Davis, N. ([1996] 1997b) 'Women, citizenship and difference', a Background Paper for the conference at the University of Greenwich, July 1996, included in *Feminist Review*'s special issue *Citizenship: Pushing the Boundaries*, Autumn 1997.

Yuval-Davis, N. (1999) 'The multi-layered citizen: citizenship in the age of globalization', *International Feminist Journal of Politics* 1, 1: 118–36.

Yuval-Davis, N. and Worbner, P. (eds) (1999) *Women, Citizenship and Difference*. London: Zed Books.

5 Becoming a person
New frontiers for identity and citizenship in a planetary society

Alberto Melucci

Becoming a person

Dramatic social changes over the last three decades have revealed the limits of the modern definition of democracy and the inadequacy of political institutions' responses to the planetarization[1] of the world system. I will argue that today's democracy requires conditions for enhancing the recognition and autonomy of individual and collective signifying processes in everyday life. Contemporary societies based on information allocate specific resources to individuals, who use them to become autonomous subjects of action; but in order to maintain themselves systems extend their control over the deep-lying sources of action and the construction of its meaning.

This chapter will deal with new forms of inequalities which prevent each individual from accessing and utilizing the tools that one needs to construct a specific self. Inclusion and exclusion refer here not to material resources, but to the possibility of becoming a person. These processes are visible in the peripheries of the planet, where millions of people are moved away from their traditional cultures. But the same processes are also visible in Europe and other 'developed' societies, where one can see an ever-growing number of people deprived from the right to participate in the decisions that will rule their cultural and symbolic worlds.

We are faced by a crisis in the modern concept of the individual (Taylor 1989, Bauman 1991, 1993, Giddens 1991, 1992, Touraine 1994) and simultaneously by a burgeoning of demands and needs which concern the realization of individuality. This is a process which becomes visible precisely at the moment when individuals acquire sufficient resources to think of themselves as individuals and act as such; when, that is, they are able to construct their own identity as something not already given, and especially as something which is not given once and for all but depends on potentialities for which each person can feel responsible (Melucci 1989, 1996a).

'Each person' should not be taken to mean all and everyone indiscriminately. Indeed, today's new inequalities stem precisely from the way in which these potentialities are distributed. No longer are they material disparities, but disparities in the chances of each individual to fulfil him or herself as a whole human being.

This availability of resources generates extensive demands which bring into play the desire and capacity of each person to be what he/she wants to and can be. Although modernity laid the basis for the autonomy of the individual subject, never until today have these potentialities been so widely available. The transformation of educational systems, changing family values, the extension of personal rights, the multiplication of cultural opportunities – these simultaneously create both needs and resources, so that people may conceive of themselves as individuals while they also possess the effective ability to construct their autonomy.

The transformation of identity construction processes and the large-scale diffusion of the potentialities of individuation force us to go beyond the modern concept of the individual. The modern individual is still a substantial entity, endowed with essence, with a metaphysical nucleus to refer to and simultaneously to struggle against in order to shake off the chains of tradition. 'Modern' individuals address the problem of change by summoning up inner energies against the resistance and opacity of the external world. They affirm themselves as individuals in a Promethean struggle against the forces of nature in order to subjugate them to the power of reason and technology, and against the social order and its traditional rules. But modern individuals also struggle against that dark side of the self which prevents reason from asserting itself as the highest form of liberty.

The image of the individual that now emerges in our society is a development of the legacy of modernity, but this modern inheritance is emptied of its substantialist dimension and propelled towards action and process. The individual is a potentiality which constructs itself as the on-going utilization and investment of resources. However, this individual has the main problem of maintaining her/himself, of guaranteeing a stable nucleus. If everything changes, if self-assertion as an individual entails constant self-redefinition, the true difficulty lies not in how to change the individual's life history but how to ensure its unity and continuity. This individual-as-process constantly endeavouring to construct the self must nevertheless safeguard limits and preserve roots in biology and society. This is an individual who must cope not only with self-realization but also with the boundaries of his/her action and constantly answer the question, 'Who am I?'.

It is a question which today concerns the whole of humanity, even that component of it apparently excluded from these processes. The opportunity is potentially open to everybody now that world culture has become universalized and organized into planet-wide patterns of information and communication. At the systemic level,[2] individuals are offered chances for self-realization unparalleled by anything in past societies. They have opportunities available which develop their cognitive and communicative capacities through education and information. The extension of civil rights expands the sphere of personal freedom and the exercise of voluntary decisions. Freedom of choice in affective relations enables them to establish bonds which depend only on themselves. The richness of associative life allows them to participate freely in numerous relational networks.

All these processes open up a broad field in which each individual may develop potentialities, make choices, fulfil his/her individuality. The more differentiated a system, the more it is forced to rely on autonomous subjects able to understand diverse 'languages', to process knowledge, to take independent decisions. Thus in the life of the great contemporary organizations or in democratic politics, individuals are required to participate and to take decisions, and the emphasis is placed on their responsibility. Individuals, for their part, ask for their rights to be recognized, they endeavour to express their independence, they advance demands regarding their personal needs, affective lives, and physical and psychological well-being.

Whether each individual is then effectively able to utilize these possibilities is, of course, a different matter: it depends on the more or less equitable distribution of resources, whose enormous disparities must be investigated at the same systemic level. Striking differences in access to these opportunities stem from potent forces excluding entire social groups and parts of the world. Within the so-called developed societies and in the peripheries of the planet, new forms of inequality arise as cultural deprivation, as the destruction of traditional cultures replaced only by marginalization or by dependent consumption, and as the imposition of lifestyles which no longer provide individuals with the cultural bases for their self-identification.

It therefore seems that contemporary systems contain a strong impulse towards the autonomy of individuals as well as tendencies towards a mass society based on exclusion, depersonalization, the manipulation of information, standardized consumption, conformism and apathy. These are, in fact, two contradictory aspects of the same process. In highly differentiated societies based on information, it is difficult to ensure integration and control. The centrifugal forces are powerful, the risks of fragmentation and the potential for conflict are very high. Power must therefore take molecular and ubiquitous action so that behaviour becomes as predictable as possible, while close constraints must be set on deviation from the norm. 'Massification' is economic and programmable, exclusion is the price for control. But the other ever-present face is a powerful thrust towards that individual autonomy without which a highly differentiated society could not function.

Which of these two processes prevails depends on the amount of openness and equity in the social system; and this, in turn, depends on political choices and on the model of democratic society that we are able to pursue. However, in conceiving of a more just and open society we are obliged to think in terms different from those of the modern age and to recognize that the social bond can no longer be taken for granted. There is no longer the obvious and natural belonging provided by established social containers. What there is instead is the individual capacity to actively recognize oneself as part of a communal identity and therefore to take autonomous action in constructing that identity and contributing to human co-existence. This brings us to the issue of difference: when identity is not given once and for all, we must become able to recognize difference as a resource and to consider it as a value to be preserved.

Difference and solidarity

Different forms of postmodern and post-national identities have emerged in recent years (Anderson 1991, Soysal 1994). They can be seen as responses to a search for meaning in societies that are unable to provide forms of membership and identification to meet the needs of individuals and groups for self-realization, communicative interaction, and recognition. Difference has become a key component in both interpersonal relations and society as a whole. The question raised is how communication and solidarity can be preserved when identity is based on irreducible differences: gender and ethnicity are extreme cases of a more general problem concerning co-existence in a highly differentiated world.

The more the space of social experience expands, the more meanings multiply and the more values diversify. Rules proliferate and there is no single frame of reference for all members of a society, of an organization, of a group, of a family. We witness the *pluralization of meaning* paralleled by the *multiplication of belongings*. Individuals are members of several systems and in each of them they deploy only one part of their identity. Finally, the environment in which they move – be it the political arena, the workplace, interpersonal relations – is unstable and this constantly confronts them with uncertainty. As citizens, as members of groups and organizations and as individual human beings, they are constantly required to make decisions and to take risks in order to reduce uncertainty.

In a differentiated society people are therefore members, citizens, persons: through these different ways of belonging, contemporary individuals are acting on the borders of different systems and they increasingly need permeable identities that allow the transition between the various regions of meaning and institutional settings. We have inherited from the culture of industrial society a strongly instrumental idea of the social, the idea that there exists a set of shared values and goals, and the social organization is simply a machine with which to achieve them (Touraine 1994). This is certainly no longer true today, if it ever was. If the social fabric is made up of a network of differentiated relations and plural interests, the achievement of unity is only the outcome of exchanges, communications and mediations.

Living with difference contains an inherently ambivalent potential (Bauman 1991, 1993). There is, on one hand, a risk of entropy, as the explosion of differences could bring disintegration, loss of the fundamental bonds that allow solidarity and the pursuit of common goals. But, on the other, differences also have great dynamic potential because they generate those synergies and connections that in a homogeneous world were not possible. A planetary society must come to terms with diversity. Given that society can no longer rely on its automatic or preordained functioning (i.e. through kinship networks, religious memberships, or community ties), it requires greater organization and more energy if its very existence is to be maintained. The social bond depends on how we make it exist and how we nourish it. This perspective entails greater margins of risk than in the past, and greater investment in rendering differences translatable. There is no inevitability about the results achieved, for they are always the outcome of processes which we ourselves have activated. A capacity for constant negotiation is required and we must be able to revise the rules that we jointly establish. The social bonds are increasingly the outcome of pacts which we are able to stipulate, such as the rules we agree to use for the solution of conflicts.

A striking example of the emergence of differences is the unexpected resurgence of ethnic and territorial conflicts in the last thirty years (Kymlicka 1995, Maffesoli 1995, Melucci 1996b). These conflicts are not a simple extension of the national questions inherited from the formation of the modern states. Of course there are aspects that perpetuate the legacy of historical nationalism and forms of action reminiscent of traditional struggles for citizenship; but these conflicts also display features which we can only understand if we acknowledge their discontinuity with the past.

Nationalism, ethnicity and territorially-based identities overlap and interweave. They generate phenomena with traditional features, attitudes which are markedly defensive and sometimes openly reactionary, but they also raise issues that pertain to the planetary integration of a society based on information. Today, the cultural models of the central[3] societies impose themselves as universal codes of behaviour and communication. They tend to cancel out cultural differences and thereby eliminate the possibility of communicating itself, which always entails equality but also diversity. The appeal to ethnic or territorial identity frequently arises from long-standing national questions, and it raises extremely complex political problems. Yet it also expresses, and conceals at the same time, new needs. In the society of global communication, individuals and groups demand the right to be different and they resist their absorption into dominant models. From this resistance stem new and dramatic challenges in laying a new foundation for society.

Ethnic and territorial claims also highlight the crisis of the international system based on the model of the nation state, which is now unable to enclose the plurality of peoples and cultures within the confines of a centralized political order. The nation states have lost their authority. From above, planetary interdependence and the emergence of transnational political and economic forces have shifted the true decision-making centres elsewhere. From below, centres of autonomous decision making (groups, organizations, local institutions) proliferate, and society acquires power which it never enjoyed during the development of the modern states.

Behind the issues raised by ethnic and national conflicts there arises a confused appeal for society to be given the power to decide its own existence and to control its own development. This requires a new set of relations to be established among the various components of planetary reality (groups, interests, cultures, nations). A new model of planetary relations no longer founded on nation states is one of the great issues that confront the contemporary world. Enormous effort is required of humankind to give political form to its planetary social life. There is an urgent need for a political arrangement able to govern the plurality, the autonomy and the richness of differences and at the same time to express our shared responsibility for the fate of the species and of the planet.

But, if the most powerful thrust in complex systems is towards self-realization and the assertion of differences, what, we may ask, ensures the maintenance of the social bond and of solidarity? What is it that still enables us to recognize ourselves collectively and as belonging to a larger entity, however this may be defined? This raises issues which concern both everyday life and the higher reaches of politics. How can a social bond be established when it is no longer founded on something which guarantees it *a priori* from outside? The very idea of 'society' does not suffice any longer to provide this foundation. The idea of society itself is the last great legacy of metaphysics, that of the social body as an organism which is kept in being by the integration of its parts, the division of functions, the reference to shared values; a body governed by a logic independent from actions and interactions of its component parts, human beings endowed with the capacity of producing meaning.[4]

If the social bond is increasingly a matter of choice, on what is it based, and what ensures its persistence over time despite the affirmation of differences and the emergence of conflicts? It is possible to refer to solidarity – a word which occurs frequently in end-of-millennium language – in terms of equality or difference. In the former case, the social bond is based on recognition of what is shared, of what it is that permits the reflection of self in the other. In the latter, the bond is founded on difference; that is, on recognition in the other of what we lack and require for our completion.

These two forms of solidarity were long thought of as distinguishing traditional society (the former) from modern society (the latter). In reality, they should be conceived as two enduring faces of the social bond. It is not true that traditional forms of solidarity disappeared to be replaced by modern ones, or that they survive today only as archaic residues. Those forms of solidarity considered to be archaic and destined to be swept away, like ethnicity or kinship relationships, instead persist in contemporary society and are indeed acquiring new vigour. They have found new space to grow and interweave with so-called modern forms of solidarity.

Solidarity by similarity and solidarity by difference therefore merge to constitute the contemporary forms of the social bond. In fact, the culture generates both individual autonomy and tendencies toward massification and depersonalization. When there is too great an emphasis on difference, identity is in danger of disintegrating. This gives rise to the counter-impulse to return to the security of similarity, of the small group, of the sect, of the territory.

On the other hand, mass society exerts strong pressure towards conformity. One may identify by similarity even in the culture of consumption and the media, increasingly homogeneous and levelled. People become fans of the last movie or TV star, they dress in a certain style, they consume the same products, music and images (Featherstone 1992). At the supermarket, in front of the television, in the concert hall and at the discotheque, people feel themselves similar to many others. Solidarity by similarity, therefore, is reborn at the heart of differentiated society. It may take the form of a search for what is immediate, close, recognizable. Primary, biological or territorial identifications offer the overwhelming security of immediate recognition. Alternatively, one may recognize oneself because one participates in the standardized culture which imposes homogeneous cultural codes from outside. The languages, styles of consumption and information technologies elaborated in a few centres of the system impose themselves on a planetary scale as new factors of unification and recognition by similarity.

Yet, as we have seen, complex society is also a society of differences. Complexity dictates that no-one can achieve their goals by themselves, by acting alone against the others, if we are to continue to exist on this planet but also to operate as a single organization, a group, a family. Only when differences are not denied does it become possible to establish that minimum set of rules whereby these differences can be negotiated and wholeness created.

Respect for differences can only be achieved if we take care of our means of communication. Difference cannot be communicated with the words of the dominant language, for it is a relational construct that implies the confrontation of (at least) two parts. Thus, we need to understand other languages and to be able to speak with different words: that is, to conceive of points of views other than our own.

Points of view

The faith of past generations in the final outcome of history has faded, and we have reached that threshold of the culture where only what human action itself is able to produce can save or condemn the culture itself. Memory occupies an important place in this scenario because it constitutes the reservoir of similarity and difference. It offers us the chance to recognize ourselves as equal and different, to establish continuity and discontinuity in our identity and relationship with others. Memory can either function only as a regressive defence of a by-now dead past, or as the source and foundation of the present. By choosing what we wish to preserve and what we agree to change, we become aware of the similarities and differences within ourselves and between ourselves and others. Recourse to the past, when it is not defensive closure, forces us to recognize our partiality because it always involves preservation and loss.

But as a second requirement, a self-limiting notion of rationality must be applied to social life when power is based on the manipulation of cultural codes and when social actors are increasingly involved in conflicts for the construction of meaning. Any new definition of citizenship must consider the necessary elements of diversity and uncertainty in basic social relations, and must include a measure of respect for all those parts of human experience that are not reducible to modern rationality.

In our approach to differences, we are still tied to the legacy of modernity, and our method of dealing with problems is still conditioned by the binary logic of 'either . . . or'. We are beginning, albeit laboriously and reluctantly, to enter a world in which the only possible logic is that of 'both . . . and'. The great revolution introduced in contemporary science by relativity and quantum physics lies precisely in the realization that the world always stands in relation to an observer. The discourse of others thus becomes crucial, no matter what 'language' they use to express their point of view. Accepting that others view things from different standpoints and that they construct a different experience of the world exposes us to doubt but also to surprise. Others reveal parts of the world to us which we cannot see from where we stand.

The passage from a linear to a circular point of view, from a dualistic logic to a global, dialogue-based logic is a qualitative leap which requires us to embrace something as yet unknown and only just emerging in the culture. A plural and dialogue-based universe, however, is not the universe of absolute relativism. On the contrary, it gives us responsibility for our point of view and for our choices, empowers us to declare them and informs us that there are other viewpoints.

Listen to others and construct a common language, this is the challenge that awaits us in the world we are about to enter; in which no-one can have monopoly over language, codes or communication. We must come to agreement, establish the point of view adopted by our interlocutors, in which part of the universe each of them is located, and which part of the universe they are able to see. We must endeavour to translate among languages while preserving their specificity.

One can easily see the new forms of power and domination now taking shape through the control of scientific language, of information and of the media. Monopolizing the meaning of communication is a way to suppress the point of view of others. But a universe of differences extends an equally forceful invitation to humility and urges us to accept our limits and tolerate otherness.

In the knowledge that the richness of the unpredictable is born of differences and that listening unlocks that part of the world which has been closed off to us, this outcome merits working for. Only thus can monopoly on the word be prevented from crushing every diversity, only thus will the variety of languages continue to remind us that in a planetary world each of us needs everyone else.

Inclusions/exclusions

Inclusion and exclusion are redefined according to new forms of inequality which relate to the production and distribution of resources for individualization. Becoming a person is a matter of capacities, rights and responsibilities which are unequally shared. The processes of planetary integration create exclusion within the most 'advanced' societies and dis-equilibria among the various parts of the world. Those excluded seem to have been abandoned to their fate. And yet they are an important part of the world in which we live, and without them there can be no survival.

The excluded have no other voice than their condition; or else they speak through the dramatic explosion of the crises that regularly affect sectors of the advanced societies or areas of the world. Class analysis is still able to interpret the mechanisms and structure of many of these inequalities, and collective action often involves the mobilization of marginalized and excluded social groups (Sen 1992, Procacci 1993). But in this case, too, we must accomplish a quantum leap in our capacity for analysis. In fact, the traditional structure of material inequalities is, in part, a new structure based on the unequal distribution of the resources typical of an information society that has a great deal to do with the ways in which we name the world. Who are the actors deciding the language used to name reality and choosing the codes that organize it? This is the central issue of power and conflict in a society in which information is becoming the core resource of social life. It applies to the world system as such, where society has become a whole. The various forms assumed by power and social conflict affect this planetary space in its entirety, albeit in different ways in different parts of the world, and as regards different social groups.

These new inequalities concern disparities in access to the means by which the meaning of action is defined, individual and collective identity constructed, and native culture safeguarded. Those who are excluded, therefore, are deprived of material resources, but even more so of their capacity to be subjects: material deprivation combines with entirely subordinate inclusion in mass consumption, with the manipulation of consciousness, with the imposition of lifestyles which destroy, once and for all, the roots of popular cultures.

New conflicts emerge that are eminently relational, dynamic and cultural because they invade the sphere of meaning formation; but they are nevertheless structural in character because they affect the forms of domination of a society based on information. The problem thus immediately arises of the relationship between these types of conflict and their empirical manifestations, which always come about in the context of concrete historical societies – that is, within a national state, a political system, a class structure, a specific cultural tradition. The problem becomes even more acute when we refer to 'developing societies', in which all these features are marked by economic dependence and by the weight of traditional power and inequality structures. Consequently the question to address is the form that these conflicts assume when they become empirically visible within a concrete society, especially those in the most deprived areas of the world.

There are apparently two important aspects to consider when answering this question: first, the nature of the political system and of the state; second, the structure of inequalities and the mechanisms that produce and maintain poverty in different countries. As regards the first aspect, the question concerns the relationship that arises between the emerging forms of collective action and their political expression. In the 'developing societies' (as well as the poorer areas of the so-called 'developed' societies), the democratization process and an autonomization of the political sphere has labouriously got under way. On the one hand, this is no longer simply identified with the state; on the other, it has escaped the grasp of the oligarchic elites that used the state as the instrument to maintain their supremacy. It is therefore impossible, in those societies, to separate collective action from struggles for citizenship, for civil and democratic guarantees, for the attainment of forms of participation which translate into new rules and new rights.

But it would be an error to collapse collective action into politics, because it is precisely towards the desacralization and limitation of politics that complex systems are moving. From the analytic perspective that I use, the political system is not coterminous with society, and the dimension of social relations is analytically broader than political relations. The latter concern the processes whereby rules and decisions are shaped by the competition and negotiation of interests. Neo-liberalism, too, seemingly proposes an approach which tends to reduce the scope of political relationships and to desacralize politics, but in fact it continues to nurture the myth that social demands can be straightforwardly translated into decision making through an allegedly open competition. This thus fosters an ever more procedural version of democracy which serves to conceal new forms of domination and power. It is instead the non-transparency of political processes that the analysis of collective action reveals to us. Collective action makes conflicts visible, and it reminds us that politics is not solely representation – it is also power. It also reminds us that the transformation of social demands into new rules and new rights is an open-ended task of democracy, a never-accomplished process. The transparent translation of social demands never occurs; a quota of conflict still persists in society to remind us of this shortfall. The distinction between systems of representation and decision making, on the one hand, and the forms of collective action irreducible to them on the other, is therefore one of the necessary conditions for contemporary complex systems to maintain themselves open.

In regard to the concrete form assumed by conflicts, the first point concerned the nature of the political system and of the state. The second point concerns the enormity of the inequality and poverty still persisting in many societies at the world scale. If class analysis is still able to explain many of these inequalities, the traditional and new forms of material exclusion are already part of a new structure based on the unequal access to the resources of a society based on information. An important task for theory and research, therefore, is analysis of this interweaving between old and new; analysis which, however, requires that categorical leap without which one remains trapped in old schemes of thought.

Poverty provides a good example of this interweaving. The intolerable poverty suffered by large swathes of the population has generated waves of mobilization involving various categories of 'the poor people' (the landless, the inhabitants of the various urban ghettos of the world, and so on). But the issue of poverty has mainly mobilized the urban middle classes, who have launched numerous organizations, campaigns, exemplary actions, etc. Poverty has thus become an issue which concerns the definition itself of rights and the notion of 'humanity' and of 'being human'. It is an issue, therefore, that certainly concerns the material conditions of the excluded, but also and simultaneously involves a typically 'post-material' cultural and ethical question: what is meant by being 'human', and who has the right to apply this definition? The matter becomes tragically important when one realizes that poverty is inevitably bound up with the 'defensive' violence unleashed by the dominant groups against the threat raised by the excluded.

This heightens the responsibility of that part of planetary society which possesses resources and capabilities. We, the 'developed' ones, are privileged not only because we possess more but also because we have in the place of all those deprived of it. Addressing the problem of 'others', of the excluded, of the vicious wars that seem millions of miles away, of ferocious and for us incomprehensible conflicts, of the unutterable misery of parts of the world where people live in subhuman conditions, can no longer consist solely in mobilizing fine sentiments, which often means silencing one's conscience. Instead, it means changing the point of view, realizing that in a planetary society there is no citizenship without human rights for everybody, without the possibility for everybody to become a person. The rest of the world is granting, mostly unwillingly, a privileged position to those 'included'. But the problem of the 'others' bears down upon us, the privileged ones, because this world will continue to exist only if the 'others' are part of it, otherwise it will slide into disaster.

Conflict has become ubiquitous in highly differentiated societies. At the same time, because of its global interdependence planetary society has become much more vulnerable than it was in the past to the destructive effects of conflicts, especially when they are violent. Analysis of the social movements which have emerged in recent decades reveals that, albeit in embryonic form, a different possibility of handling conflicts at the symbolic level is already manifest in complex societies. Within the overall picture of the contemporary world riven by violent conflicts and local wars, there have also emerged forms of social conflict which are symbolic in nature and which seem to revive experiences that human cultures have already lived through. History testifies to the fact that conflict is not always expressed through physical violence; it may also arise with a symbolic force that does not diminish its range or its intensity.

The novel feature of some of the movements that have arisen in complex societies over the last few decades (youth, women's, pacifist, environmentalist, anti-racist movements) is precisely that they have shifted conflict to the symbolic arena (Melucci 1989, 1996b). Modern society has schooled us in the belief that conflicts aim to overthrow the state and the economic order by means of violent mass action. Although many of the conflicts of the last thirty years have not directly dealt with the state, the market and the political system in the first place, they have produced immense and far-reaching changes which have then had major effects on economic and political structures.

If social conflict can assume forms other than physical confrontation and recourse to violence, it becomes important to ask what forms of political organization and of controversy management make it possible to absorb a proportion of the potential violence always implicit in conflicts and enable such violence to express itself, at least mainly if not wholly, at the symbolic level. There is no simple answer to this question, for it directly involves the definition of democracy in complex systems and in planetary society as a whole. Analysis of democracy today entails examination of how differences and the conflicts that they engender can be handled with the least possible amount of actual violence. Asking ourselves through which forms of action and within which boundaries differences can today be negotiated, means to specify the new space for democracy in a totally interdependent system.

The space for democracy

The stand-by option of legitimate violence or even war provided the modern state with one of its crucial working mechanisms, both in the management of internal conflicts and in international relations. The possibility of resorting to this *ultima ratio* has always been part of the political game. Now that this option implies escalation towards catastrophe, and now that the alternative is either jointly-negotiated survival or self-induced destruction, the logic governing the decision process cannot be the same.

This situation does not eliminate risk, but it changes the manner in which the task of joint decision making can be approached. It pushes us to reach agreement on a limit which is the condition itself for us to begin to decide. Not to insist on differences to the point of catastrophe, and respecting differences so that their denial does not produce catastrophe: these are the two imperatives of democratic politics in a global society which encompasses all human beings and fashions the possibility of a new pact. This does not exclude the possibility that some player may refuse to abide by rules of the game; an eventuality which means that we cannot rely on the game's positive outcome, nor on the guarantee of being able to keep together freedom and co-existence. It is evident, however, that democracy can no longer consist simply of representation mechanisms or competition for government resources. Opening the channels of representation to excluded interests, and rendering decision-making processes more transparent, are still the fundamental tasks that democratic political action has inherited from the modern age. In addition to these tasks, however, there is a further responsibility.

The crucial factor which changes the meaning of democracy is that, without the recognition of differences and without agreement on the limits to set upon them, there will no longer be room for either differences or for decision making, but only for catastrophe. Democracy must therefore constantly endeavour to create new space for negotiation and to keep it within the confines that only the democratic process can define.

There are two major consequences of this change. The first is the profound secularization of political processes, in the sense that they can no longer promise happiness, freedom and the perfect society; they are only the temporary point of agreement which, within our limits, we are able to reach. The other aspect of these limits is that whatever passes through politics is only a part, and perhaps only a small part, of the richness of this planet's social and cultural life. There is always another side of the moon which is not mediated by the institutions and which the modern age regarded as the pathology, as the concealed residue which escaped the control of the political process. We should instead begin to consider the social as truly the other side of the moon, as that part of our communal life which constantly pushes to emerge and which reminds us of the limits of our representation mechanisms and decision-making processes.

Social demands and needs, even when they are conflictual, can be recognized as a physiological dimension of the social, the other face of political processes which renounce their claim to totality and self-restrict themselves. Hence democratic life concerns both procedures and the definition of an open space of guarantees and rights so that whatever does not pass through politics is not reduced to the rank of residue or pathology.

The crucial problem is the translation of this hidden dimension into new rules and new rights: how to pass from the immediate identification of new needs to the definition of a shared space in which differences can be posited for everyone. This shared space largely depends on the way in which public discourse is constructed. In societies in which information is the crucial resource, then power is also exercised by controlling the hidden codes through which meaning is created and communicated. Consequently, democracy is measured by the degree of openness of the arenas in which public discourse is produced and disseminated, even when the game is not played on an equal footing. In the awareness that the power of information consists primarily in the power to name, democracy should work to prevent the monopolization of language and to safeguard the 'right to the word', of which our age has urgent need: that is, the freedom of individuals and groups to establish the meaning of what they are and want to be.

From this perspective, action can be taken to turn public discourse into a true 'public space', an arena of languages in which the meaning, the priorities and the goals of communal living are named and compared. The distinguishing feature of the complexity of the contemporary world is that it comprises problems to which there are no solutions. There are polarities between which it is impossible to choose because the equilibrium of a highly differentiated system can be ensured only if they are kept together. There are problems which it is impossible not to attempt to solve, but whose solution only temporarily alleviates uncertainty.

We address uncertainty and we attempt to reduce it by means of political decisions. But political decisions tend to disguise the fact that there is no solution to the great dilemmas behind techniques and procedures. They can only make temporary adjustments, which will be more democratic the more they are equitable and amenable to the possibility of change. For instance, it is difficult to choose between autonomy and control. There is today a tendency to give priority to individual skills and choices, and the counter-tendency to create close-knit systems of behaviour control which invade the brain, motivations, and the genetic structure itself.

There is a similar tendency towards increased intervention in society and nature by means of science and technology, which is matched by the need to respect the constraints of nature within and around ourselves. A further dilemma arises from our potential for self-destruction, which depends on irreversible scientific progress which cannot be erased (unless some catastrophe wipes out the human race at its present stage of evolution). But the use of this knowledge depends, in turn, on the choice of energy, scientific and military policies which do not produce catastrophic and irremediable effects.

The expansion of society to encompass the planet eliminates all external space. By including all territories and cultures, it squeezes every difference out of them. The centres which elaborate cultural codes for the world market of the media impose languages and lifestyles, but, as a consequence, marginal cultures are progressively reduced to silence. These great dilemmas are often concealed and neutralized behind the technical guise of decision-making procedures. Thus many of the issues that affect the lives of each of us, the destiny of the species, and the quality of possible evolution are removed from debate and from control by society. Democracy in a complex society is measured by the capacity to bring these dilemmas to the surface, make them visible and collective and define new rights around them. Recent debates on 'civil society' have opened the conceptual space for this urgent leap, even if our language is still that of modernity and the notion of citizenship itself is deeply tied to the historical formation of the modern state (Cohen and Arato 1992, Kymlicka 1995, Somers 1995, Tilly 1995).

An open society may assimilate the dilemmas of complexity by subjecting them to negotiation and decision making, thereby transforming them into temporary rules for co-existence, but without annulling the specificity and the autonomy of the subjects involved. A democracy thus understood renders nameable, and therefore susceptible to collective decision making, those dilemmas that otherwise remain concealed and therefore neutralized within the procedures of pluralistic political systems. Hidden behind the formal rules of the democratic game are processes of selection and exclusion which stifle fundamental dilemmas. The presence of conflicts and the action of the movements that express them bring these dilemmas to the surface and enable them to be named. This function is crucial for human freedom and human rights in complex societies.

Whether both poles of society's dilemma can be maintained in acceptable equilibrium, if not resolved, depends on the extent and the solidity of this democratic space. It is the arena in which the great choices required of the collectivity become visible, and in which action can be taken to reduce to the minimum the exclusion and the silence that complexity produces. In this sense democracy becomes increasingly the space of language, where the diversity of the social raises its voice and encounters its limits.

Notes

1 I deliberately use the term 'planetary' instead of other terms such as 'global' or 'mondial'. With this choice I want to highlight the reference to the Planet Earth as a physical place: right now, it is the only place we can inhabit.
2 By 'systemic level' I mean a structural perspective that comprises the complexity of the whole system.

3 The adjective 'central' loses here its physical or geographical meaning: it refers to any society following the western capitalist model of organization. 'Central' societies may be found in Europe as well as in geographically remote places such as Singapore or Hong Kong.

4 This basic idea, common in classical sociology, has its roots in nineteenth-century theory. Even the fathers of sociology as a science (let us think of Comte or Durkheim) shared a belief in society which hides a metaphysical essence.

References

Anderson, B. (1991) *Imagined Communities*. London: Verso.

Bauman, Z. (1991) *Modernity and Ambivalence*. Cambridge: Polity Press.

Bauman, Z. (1993) *Postmodern Ethics*. Oxford: Blackwell.

Cohen, J. and Arato, A. (1992) *Civil Society and Political Theory*. Cambridge, MA: MIT Press.

Featherstone, M. (1992) *Consumer Culture and Postmodernism*. London: Sage.

Giddens, A. (1991) *Modernity and Self-Identity: Self and Society in the Late Modern Age*. Cambridge: Polity Press.

Giddens, A. (1992) *The Transformation of Intimacy*. Cambridge: Polity Press.

Kymlicka. W. (1995) *Multicultural Citizenship. A Liberal Theory of Minority Rights*. Oxford: Oxford University Press.

Maffesoli, M. (1995) *The Time of the Tribes*. London: Sage.

Melucci, A. (1989) *Nomads of the Present. Social Movements and Individual Needs in Contemporary Society*. Philadelphia: Temple University Press.

Melucci, A. (1996a) *The Playing Self. Person and Meaning in the Planetary Society*. Cambridge: Cambridge University Press.

Melucci, A. (1996b) *Challenging Codes. Collective Action in the Information Age*. Cambridge: Cambridge University Press.

Procacci, G. (1993) *Gouverner la Misère*. Paris: Seuil.

Sen, A.K. (1992) *Inequality Re-examined*. Oxford: Oxford University Press.

Somers, M. (1995) 'Narrating and naturalizing civil society and citizenship theory: the place of political culture and the public sphere', *Sociological Theory* 13, 3: 229–73.

Soysal, Y.N. (1994) *Limits of Citizenship. Migrants and Postnational Membership in Europe*. Chicago: University of Chicago Press.

Taylor, C. (1989) *Sources of the Self: The Making of the Modern Identity*. Cambridge, MA: Harvard University Press.

Tilly, C. (1995) *Citizenship, Identity and Social History*. Cambridge: Cambridge University Press.

Touraine, A. (1994) *Critique of Modernity*. Oxford: Blackwell.

Part II

Exclusions and inclusions in work and welfare

6 The paradox of global social change and national path dependencies

Life course patterns in advanced societies

Karl Ulrich Mayer

Introduction

When did I personally give up the conviction that Western advanced societies and the socialist countries were following alternative paths of development and modernization? It was in the spring of 1982 when a plane which brought me from Moscow to Tallin in Estonia touched the runway and the passengers applauded not only the success of the landing but also the music erupting from the intercom loudspeakers: 'By the rivers of Babylon ...'. Of course, in English. That Western pop culture was able to invade Aeroflot not only demonstrated global cultural hegemony. It also suggested that state socialism could probably not isolate itself sufficiently to follow its own developmental pattern in other important respects as well.

By 1989, that issue was settled (Zapf 1996). The idea that one could distinguish two major pathways of development – the modernization of Western liberal democracies in contrast to the development of state socialist societies – had collapsed. But if – with some minor remaining doubt in regard to China – socialism could not represent an alternative developmental goal and trajectory, then the assumption that advanced societies could be grouped together as changing in a broadly similar manner regained strength.

In the years after 1989 this tacit assumption that Western advanced societies are both subjects to and agents of broadly similar, global socio-economic developments has become even more widespread. I use the term 'global' here in a restricted sense. I do not want to talk about globalization in general, but hope to pick out two implications of this thesis. First, that the major socio-economic changes of advanced present-day societies are of essentially the same kind. And second, that the intensification of international market competition and the accompanying loss of national regulatory power are the underlying cause and mechanism of recent changes. Global social change, then, relates to the belief that globalization creates a set of similar pressures and challenges which allow or force similar responses. Some will be faster, some will be slower, but they all move on the same road. Moreover, these forces and trends will make societies ever more similar to each other.

Among these current social changes common to all advanced societies, the following are frequently taken to be most salient:

- increasing exposure to international market competition in trade, manufacturing, finance capital and services;
- a restructuring of occupational and organizational structures horizontally between sectors and firms and vertically between skill levels (upgrading/ skill shortage);
- the spread of both information technology and mass media culture;
- an increasing participation of women in education, training, employment and careers;
- a weakening of union power and employer–union coordination;
- a deregulation of labor markets partly induced or made possible by increasing international labor migration;
- a decreasing ability of national governments to carry through effective macroeconomic regulation beyond the control of money flow;
- a decreasing ability of national governments to influence collective bargaining;
- a decreasing ability of national governments to maintain a sufficient tax base for public investment and redistribution;
- pressures to reduce public spending for welfare programs despite increasing financial burdens due to the ageing of populations.

However, we as sociologists with the same degree of conviction also share a second belief, namely that major institutional, structural and cultural differences, partly based on century old historical foundations, do in fact exist. They exist not only between the former Western and the former socialist or between the Western and Asian countries, but also within the family of Western advanced societies. Because of such deeply set distinctions, these countries can be expected to change on their own different tracks for a long time to come. Even if pressures and challenges of global social change may to some degree be similar, the responses will vary widely given the diverging institutional configurations existing in any given country. Again let me give a preliminary list of such national characteristics:

- Countries differ markedly in the mean and the variance of the scope and quality of schooling and vocational/professional training and thus in their ability to supply the kinds and levels of skills required under newly-emerging divisions of labor (Tessaring 1998, Shavit and Müller 1998).
- The degree of political protection and subsidization of agriculture has a differential accelerating or delaying impact on the flow of the labor force from agriculture to manufacturing and services (Esping-Andersen 1999).
- Countries diverge in their degree of corporatist coordination: membership in unions and employers' associations, the respective rights of workers' councils (e.g., in case of dismissals), the legal rights in the protection of

workers and the extent of automatic coverage of collective bargaining agreements (Traxler 1996).

- The public sector plays a vastly different role in providing and setting standards for employment. For example, regarding women's employment, in some countries it provides few jobs altogether, while in others the public sector opens opportunities for the best skilled jobs for women, while in still other countries, it offers low qualified and low paid jobs for women (Esping-Andersen 1990).
- Welfare states differ in the scope of entitlements as well as in the kind and generosity of provisions. They differ, for instance, in regard to family allowances and family services (Gauthier 1996).
- National economies differ widely in their degree of export and import quotas, in the relative dominance of foreign or multinational corporations, in the forms of ownership, financing and managerial control.
- Cultural conceptions of gender roles change slowly and also lead to diverging patterns of female labor force participation and relative career commitments (Blossfeld and Hakim 1997).
- Finally, the definition of citizenship rights and access to them on the one hand and the degree of exclusion and inclusion into the boundaries of welfare state solidarities, but also spatial affinities and migration traditions, on the other hand, lead not only to varying relative proportions of populations of foreign descent, but greatly affect the degree and speed of assimilation and integration (Soysal 1994).

If one wants to understand why these nationally specific institutional configurations tend to be historically highly stable, the theoretical notion of 'path dependencies' might be helpful. Path dependency implies a bundle of ideas (see also North 1990a,b, North 1993, Arthur 1994, Pierson 1996):

- Basic choices between institutional alternatives, partly made a long time ago, tend to lock societies on to given tracks. They are often very difficult to reverse. Thus, small events can lead to high directionality and high inertia.
- Path dependencies often relate to processes of long-run, positive and increasing returns. However, they do not need to represent the best possible solution in the early stage of the process, nor do they need the final outcome to be beneficial.
- Even serious external pressures will not easily lead to change especially in politically regulated institutional systems, because high fixed costs, ingrained feedback processes, reduced coordination and transaction costs, action expectations adapted to the institutional set-up and in-built positive incentives tend to maximize the reproduction of the existing order.

These two cherished beliefs of, on the one hand, the uniformity of global change and of, on the other, highly stable national diversity are logically and empirically incompatible. Therefore, they present an unresolved paradox for sociological theory. I further believe that these apparent contradictions are not merely a matter of varying levels of generality or abstractness, but that – at least in the way they are usually presented – only one of the two views can be adequate.

As sociologists we tend to stress similar change across advanced countries when we look at longer time periods and we tend to highlight differences between countries and their relative stability when we compare societies at a given point in time.

In abstract, there could be the following solutions to this paradox. Solution 1 would show that the hypothesis of the pervasiveness and homogeneity of global change is adequate, no different or diverging pathways can be observed, but – at best – pioneers and latecomers. Solution 2 would show that the hypothesis of global change is wrong: diverging national pathways would then be the unsurprising observable consequence. Solution 3 would accept divergence for the past and convergence for the present: that increasing interconnection and competition will eradicate institutional and cultural differences. Solution 4 would accept that the processes of globalization exert roughly similar pressures and challenges for all advanced societies, but that historically ingrained, nationally specific institutional set-ups will lead to very different and nationally varying responses to similar pressures.

In the remainder of this chapter I will use the competing hypotheses of global social change and national path dependencies as a background for my examination of one particular aspect of modern societies: patterns of the life course. These include specific forms of educational pathways, employment biographies and family trajectories. Moreover, patterns of the life course also refer to diachronic aspects of social and economic inequalities across the life time as cumulative, cyclical or unstable and to nationally specific forms of social exclusions and of welfare entrapment. To the extent to which these various aspects of individual lives can be seen as being both interdependent and institutionally regulated, they can be understood as manifestations of particular life course regimes (Myles 1992, Mayer 1997).

In the following I shall first sketch the present state of theory on recent historical changes in the life course patterns of advanced societies. This theory quite perfectly fits the assumption of uniform and global social change as elaborated above. Second, I will reconstruct diverging national patterns of life course regimes. Here again it will become obvious that the latter constructions fall under the domain of our second general belief about national divergencies. It will also become apparent that each construct of both historical and national patterns of life courses implies specific conditions and forms of social exclusion and inclusion. Third, on this more concrete basis, I will again confront our paradox and ask whether and how it might be resolved.

Historical changes in life course regimes

There exists by now a stylized history of the development of life courses which – in different versions – has been well described, e.g., by Modell *et al.* (1976),

Hareven (1982), Anderson (1985), Kohli (1985), Held (1986), Mayer and Müller (1986), Buchmann (1989), Myles (1990, 1992) and Mayer (1998). Life courses are said to have developed from a traditional/pre-industrial to an industrial regime and after that to a post-industrial regime. The latter two regimes have also been labeled Fordist and Post-Fordist life cycle or the standardized and de-standardized life course. Let me stress here very strongly that these historical periods are theoretical constructs rather than validated empirical generalizations. Therefore not only are their boundaries as historical periods far from definite, but also their correspondence to actually lived lives. Persons can have lived various parts of their lives under the conditions assumed for different life course regimes.

Under the traditional, pre-industrial life course regime, life is assumed to center around the family household and its collective survival. Schooling was non-existent or short (only in winter when children were not needed on the farm), training was part of family socialization in one's own or other families as servants. Marriage was delayed until either the family farm could be inherited or a farm heiress be married or until a sufficient stock of assets could be assembled to establish a household, build a house, lease some land, etc. Life was unpredictable due to the vicissitudes of nature in harvests, and the probability of sickness and early death (especially for women in childbirth). Economic dependency and debts were widespread. The subjective counterpart of such a life course regime was a collective rather than individual identity, fatalism and religious complacency.

The early industrial life course regime is well-captured in Rowntree's (1914) image of a life cycle of poverty. Industrial workers rose only for a short time in their life above poverty, when the family was still small and physical working capacity at its peak. Schooling was compulsory, but ended at a relatively early age. Work started at the age of 12–14 and ended only with physical disability in old age. Marriage was delayed until sufficient resources for establishing a household (furniture, dowry) were accumulated and until employers were prepared to pay a family wage. Unemployment was frequent.

The next stage is postulated to be the industrial, Fordist life course regime. It is characterized by distinct life phases: schooling, training, employment and retirement with stable employment contracts and long working lives in the same occupation and firm. A living wage for the male breadwinner could allow women to stay at home after marriage. The risks of sickness, unemployment, disability and old age were covered and softened by an evermore comprising system of social insurances. Age at marriage and first birth decreased into the early twenties. Families could accumulate savings to buy their own housing and wages were age-graded. Real incomes and purchasing power increased for a good part of the working life and then stabilized until retirement when pensions and low rents or mortgage payments ensured a standard of living comparable to the one of the active years. Relative affluence allowed at least children to receive more education and training than the parental generation and parents could afford to support property acquisition of their children.

Table 6.1 Historical changes in life course regimes

Life course regimes	Traditional – c. 1900	Industrial – c. 1900 to c. 1955	Fordist/welfare state – c. 1955 to c. 1973	Post-fordist/ Post-industrial – c. 1973–
Unit	Family farm/ firm	Wage earner	Male breadwinner, nuclear family	Individual
Temporal organization	Unstable, unpredictable, discontinuity	Life cycle of poverty, discontinuity	Standardized, stabilized, continuity, progression	De-standardized, discontinuity
Distribution	Estate hierarchy	Class hierarchy	Middle-class integration, status distinctions	Classless, differentiation
Education	Minimal elementary	Medium compulsory	Expansion of secondary and tertiary education and of vocational training	Prolonged, interrupted, lifelong learning
Work	Personal dependency, family division of labor	Wage relationship, firm paternalism, unemployment	Full lifelong employment, upward mobility, income progression	Delayed entry, high between firm/between occupation mobility, flat income trajectories, unemployment
Family	Partial and delayed marriage, instability due to death, property centered, high fertility, early death	Delayed universal, fertility decline	Early universal marriage, early childbearing, medium fertility	Delayed and partial marriage, pluralized family forms, low fertility, high divorce rate, sequential promiscuity
Women	Family workers	Low-skilled supplementary wage earners	Housewives	Career employment

Table 6.1 Continued

Life course regimes	Traditional – c. 1900	Industrial – c. 1900 to c. 1955	Fordist/welfare state – c. 1955 to c. 1973	Post-fordist/ Post-industrial – c. 1973–
Retirement/ old age	With physical disability, old age dependency, early death	Regulatory or by disability, low pensions	Regulatory: medium pensions	Early retirement, decreasing pensions, increasing longevity, increasing chronic illness
Social policy risks	Debt, poverty, morbidity	Poverty, unemployment, disability, large families	Women's old age, poverty	Low skills, unemployment, solo mothers, early adult marginality
Institutional configuration	Rural economy, high fertility/high mortality	Capitalist economy, high labor supply, weak unions	Mass production/ consumption, strong unions, macro-economic regulation, welfare state expansion	Educational expansion, women's movement, value changes, weak unions, globalization, demographic ageing

The subjective hallmark of such a life course regime was material progression and accumulation, but also conformity to given roles within the economy and the family. Its logic followed the logic of division of labor within the nuclear family and of the family welfare as a joint utility function of the family members. Social identities were well-defined and stable. Stratification was homogenized and workers were integrated into society socially, economically and politically.

The standardized linear and homogeneous life course that emerged in post-World War II society is generally attributed to the coming together of two forces: Fordist industrial mass production in which a materially relatively secure working class became established, and the welfare state's guarantee of income across the entire life cycle of the family. The standardization of the life course meant in a sense that workers' life chances became 'middle class'.

The construct of a post-industrial, post-Fordist life course regime has, in contrast, been characterized by increasing de-standardization across the lifetime and increasing differentiation and heterogeneity across the population. Education has expanded in level and duration, vocational and professional training as well as further training has proliferated. A number of life transitions have been delayed or prolonged. With increasing age variance, the degree of universality and of sequential orderliness have decreased. Entry into employment is believed to have become more precarious, first work contracts are often temporary, employment interruptions due to unemployment, resumed education or training or other times out of the labor force have increased. The rate of job shifts increases and occupations are increasingly not life-long. Careers become highly contingent on the economic fates of the employing firms, therefore, heterogeneity across working lives increases. Downward career mobility increases relative to upward career opportunities. Working lives shorten due to later entry and frequent forced early retirement. The experience of unemployment becomes widespread, but is concentrated among women, foreign workers, young people and older workers. Age at marriage has increased. Non-marital unions become a normal phase before marriage. Parenthood is delayed and, for a significant part of the population, never comes about. Divorce increases as well as the number of children growing up in a single-parent household and/or without a father present in the household. Women overtake men in their share of general education and greatly increase their occupational qualifications. Women want to work life-long and they have to work to augment the family budget or support themselves as solo mothers. The standard of living in old age is threatened by reduced pension entitlements. The relationship between the home and the working place is changing rapidly. Women are out of the house most of the day.

The subjective counterpart is hedonistic individualism where all persons – even within a family – have their own life designs and life projects or, rather, follow egoistically the shifting material incentives and consumption idols from situation to situation.

These life course regimes also imply differences in the manner in which the lives of women and men are regulated. Under the traditional life course regime, gender roles were differentiated horizontally and functionally within the family as an economic unit and vertically according to the patriarchy of marriage and lineage. Women's lives were stratified according to their marriage opportunities and subject to the deathly risk of childbearing. Under the industrial life course regime, the widespread exclusion of women from continuous employment maximized the differences in gender roles and the resulting life course patterns. For post-industrial life course regimes there is some indication that despite persistent inequities in labor income and career opportunities, educational pathways and working lives of men and women tend to become more similar to each other.

Which institutional configurations shape these various life course regimes? The following is a preliminary suggestive list.

The traditional life course regime was regulated by the demographics of high mortality and high fertility, by the prerequisites and vicissitudes of a rural economy without the benefits of the agrochemical fertilization of soil and scientific animal husbandry.

The industrial life course regime was, in its early periods, subjected to an untamed capitalist economy with a weak labor movement and a high supply of labor (due to the first demographic transition as well as to the turbulence of the

Great Depression). In its later period after World War II, the industrial life course regime was made possible by an effective coordination between capital and labor, mass production and mass consumption, macro-economic policy intervention stabilizing economic cycles, full employment, rising real wages and standards of living, and, finally, welfare state expansion.

For the post-industrial, post-Fordist life course regime or life course disorder, a manifold of causes is named: educational expansion and its unintended effects, the women's movement, value changes, individualization and self-direction, weakness of unions, de-industrialization, the labor market crises with spiraling structural unemployment, globalization of economic markets, and the demographic crunch produced by the low levels of fertility and decreasing mortality.

Nationally varying political economies and diverging life course regimes

How plausible is the assumption of a common history of a sequence of life course regimes? Not only are the overall trends contested, but also the relative timing of the onset of new regimes and their duration are seen as varying widely between countries. One of the backbones of the developmental construct is the nature and timing of the shifts in the sectoral and occupational distribution of the labor force. De-ruralization was already far advanced in the last century for the United Kingdom, while for Germany the major shifts were delayed both by the Great Depression and World War II and its aftermath until the 1960s. For Italy, Spain and Ireland the exodus from agriculture extended well into the 1970s and 1980s. Likewise, de-industrialization and the exodus from manufacturing in the last decades started much earlier in the United States, but were delayed in Germany due to both its export-oriented manufacturing industry and its politically negotiated subsidies for the coal, steel and ship-building industries. Educational expansion and the labor force integration of married women took off at least a decade earlier in the Scandinavian countries than in Germany and came about even later in the Southern European countries. The welfare state was well-established in most advanced countries by the 1970s, albeit on differing levels and different forms, while Germany and Britain had their major expansions already in the aftermath of World War II (Esping-Andersen 1998).

Despite all these reservations, the commonality of something like a 'Golden Age' of post-World War II Western development is hardly disputed. The social integration and the relative affluence of the working class, employment and occupational stability, increasing real wages and standards of living, the extraordinarily good times for family formation and childbearing are characteristic even if the timing differs. It is also hardly contested that all of the advanced countries faced major changes in the temporal and social organization of the lives of men and women from the early 1970s until today.

My major thesis is that the impacts of the current shared processes of de-industrialization and globalization on life courses will crucially depend on the institutional configuration and dominant political economy in given countries. Not only will the degree of period inequalities typically differ, but also the distribution and temporal patterns of inequalities across the life time (Esping-Andersen, Mayer and Myles 1997). Moreover, Esping-Andersen in his recent book (1999) has advanced strong arguments that institutional configurations may lead to differing and deducible forms of what he calls 'welfare entrapments'.

The leading idea resembles closely what Glen Elder (1974) in his classic study on the 'Children of the Great Depression' has called accentuation. How families coped with the effects of the Great Depression depended highly on their initial competencies and resources. Poor competencies and poor resources easily led to 'vicious circles' of deprivation and marginalization, whereas good competencies and good resources allowed one to cope with the effects of the Great Depression quite successfully. As a result, heterogeneity and inequality between families increased.

Likewise, we might assume that in the good times of the post-war 'Golden Age', differences between countries and between persons within a country in basic resources, institutional options and restrictions mattered less than in times of shortage and decline. Therefore, it is reasonable to assume that, in the current period, national characteristics will have a greater impact on life course regimes than in the 1960s and early 1970s. We would, therefore, expect a growing divergence between countries as well as a growing heterogeneity and inequality within countries.

To examine this thesis, I will now proceed in three steps. First, for seven countries – Germany (West), USA, Great Britain, Denmark, Sweden, Italy and France – I will demarcate those institutions which are most decisive for life course outcomes. Second, I will group these countries into four major types and look at various aspects of the life course. Third, in doing so I will develop hypotheses on the likely outcomes, i.e., the degree of convergence or divergence in life course regimes between countries to be expected in the near future. Most of the relevant information is condensed in Tables 6.2, 6.3 and 6.4 and, due to space considerations, only partial comments are included in the text.

In regard to schooling and training, the most important institutional distinction is probably the one between countries with hierarchically segregated secondary schools and an apprenticeship system, on the one hand, and countries with universal secondary schools on the other hand. This distinction separates Germany (together with Austria and the German-speaking parts of Switzerland) from the rest of our countries. If we then look at the degree of institutional linkage between education, training and the early occupational career, we find a close and hierarchical coupling in Germany and France. These are based on educational ladders in Germany and on organizational ladders in France. There are much looser or more varied connections in the UK, Scandinavian and the Southern European countries (Shavit and Müller 1998).

The protection of workers in the labor market is low in the UK, but relatively rigid in the others. Low protection makes the reallocation of workers between firms easier and thus allows economies to adapt faster to external

Table 6.2 Institutional variation and life course outcomes

Macro-variates		GER	USA	UK	DK	SWE	IT	FRA
School								
Schooling			✗	✗	✗	✗		✗
Training		✗			✗			
Education – occupation link								
Loose			✗	✗	✗	✗	✗	
Educational space		✗			✗			
Organizational space					✗			✗
Labor market								
Regulated		✗			✗	✗	✗	✗
Deregulated			✗	✗				
Labor market flexibility								
Internal	High	✗						
Within firm	Low		✗	✗	✗	✗	✗	✗
External	High		✗	✗				
Between firms	Low	✗			✗	✗	✗	✗
Welfare state								
Private protection insurance			✗	✗				
Collective protection		✗			✗	✗	(✗)	✗
Public employment policies					✗	✗		(✗)
No employment policies		✗	✗	✗			(✗)	
Good family services					✗	✗		✗
Bad family services		✗	✗	✗			✗	
Means-tested, targeted			✗	✗			✗	
Universal		✗			✗	✗		✗
Employment based		✗						✗
Citizenship based					✗	✗		
Low			✗	✗			✗	
Economic relations								
Market			✗	✗				
Macro-corporate		✗			✗	✗		✗
Micro-networks							✗	
Role of state								
Non-interventionist			✗	✗				
Regulatory		✗			✗	✗		
Public ownership							✗	✗
Continental conservative welfare state		✗						✗
Liberal market state			✗	✗				
Scandinavian social democratic welfare state					✗	✗		
Southern Europe welfare state							✗	

changes. Here, the UK seems to have an advantage. However, this is only one aspect of labor market flexibility. The other aspect concerns the ability of firms to flexibly reassign tasks within the firm – and here the countries with a well-developed training system should have an advantage (Rhodes and van Appeldoorn 1997).

Welfare states and the corresponding provisions differ from each other in various important aspects. Are legal entitlements primarily based on citizenship or employment? Are insurances mainly collective or private? Are provisions legally defined and universal or means-tested? Do countries provide good family services or bad? Do they pursue full employment policies or not? On these dimensions, our countries show very different welfare mixes. For example, French and Scandinavian women can rely on good child care facilities. Scandinavian women can also count on the public to care for the elderly. Unemployed Scandinavian young adults until recently had claims on a social wage independent of preceding employment. Germans cannot count on aggressive public employment measures but on fairly generous unemployment, sickness and disability compensation. With some notable exceptions such as old age pensions in Italy, Southern Europeans must primarily rely on their families (Esping-Andersen 1990, 1999; Lessenich/Ostner 1998).

These variants in the organization of the welfare state show a fair degree of correspondence to the manner in which these societies achieve coordination in their economic systems. The Liberal Market States are reluctant welfare providers, while countries with a high degree of corporatist coordination between employers and unions rely on the welfare state to provide social wages for the unemployable or to offer public employment. Where micro-networks of family, kinship and locality play an important role in the internal and external relations of firms, the family must also act as a buffer for those who can neither succeed in the private sector nor exploit the state as an employer.

Even such a crude representation of the institutional configuration of the societies under consideration raises some serious questions about the adequacy of putting given countries in the correct boxes. There are important differences between the countries classified together. The centralized étatiste France is almost a type of its own, as is probably Germany. But to be able at all to relate institutional configurations to life course regimes, I will nonetheless simplify matters by collapsing our countries into four categories: the Liberal Market States, the Continental Conservative Welfare States, the Scandinavian Social Democratic Welfare States and the Southern European Welfare States. These are then the 'Three Western Worlds of Welfare Capitalism' depicted by Gøsta Esping-Andersen (1990) augmented by Italy and Spain (see also Esping-Andersen 1999; and for severe conceptual and empirical critiques of the Esping-Andersen typology, Lessenich and Ostner 1998; for other attempts to classify advanced societies, see Soskice 1991, Allmendinger and Hinz 1997, Mayer 1997, Hakim 1999). Thus, the major thrust of my argument here is *not* whether and how countries can be grouped together into types of welfare state regimes, but that I can make plausible in an exemplary manner that institutional configurations and life course regimes co-vary in a systematic manner, and in what way this occurs. The success of the latter does not depend on the feasibility of welfare state regimes, but on the feasibility of the institution–life course outcomes linkage. They are introduced here basically as a short-hand device to concentrate in a chapter what otherwise would have to be a lengthy monograph.

Liberal Market States are taken to be characterized by the following institutional configuration: little stratification in the school system, no well-developed institutions for vocational training, a poor performance in training the work force for skilled labor, high labor market flexibility in reallocating workers between firms, a relatively low level of welfare income redistribution, low social insurance levels, citizenship based and targeted, means-tested social provisions, poor family services.

The Continental Conservative Welfare State for which Germany is our major example has developed institutions which make for stratified and selective schooling, a well-developed training system, a good performance in skill formation and therefore high internal labor market flexibility, but highly segregated, segmented and rigid labor markets. Social insurance is, in comparison, at relatively higher levels and is mostly based on entitlements derived from employment. Family services are relatively poor and therefore make it difficult for women to maintain continuous work careers.

The Scandinavian Social Democratic Welfare States do not stratify and segregate their secondary school system and are relatively efficient in providing vocational training within the school system. Their citizens enjoy very high levels of social insurance based on universal citizenship rights and the general tax base. Family services are excellent and therefore allow women to become fully integrated into the labor market, not least in the family services themselves.

Finally, the Southern European Welfare States have stratified schooling systems, a mixture of school and firm-based vocational training, low transfers except for pensions and high labor market rigidity.

What are the consequences of these four institutional configurations, and different political economies for the predominant life course regimes? To capture essential aspects of such life course regimes I have selected twelve variables:

- leaving the parental home,
- the age of leaving school or formalized training,
- the process of labor market entry,
- the rate of fluctuation as work life mobility between firms,
- the rate of work life mobility between occupations,
- the shape and distribution of income trajectories,
- the rate of unemployment,
- the labor force participation of women,
- the degree of career involvement of women,

- fertility and the stability of families,
- median and dispersion of the age at retirement, and, finally,
- the specific life course risks, the manner of negative entrapment related to each of the life course regimes.

What are the life course profiles for each of the political economy types? At this preliminary stage of theory building, they cannot be put forth with strong claims as to their proven validity. They should be taken therefore as initial hypotheses or stylized facts (see also Esping-Andersen 1997).

Table 6.3 Political economies and life course outcomes

	Liberal market state	Continental conservative welfare state	Scandinavian social democratic welfare state	Southern European welfare state
Leaving home	Early, high variance	Medium, high variance	Early, low variance	Late, high variance
Age leaving school/training	Medium homogeneous	High stratified	Medium	Low stratified
Labor market entry	Early, stop-gap, low skill	Late, integrated, high skill	Early, integrated	Late, marginal
Firm shifts	High	Low	Low	Low
Occupational shifts	High	Low	High	Low
Income trajectories	Flat, high variance	Progressive, low variance	Flat, low variance	Progressive, high variance
Unemployment	Low	High	High	High
Employment of women	High	Low	High	Low
Careers of women	High, continuous	Low, interrupted	Low, continuous	Low, dualist
Family	Unstable, medium fertility	Stable, low fertility	Stable, medium fertility	Stable, low fertility
Retirement	Low replacement, high variance	High replacement, low variance, early	High replacement, low variance, late	Late, high variance
Entrapment	Low skill, low wage, employed, poverty	Unemployed, out of labor force, early retirement	Low skill, female public employment, welfare careers	Youth unemployment, old age care

Universal and comprehensive schooling without institutionalized appren-
ticeships in the Liberal Market states makes for a median and fairly standardized
age at leaving school. There is some variance (due to high school drop-outs in
the US and the private school sector in the UK) and due to the differences
between O- and A-levels in Britain, but in comparison non-selective, comprehensive school systems standardize the length and finishing age of the formative
period. Labor market entry comes early even for college graduates but the transition between education and full labor market integration is often marked by a
sequence of stop-gap jobs (Allmendinger 1989, Oppenheimer and Kalmijn
1995). Low paid and marginal employment as well as unemployment is widespread among young workers. Educational certificates are of minor importance,
occupational identities are weak and therefore work lives are primarily structured by individual attempts to make good earnings. Commitment to given
firms is low and job shifts between firms are frequent. Deregulated labor markets
foster employment, but depress wages. Mean income trajectories are fairly flat
across the working lives because efficiency wages and seniority premiums are
weak and effects of the business cycle are stronger than age effects. Labor
income inequality is high, but the stability of relative income positions across
the working life is low. Employment opportunities for women are good and
employment trajectories are highly continuous, but women's work is hardly
optional, because their contribution to the family budget is badly needed. There
are many opportunities for a variable length of the working day for women. But
this, of course, also means that full-time employment is scarce (Blossfeld and
Hakim 1997, Hakim 1999). Probably because of the relative economic
independence of women, divorce rates are high, but so are remarriage rates of
women with children who could hardly cope otherwise. Nonetheless, and
despite poor family allowances and services, fertility among these countries is
not low. At retirement, the replacement rate of pension income compared to
the final wages is relatively low and there is a high variance of the median age
at retirement, because on the one hand, older workers can be fired easily, and
on the other hand, older workers continue to work even at lower wages because
of the low level of expected pension income. What are the major risks in this
life course regime, i.e., what are likely conditions of social exclusion? Low skills,
low wages and life as a working poor person below or close to the poverty level.
For a considerable proportion of the population the threat of a cumulative cycle
of disadvantage is very real.

Continental Conservative Welfare States stratify school and training tracks
and thus induce a higher variance in the ages at which young adults leave the
formative period. A prolonged educational period also pushes the age of leaving
home upward, but its variance is tied to educational and training decisions.
To the extent to which training is organized within firms, transitions to
employment are smoother and integrated along the lines of occupational tracks.
Training investments by both firms and young people are high and therefore the
attainment and the later use of certified skills play a large role in young people's
lives. Job shifts between firms are rare and changes between fields of

occupational activities are even rarer. For those who successfully manage their labor market entry, mean income trajectories are progressive up to the early forties and then flatten out. Efficiency wages and seniority schemes are widespread even in the private sector. The industry-wide binding character of collective agreements and informal wage coordination between industry unions ensures relatively low degrees of wage inequality. Labor market rigidities go hand-in-hand with high rates of unemployment, especially for younger workers of foreign descent, women and older workers who become laid off. Although the labor force participation of women has been increasing rapidly, the opportunities for married women with younger children are limited. Career interruptions in the early years after childbirth and later part-time work are normatively expected and institutionally supported by restricted child care and child leave options. Marriages are comparatively stable, but fertility is low. Especially for women with higher education, a dualistic behavior pattern is observable: either high career commitment with no children or career withdrawal and two children. Retirement comes early because firms try to get rid of more expensive older workers, but this practice is increasingly limited by tighter disability and old age pension rules. The major life course risks in this political economy are long-term unemployment and being pushed into the group of labor market outsiders.

I should add that this primarily refers to (West) Germany. France is a deviating case especially in regard to its good family allowances, good child care facilities and high rates of full-time employment of women. East Germany has been remodeled institutionally along the lines of the old Federal Republic with a resulting dramatic reduction of the employed labor force especially via forced early retirement, but still maintaining higher levels of women's labor force participation.

Life courses in the Scandinavian Social Democratic Welfare States are distinct, especially regarding the full-time, full working life integration of women into the labor force, a somewhat higher level of fertility until the nineties, the non-temporary character of non-marital unions, the public support for active labor market integration policies, and, finally, relatively late ages at retirement. The major life course risks are the transitions from comprehensive school to employment resulting in relatively high levels of youth unemployment (or youth in public employment programs), and the entrapment into low wage, low skill employment in the public sector for women. Another risk is the one of becoming dependent on welfare payments for a longer period of life.

Life courses in the residual welfare states of southern Europe for both women and men are closely tied to the fortunes of the larger family. Not only is access to employment highly dependent on family and kinship connections, but most of the welfare burdens are put on families. A large number of unemployed or marginally employed young people live with their families longer than anywhere in Europe. Care for chronically ill old people is left almost exclusively to families. Women have caught up with men in their educational attainments and occupational qualifications and many of these qualified women delay or renounce child bearing to escape the burdens connected with motherhood. In family patterns, marriage is still almost universal, but child bearing diverges greatly between North and South, city and country and according to the educational level of women. As a consequence, inequalities between families are high and for individuals, they tend to be cumulative across the life course. Only in regard to pensions for certain occupational groups does the Southern European Welfare State show surprising generosity in level and in regard to the early age of eligibility.

We can summarize these life course regimes as ideal types according to four dimensions:

- Which is the unit around which life courses are primarily organized in the four types of political economies?
- What is the predominant temporal organization of states and events across the lifetime?
- How heterogeneous and unequal are life courses between social classes and between men and women?
- How do inequalities within birth cohorts develop across their collective lifetime?

In the Liberal Market States the basic unit and actor in the life course is the individual. The organization of life time is not particularly standardized and exhibits a fair degree of discontinuity. Income inequalities are on a high level in comparison and increasing across time. They are accentuated by highly unequal and dualistic access to social insurance. Those who can afford private insurance are well-covered and those who cannot afford private insurance are at risk of falling into poverty. The high labor market integration of women, in contrast, tends to favor equity between men and women. The relative income position across the life course is quite unstable, but still tends to result in cumulative cycles of privilege and disadvantage and, thus, increasing inequality across the life course.

Continental Conservative Welfare States organize life courses around the nuclear family (although with increasing parts of the life time and for increasing groups outside). In comparison life courses are still highly continuous and standardized. Cross-sectional inequalities are in the medium range and fairly stable across worklife and retirement. Inequalities, however, increase between those integrated into the highly protected labor market and those who either have a hard time entering or are being phased out into early retirement via temporary unemployment or are being kept out (at least partially in life time and in working hours) such as women. Some of these outsiders are cushioned by social wages and others by their families. Gender inequalities are decreasing somewhat – more obviously in general education, less in occupational training, tertiary education and employment, and much less in occupational careers. But these gains are threatened when external pressures increase, and risks are again disproportionately shared by women (as well as foreigners).

Table 6.4 Political economies and life course regimes

	Unit	Temporal organization	Inequalities; heterogeneity	Intra cohort/time inequalities
Liberal market state Low stratified schooling No training Low skill High external flexibility Low transfers Low protection Targeted, need Citizenship based Low family services	Individual	Discontinuity, de-standardized	High, dualism: private protection/ excluded, gender equality	Unstable, cumulative and high inequality
Continental conservative welfare state Stratified schooling Training/high skill High internal flexibility High transfer High protection Employment based Low family services	Family	Continuity, standardized	Medium, male dominance	Stable, medium inequality Insiders/ dependents/ outsiders
Scandinavian social democratic welfare state Low stratified schooling High skill High protection Citizenship based Good family services	Individual	Continuity, standardized	Low, homogeneity, gender equality	Stable, equality
Southern European welfare state Stratified schooling Low transfers Low protection	Family	Continuity, de-standardized	High, male dominance	Unstable, cumulative and high inequality

Scandinavian Social Democratic Welfare State societies favor the individual as unit and agent of the life course. Their high degrees of social protection support continuity across life and tend to standardize life courses. Although disparities increase, the income distribution is still quite equitable and transfer incomes stabilize and equalize income trajectories.

In the Southern European Welfare States the bulk of increasing risks of unemployment and of an ageing population is loaded onto the families. Thus, the individual life course depends highly on the relative ability of families to cushion risks. This should increase cross-sectional and life course inequalities.

The paradox reconsidered

In the beginning of this chapter, I confronted two major and conflicting perspectives on the development of advanced societies: the commonality of global change and the institutionally based national path dependencies. A closer inspection of one 'dependent variable' for both of these processes – life courses – can help to resolve this paradox. The big issue is what kind of transformation in institutional arrangements and life course outcomes we should expect under the impact of the global changes outlined above. This chapter can, at best, help to set the stage for starting to answer this question. What I have attempted to document here is not only the considerable degree of variation in institutional arrangements, but also their close linkages to life course outcomes. Following this premise any impacts of global changes must necessarily be mediated through the initial institutional configurations. We may therefore expect diverging rather than converging life course regimes in the countries under consideration. Even if institutions will also come under pressure for reorganization and will have to adapt eventually, this process will likely be much slower than the intermediate redistribution of life chances under the condition of existing institutions.

What will be the likely outcome of those processes for social exclusion? On the one hand, we find worsening conditions for a number of social groups which are, to some extent, common to all the countries under consideration here such as: young adults without training and qualifications, young adults from migrant worker families, single mothers and young families with more than two small children. These groups tend to lose both in relative and absolute terms.

On the other hand we also find different and probably increasingly divergent outcomes in the way social exclusion manifests itself. In Liberal Market States cycles of disadvantage concern entrapment in a condition of 'working poor' when wages do not guarantee a life above poverty level. For marginal groups, these forms of entrapment are accompanied by high rates of violence, self-destructiveness and imprisonment. Whether new kinds of policies like the Earned Income Tax Credit in the US will be able to counteract these tendencies effectively remains to be seen. In Continental Conservative Welfare States social exclusion typically takes the form of exclusion from the labor markets. This applies to young adults, but in varying degrees – e.g., higher in France and lower in Germany. Most frequently, however, it is older workers who are channeled out of the labor force via long-term unemployment. An additional form of social exclusion exists for that heterogeneous conglomerate of persons who are waiting between various forms of social wages, e.g., between unemployment benefit and disability pension. Scandinavian Social Democratic Welfare States remain fairly efficient in preventing permanent social exclusion, since they can still rely on a broad consensus for redistribution and interventionist policies. In the Southern European Welfare States social exclusion accumulates massively among the ranks of the unemployed young adults.

There are counteracting tendencies to such an increasing divergence. One impressive example is the Youth Training Initiative financed by the European Social Fund which, in 1999, reached hundreds of thousands of young adults throughout the European Union. But whether its effects will be more than temporary will depend greatly on whether the European financing is substituted by permanent national programs and whether subsidized training leads to permanent employment or not.

Finally, a concluding remark is in order on how the research program outlined in this chapter will have to proceed. A first further step will be to validate the cross-sectional country profiles in regard to institutional configuration, life course outcomes and their inter-linkages. A second major step will have to transform both the institutional configuration and the life course outcomes into diachronic accounts across time, i.e., into accounts of institutional and behavioral change. As a third step, comparative micro-analytic longitudinal studies will have to be employed to unravel the causal linkages between institutional setups and life course regimes.

Acknowledgments

This chapter is closely related to research carried out in two on-going projects: The German Life History Study at the Max-Planck-Institut für Bildungsforschung Berlin, Center for Sociology and the Study of the Life Course, and the POLIS-Project (Political Economies and Life Courses in Advanced Societies) coordinated at the Robert-Schuman-Centre of the European University Institute in Florence. I especially want to thank my co-principal investigators in the POLIS-Project – Gøsta Esping-Andersen (Trento), John Myles (Tallahassee) and Richard Breen (Florence) – for many of the ideas in this chapter. Our jointly developed proposal for the POLIS-project and our debates during the academic year 1996–7 are the basic source for the views and information in this chapter. I gratefully acknowledge the support of the Robert-Schuman-Centre at the European University Institute in Florence and of the Max-Planck Society for the Advancement of Science for my stay in Florence in the framework of the Jean-Monnet-Chair during the academic year 1996–7.

References

Allmendinger, J. (1989) 'Educational systems and labor market outcomes', *European Sociological Review* 5: 231–50.

Allmendinger, J. and Hinz, T. (1997) 'Mobilität und Lebensverlauf: Deutschland, Großbritannien und Schweden im Vergleich', in *Die westeuropäischen Gesellschaften im Vergleich*, S. Hradil and S. Immerfall (eds). Opladen: Leske and Budrich, pp. 247–85.

Anderson, M. (1985) 'The emergence of the modern life cycle in Britain', *Social History* 10: 69–87.

Arthur, B.W. (1994) *Increasing Returns and Path Dependence in the Economy*. Ann Arbor, MI: University of Michigan Press.

Blossfeld, H.-P. and Hakim, C. (1997) *Between Equalization and Marginalization. Women*

Working Part-Time in Europe and the United States of America. Oxford: Oxford University Press.

Buchmann, M. (1989) *The Script of Life in Modern Society. Entry into Adulthood in a Changing World*. Chicago: University of Chicago Press.

Elder, G. (1974) *Children of the Great Depression*. Chicago: University of Chicago Press.

Esping-Andersen, G. (1990) *The Three Worlds of Welfare Capitalism*. Princeton, NJ: Princeton University Press.

Esping-Andersen, G. (1997) 'The comparative political economy dimension. Life course profiles within different welfare regimes'. (Paper prepared for the 1st International POLIS project workshop, February/March, European University Institute, Florence.)

Esping-Andersen, G. (1998) 'Social foundations of postindustrial economies', (Manuscript), University of Trento.

Esping-Andersen, G. (1999) *Social Foundations of Postindustrial Economies*. Oxford: Oxford University Press.

Esping-Andersen, G., Mayer, K.U. and Myles, J. (1997) 'Political economies and life courses in advanced societies (POLIS-Project). A research project outline', Florence. Robert Schuman Centre, European University Institute.

Gauthier, A.H. (1996) *The State and the Family. A Comparative Analysis of Family Policies in Industrialized Countries*. Oxford: Clarendon Press.

Gauthier, A.H. and Furstenberg F.F. Jr. (1999) How do young people use their time? A cross-national comparison of time budget surveys. (Paper presented at the Conference 'Transition into Adulthood', Philadelphia, 9–11 April 1999.)

Hakim, C. (1999) 'Models of the family, women's role and social policy', *European Societies* 1, 1: 33–58.

Hareven, T.K. (1982) 'The life course and aging in historical perspective', in *Aging and Life Course Transitions: An Interdisciplinary Perspective*, T.K. Hareven and K.J. Adams (eds). London: Tavistock, pp. 1–26.

Held, T. (1986) 'Institutionalization and deinstitutionalization of the life course', *Human Development* 29: 157–62.

Kohli, M. (1985) 'Die Institutionalisierung des Lebenslaufs. Historische Befunde und theoretische Argumente', *Kölner Zeitschrift für Soziologie und Sozialpsychologie* 37: 1–29.

Lessenich, S. and Ostner, I. (eds) (1998) *Welten des Wohlfahrtskapitalismus. Der Sozialstaat in vergleichender Perspektive*, Frankfurt am Main: Campus.

Mayer, K.U. (1997) 'Notes on a comparative political economy of life courses', *Comparative Social Research* 16: 203–26.

Mayer, K.U. (1998) 'Lebensverlauf', in *Handwörterbuch zur Gesellschaft Deutschlands*, B. Schäfers and W. Zapf (eds). Opladen: Leske and Budrich, pp. 438–51.

Mayer, K.U. and Müller, W. (1986) 'The state and the structure of the life course', in *Human Development and the Life Course: Multidisciplinary Perspectives*, A.B. Sørensen, F.E. Weinert and L.R. Sherrod (eds). Hillsdale, NJ: Lawrence Erlbaum Associates, pp. 217–45.

Modell, J., Furstenberg, F.F. and Hershberg, T. (1976) 'Social change and transition to adulthood in historical perspective', *Journal of Family History* 1: 7–32.

Myles, J. (1990) 'States, labor markets and life cycles', in *Beyond the Marketplace: Rethinking Economy and Society*, R. Friedland and A.F. Robertson (eds). New York: Aldine de Gruyter, pp. 271–98.

Myles, J. (1992) 'Is there a post-Fordist life course?' in *Institutions and Gatekeeping in the Life Course*, W.R. Heinz (ed.). Weinheim: Deutscher Studien Verlag, pp. 171–85.

North, D.C. (1990a) 'A transaction cost theory of politics', *Journal of Theoretical Politics* 2: 355–67.

North, D.C. (1990b) *Institutions, Institutional Change and Economic Performance.* Cambridge: Cambridge University Press.

North, D.C. (1993) 'Institutions and credible commitment', *Journal of Institutional and Theoretical Economics (JITE)* 149: 11–23.

Oppenheimer, V.K. and Kalmijn, M. (1995) 'Life-cycle jobs', *Research in Social Stratification and Mobility* 14: 1–38.

Pierson, P. (1996) 'Path dependence and the study of politics'. (Paper prepared for presentation at the American Political Science Association meetings, San Francisco, September 1996.)

Rhodes, M. and van Apeldoorn, B. (1997) 'The transformation of west European capitalism?' in *Developments in West European Politics*, M. Rhodes, P. Heywood and V. Wright (eds). London: Macmillan, pp. 171–89.

Rowntree, B.S. (1914) *Poverty. A Study in Town Life*. London et al.: Nelson (first published 1901).

Shavit, Y. and Müller, W. (1998) *From School to Work: A Comparative Study of Educational Qualifications and Occupational Destinations*. Oxford: Clarendon Press.

Soskice, D. (1991) 'The institutional infrastructure for international competitiveness: a comparative analysis of the UK and Germany', in *The Economics for the New Europe*, A.B. Atkinson and R. Brunetta (eds). London: Macmillan, pp. 45–66.

Soysal, Y.N. (1994) *The Limits of Citizenship: Migrants and Postnational Membership in Europe*. Chicago (u.a.): University of Chicago Press, 244 S.

Tessaring, M. (1998) *Training for a Changing Society. A Report on Current Vocational Education and Training Research in Europe*. Thessaloniki: CEDEFOP-European Centre for the Development of Vocational Training.

Traxler, F. (1996) 'Collective bargaining and industrial change: a case of disorganization? A comparative analysis of eighteen OECD countries', *European Sociological Review* 12: 271–87.

Zapf, W. (1996) 'Die Modernisierungstheorie und unterschiedliche Pfade der gesellschaftlichen Entwicklung', *Leviathan* 24: 63–77.

7 Reconsidering the socialist welfare state model

Mojca Novak

Introduction

Post-socialist countries share many common factors and features of development. Among other things we find the lack of a significant social policy that has been accompanied by an overwhelming and excessive concern for welfare from cradle to grave (Ferge, in Ferge and Kolberg 1992) that rendered people socially helpless. Social policy under socialism repeatedly showed itself to have been used as a reward for those classes that showed themselves to be politically loyal, while social rights themselves remained an unachievable ideal. Moreover, these welfare state regimes revealed themselves as a fusion of both economic and social sectors, concentrating on the 'work sector' that brings them close to the Bismarckian concept of welfare (Marklund 1993). Despite its orientation to work, this application of the term 'welfare state' pays homage to those universal schemes which encouraged the belief that social austerity under socialism could be transcended. Insofar as we find poverty and social insecurity used as an instrument to undermine those 'disloyal' citizens and social classes that were defined as being 'incompatible' with socialism, such as farmers and artisans, there was, nevertheless, no particular official concern expressed. Moreover, the data on poverty remained secret for official reasons (Szalai 1992). In contrast, as soon as the social classes that were supposed to be protected by social policy programmes began to lose their fight against poverty and social insecurity, they became a topic of growing political concern. It was unexpectedly revealed in the 1980s that socialist societies were far from achieving success in the fight for welfare and well-being. The lived reality was closer to an 'austerity' society than to an 'affluent' one, and this fact initiated a re-awakened interest among both politicians and experts for the social malady of social insecurity. Criticism of social policy under socialism was launched. It tried to prove the existence of omission and to demonstrate the inefficiency of the 'socialist' welfare state.

However, other views can help in building a different analytical framework for the re-consideration of the development of welfare regimes under socialism. If the formation of these regimes is viewed in the perspective of a century as an intensive process of interweaving influential ideas from neighbouring countries with traditional settings, then new aspects of the roots of 'socialist' welfare emerge. Welfare under socialism appears as a solid structure that has fuelled its engine with the characteristics of welfare from the pre-socialist stage of its development. When we reconsider it over a longer perspective, we see it proves to be reluctant to undergo significant changes. Schemes of provision could be extended, they could also be reduced, but its basic character remained preserved. Viewing the development of the 'socialist' welfare state in this perspective, some other issues also dot this mural, proving that the resistance to major changes is a widespread commonality among these regimes. Pioneering ideas and initiatives are powerful and instructive but if they fail to complement the welfare tradition and class-coalitions, they find only minor support from the political elite.

The development of welfare state regimes can be seen from various perspectives. It can be perceived as a controlling mechanism of the adversity and deficiency of industrialism (De Swaan 1988). It could be viewed as an innovative European completion of nation state building (Flora 1986). Finally, it could be considered as a system of social agents (Baldwin 1990), aiming at welfare redistribution. This variation in possible analytical frameworks brings the author to the core of her intentions to reconsider the development of welfare state regimes in Central Europe opposing the myth of their dominant socialist character. For this purpose, the analysis will be launched by highlighting certain major features of the transition period as they are reflected on the welfare sector and the social policy of the former 'socialist' regimes. Some reflection on the most outstanding properties of welfare state development in general will follow. The analysis of a set of selected Central European welfare regimes constitutes the centre-piece of this venture, and focuses on Hungary, the Czech Republic and Slovenia. The findings lead to conclusions about commonality and divergence among the welfare fabrics considered. Such sifting of the available empirical evidence on the subject concerned should enable us to learn from the past. As French writer and philosopher Andre Malraux, who showed a profound inclination towards embroidering the sociological perception into his 'royal' and 'conquering' novels on 'human fate' inspires us, 'If one wants to read the future, one should first read the past.'

Transition from socialist to post-socialist welfare regimes

The basis of the socialist welfare philosophy was the premise that it is in the best interests of society to alleviate poverty and to assist those who are unable to care for themselves, by increasing production, rather than by embarking on a protective policy of income distribution. The close link between welfare and a work incentive policy could also be seen as a means of steering the distribution of resources towards those most in need, but primarily, it was an instrument for the promotion of economic development and the consolidation of socialism (Dixon and Macarov 1992: 2–3). The distribution of benefits was heavily focused on enterprises with a monopolistic structure of production and distribution, and these were generally associated with a monopolistic control of the generation and distribution of social services. Because employment was guaranteed, the existence of unemployment was officially denied. Although people had jobs, they were frequently under-employed. Regardless of being dependent on the work-record, the old (socialist) system of welfare was also de-commodified (Deacon 1992: 178). The state played a major role in social policy, establishing it as an integrative part of the economy (Marklund 1993: 108). The original vision of the welfare system was very idealistic, although, ultimately, it failed to prosper. After decades of implementing socialist principles of welfare, an over-centralised, non-democratic, paternalistic state evolved, which 'spoilt' its people by making them totally dependent on its provision of social services (Ferge 1991: 431). Regardless of non-impressive results and many failures, these welfare systems did work. There was a widespread social security in terms of broad and secure access to basic services, at least for the fully employed (Ferge 1996).

Since 1989, social policy in Central and Eastern Europe has painfully experienced the post-socialist transformation, undergoing major and significant distortions. A substantial reduction of benefits on the one hand, and increasing demands for independent social initiatives on the other, are features which all revealed a wide divergence of problems. 'Ad-hoc-ism' in providing new services and the privatisation of some 'old' ones accompanied a demanded withdrawal of the state (Deacon 1992: 189–90). The future prospects for a post-socialist welfare and social policy thus significantly depend on economic restrictions and on the lack of strong countervailing social forces (Marklund 1993: 112). For the first time in history, international agencies will substantially influence redistribution objectives and outcomes, accompanying the disruption of economy (Marklund 1993: 112). For these reasons, the power elite advocates a major reduction of the welfare state, encouraging family support, local help, self-help and charity (Ferge 1991: 431). The new system of social policy should be shaped precisely against the perceived failures of the old, socialist system. This means that it will be highly commodified and will generate a new system of inequalities in which different coalitions among the old *nomenklatura*, new entrepreneurs, and privileged sections of the working class can emerge (Deacon 1992: 192).

Regardless of how sincere and well-argued the criticisms of the welfare state under socialism and its post-socialist prospects were, they were inadequate in revealing its complex nature. They mostly provide a uniform outlook on socialist social policy and its post-socialist revision. A review of a socialist model of welfare state development was carried out from a limited time perspective that is solely under socialist conditions. The results produced an invalid impression of their major features and properties. From such a perspective, a hundred-year overview of their development was repeatedly missing as the cornerstone in such a context. In order to overcome this constraint, a proposal to look at welfare state development in Central Europe in its total timing and insertion seems to be a reasonable approach.

Welfare state development: a brief overview of the contextual framework

One hundred years later the welfare state has been commonly accepted. The implementation of social insurance as an innovative principle of managing social malady started a new trend in politics at the turn of the nineteenth century. The idea of the pacification of a politically well-organised and powerful industrial working class was initiated and hesitatingly implemented in Germany under the Bismarckian regime. It soon became widely accepted, with or without major adaptations, either for short interludes or as a leading principle of 'scientific philanthropy' (De Swaan 1988: 252). Although operating at a considerably high level and according to local conditions (Roebroek 1992), charity was finally confronted with 'nation-wide, compulsory and collective arrangements to remedy and control the external effects of adversity and deficiency' (De Swaan 1988: 218) of massively proliferating industrialism. This social innovation spread immediately further in Europe and other continents, but it remained a European set of concepts, primarily dealing with how to 'reflect and evanesce problems of capitalist societies' (Klein, in Jones 1993: 7). Since then, a broad variation of local applications were substantially influenced by specific relations between the social structure and social actors.

In various in-depth analytical considerations of this mobilisation for total welfare, managed by the rapidly growing state administrations, different highlights emerged and resulted in different ways of labelling welfare state regimes. If classifications follow the orientation of the post-World War II political regimes, then welfare state models are labelled as liberal, conservative corporatist, and as social democratic (Esping-Andersen 1990). In this frame, the (former) socialist countries would join such classifications as the 'socialist' welfare state. Titmuss' classification of social policy models concentrates on three basic models, revealing prototypes such as the residual model, developed in Great Britain; the corporatist industrial achievement model, developed in Germany; and the institutional, redistributive model, developed in Scandinavia (Novak 1996). Following this classification, the (former) socialist countries can be recognised as a particular mixture, in which both the corporatist model and the institutional redistributive model intervene. The Latin rudimentary model (Leibfried 1991) can also be incorporated in this frame. If a half century perspective dominates the consideration, then the significant impact of social-democratic political ideas and the decisive 'push' from below, from the working class, particularly in Northern Europe, can be framed as its major features. Eastern Europe, considered in a similar time span, reveals the dominant influence of communist ideology.

In a century-long perspective of the development of the welfare state, it becomes more than evident that the German social innovation of social insurance has a central position. This idea could be given short shrift, as, for example, at the beginning of the century in Great Britain. Its application was also proposed by the social-democrat political forces, but failed to be accepted, as was the case in Sweden, where the idea of universalistic social welfare was put into operation some decades before its elaboration by Beveridge. Gradually expanded welfare schemes across Europe were included by the opposition in negotiations and bargaining in the Parliament. This resulted in the improvement of the well-being of industrial workers, but also succeeded in toning down their revolutionary demands. In this temporal frame, it also became evident that the social structure and social power of certain groups had a significant impact. At first glance, politically, welfare programmes transparently incorporate solidarity and charity, and a defence against social austerity. Looking at them from the perspective of social groups and political interests, it unequivocally appears that the extent and essence of welfare solidarity is the outcome of hard and protracted political fighting, where self-interest and egoism of social actors appears as a leading principle. Social justice and morality are only ostensible motives for this practice, which can and should be explained in the framework of political and social struggle (Baldwin 1990).

Extending Esping-Andersen's three-fold typology of welfare state models, the Central and East European welfare state models are constantly labelled as 'socialist' by the Communist regime, though lately a 'conservative corporatist' labelling dominates (Deacon 1992, Ferge, in Ferge and Kolberg 1992, Marklund 1993, Ferge 1996). Although it is far from being neglected, the focus on certain welfare schemes during a limited time perspective (the last few decades) poses a substantial limitation on including it in the present contextual framing. This analysis aims at the timing and the insertion of welfare state programmes in separate countries, paying particular attention to its social agents: the actors and factors. This leads this author to frame her analysis by concepts which differ from those outlined above. Generally speaking, the framing will concentrate on the inspiring ideas of Baldwin (1990) and Flora's associates (1986) who primarily stressed the significant impact of social structure and social actors, and the development of welfare institutions over the last century. What counts substantially is not the current structure of welfare state institutions, but which actors (meaning the elite and groups) and factors had the greatest impact on their development. What matters is not the current state of affairs, but the process by which the present status of welfare has been developed. Thus, the development of the Central European welfare state will be re-considered in the contextual framework of a decisive role of the social actors, stressing particularly the class-coalition between the elite and a certain social class (Baldwin 1990).

Unlike modernisation and industrialisation that had stratified Europe in different zones of adaptation, the dissemination and local adaptations of the welfare state concept followed its inception in Germany without any delay. Though dominated by the corporatist principle of welfare, the dissemination of this initiative varied in insertion but not in timing. As elsewhere, social agents, meaning factors and class-coalitions, substantially shaped the nature of these welfare state regimes. Using a planned analytical approach we can examine the following hypothesis:

> Pre-socialist welfare agents – factors and actors – had a significant impact on future welfare trends.

Taking into consideration the cornerstones outlined above, this analysis will focus on analysing welfare state development in the Czech Republic, Hungary and Slovenia. The major rationale behind this selection is that they share, firstly, the experience of Communist rule and secondly, the legacy of the Habsburg Empire. In contrast to the territory which constitutes present-day Slovenia and was exposed, either directly or indirectly, to Germanic influence during the last millennium, the Czech territory and Hungary had a long tradition of sovereign kingdoms. Since the Mohacz battle in 1526, the Slavonic regions, neighbouring the Habsburg territory such as the Czech lands, and Slovakia lost their autonomy, and were exposed to Habsburg supremacy until the end of World War I. The Mohacz battle was also crucial for Hungary, dividing its territory between the Ottoman Empire and the Habsburg Empire. After a successful war against the Ottomans in the late seventeenth century, the territory was reunited under the Habsburg Crown, ensuring Hungarian nobility substantial privileges. Secessionist political interests under the leadership of Kossuth in 1867 resulted in political dualism, dividing the empire into the Austrian and to Hungarian spheres of influence, thus converting the Habsburg Empire into the Austro-Hungarian Empire. The Czech lands and Slovene lands remained under Austrian supremacy while Slovakia, among others, was exposed to Hungarian supremacy. Following the break-up of the Empire, a number of new nation states were constituted on its ashes. The Czech lands constituted Czechoslovakia with Slovakia, while Slovene lands constituted the State of Slovenes, Croats and Serbs and a few months later the Kingdom of Serbs, Croats, and Slovenes, turning to Yugoslavia in 1929. Meanwhile, Hungary was restricted to the territory within its current borders.

Our analysis of historical empirical evidence concentrates on:

- certain 'pre-socialist' welfare state institutions, accompanied by their major features as developed under socialism,
- major properties of social structure particularly from the launching stage of the welfare regime, and
- interests of the ruling elite and of other social groups.

Before embarking on such an analysis, the reader should keep in mind the major frame of comparison. The consideration of each welfare regime's development separately is aimed at clearly showing the similarities between its pre-socialist features and their socialist follow-up. Moreover, it will be argued that apparent 'socialist' features are nothing but an extension of their pre-socialist fabrics at large. In this respect, work and employment are central to social security and welfare under socialism and the exclusion of certain groups from it is far from being a Communist invention *per se*. It appears to be more an adoption of rules that have been already in operation than the building of a new system from scratch. Thus, the major concern is the welfare fabric in the designated territories before the socialist era and under socialism. It might be similar to plans in Vienna (and Budapest) but it might be different as well. Seeking any such comparison beyond that described above might lead the reader to misleading conclusions.

Welfare state development in Central Europe

On the advent of the twentieth century, Bismarck's regime in Germany and Taffe's in the Austro-Hungarian Empire used state power to lead social policy primarily as a precaution against the revolutionary impact of such incidents as the Paris Commune. While the organisational strength of industrial workers was constantly increasing and threatened both regimes, new strategies were designed to protect the existing political and social order. This gave the impetus to pioneer the idea of fighting against the social maladies which accompanied the demographic and economic changes at the end of the nineteenth century by means of social insurance. Thus, the welfare state in the Austro-Hungarian Empire began to be launched in the 1880s, in a period of economic depression. It was conceived by a coalition against big industry, drawing support from clerical, feudal and middle-class forces, as well as from the Slavonic ethnic groups in the Empire. Sickness and accident insurance for industrial workers were financed by workers and employers, and jointly administered by them through self-governing bodies (Esping-Andersen and Korpi, in Goldthorpe 1984: 179–80). This was the general rule in the Empire, which then underwent specific adaptations in certain regions as a result of local welfare legacy and social structure.

The Czech territory: a long tradition of social insurance

In its Habsburg and Austro-Hungarian period (until World War I), the Czech lands followed the institutional agenda of the Viennese Government. However, certain traces reveal that it undertook its own unique steps, too. Some evidence shows that certain social insurance schemes, though in a very rudimentary form, have been in operation even a century before (in the 1770s and in the 1780s) their broad application in neighbouring regions. By contrast to the Bismarckian principle of welfare policy, these schemes were primarily aimed at social security of the state and public employees, later being extended to miners, too (1856). After becoming state policy in the Empire, different schemes of social insurance were implemented in its constituent lands as well: first, sickness and accident insurance at the end of the nineteenth century and then pension insurance for the salaried (1909), completing the first stage of this newly-implemented scheme (Dixon and Macarov 1992: 79).

In 1918, the Czech lands and Slovakia constituted the new nation state of Czechoslovakia, thus meeting their long-lived desire for national autonomy and sovereignty. The state administration put certain effort into the improvement of working conditions and labour legislation. In contrast, the 1920s were far from being a period of high levels of social security and welfare for industrial workers. The length of the working day was reduced to eight hours (1918) and comprehensive social insurance legislation was implemented (1924), including pensions for industrial workers. Conversely, unemployment remained high over the whole decade (approximately 14 per cent). A social insurance scheme, to which employers and employees contributed in equal measure, was framed by a compromise between the bourgeois and reform coalitions, covering the basic contingencies of old age, invalidity, widowhood, being orphaned, sickness, and accidents. In the 1930s, when an economic crisis brought about increasing unemployment and decreasing wages, the state reacted with a double strategy. This involved increased subsidies for unemployment benefits and the implementation of different programmes, such as retraining schemes and the establishment of 'work camps' and 'work houses'. World War II halted the development of these schemes. Before the war ended, some elements of the universalistic and uniform insurance system were launched to be implemented in 1948 on a national scale (Castle-Kanerova, in Deacon 1992: 95–7).

In the first two decades of Communist rule (in the 1950s and in the 1960s), the prospects of the newly-implemented social insurance were curtailed and altered by a new approach to social policy in the 1950s, which also included comprehensive medical care. Under the new concept of social policy, which incorporated a housing policy that was particularly favourable to newly-weds who promised to have large families, different hardships such as poverty, and unemployment were set to disappear. The reality was, however, far from these ideological projections. This became particularly evident in the 1970s, when faster growth in wages was favoured, though accompanied by a faster increase in prices. Lower income earners, including increasing numbers of pensioners in particular, could not cope with these trends. They therefore expected a greater participation in welfare schemes. During the second part of Communist rule, from 1970 to 1988, the number of recipients of different cash benefits doubled, increasing the total sum of benefits four-fold (Castle-Kanerova, in Deacon 1992: 98–103). It has to be noted that access to social welfare was not universal, as the self-employed and farmers were excluded. This combination of welfare principles was perceived as a mix of universal elements and a strong work orientation (Vecernik, in Marklund 1993: 109). This is also perceived as a major reason for pensioners to act as the major supporters of Czechoslovak social policy. Conversely, impoverished women remained outside welfare's concern, since it was taken for granted that they have participated in social security, guaranteed by employment and enterprise (Castle-Kanerova, in Deacon 1992: 115).

At the dawn of the independent state, in the first decades of the twentieth century, social policy followed the pioneering European welfare trends, such as the improvement of working conditions and the reduction of the working day in order to reduce unemployment. Unsurprisingly, post-socialist reformers in social policy intended to combat post-socialist problems and hardships by recalling the successful collaboration between the bourgeoisie and the working class in the 1920s and building it into a new, post-socialist projection. The results of this venture are thus far unknown (Castle-Kanerova, in Deacon 1992: 115).

Hungary: welfare provision for civil servants and industrial workers

Hungarian welfare institutions are also seen as part of an old indigenous tradition, pregnant with social struggles that accompanied their initiation and implementation (Ferge 1996: 107). In its century-long duration (Ferge, in Ferge and Kolberg 1992), the Hungarian welfare state regime can be seen primarily as a corporatist welfare system that has been initiated as a state-supported reaction to the vigorously 'marching' capitalism in the last decades of the nineteenth century. While a new form of production (i.e. industrialisation) was firmly implemented, the social composition of the population failed to keep pace with progress. Agricultural production on the great estates still dominated the economy, and cheap agricultural labour dominated a labour force that was repeatedly endangered by impoverishment. However, as an occupational group, they were supplied by selective schemes solely for health care, with no cash benefits or social insurance scheme. By contrast, though representing a smaller section of the population compared to farmers and workers in agriculture, civil servants and industrial workers took priority in welfare schemes. State and civil servants also gained 'ideological' support from nobility and from the Catholic Church as the major cornerstones of conservatism. Moreover, if the large estates, still manufacturing in a feudal mode, had not offered enough revenues to nobility, this same nobility would have enlarged its income by serving the state administration. By means of these strategies, which favoured its interests over those of other groups, the nobility established and maintained a separate and privileged welfare system. At the turn of the century (in the 1880s), industrial workers, who were less numerous than those in other social groups, but were nevertheless powerful because of their efficient political organisation in trade unions and supporting political party, made the implementation of the Bismarckian concept of social insurance possible. Conversely, it was left to the class of entrepreneurs to rely on the market provision of welfare, although the middle class established its own segmented and hierarchical private insurance scheme. This social setting showed certain ethnic particularities, though. The fact that immigrants, largely Germans and Jews, represented the greater part of this social stratum on the eve of the new century, includes an additional feature in the initial framing of the Hungarian welfare state, revealing it to be fragmented in the social and ethnic dimension. Moreover, the initial stage of launching and development indicates that the German concept of social insurance, concentrating on industrial workers alone, had amalgamated with traditional welfare schemes for civil servants. By contrast, workers in agriculture, small-holding farmers, and entrepreneurs, who apparently did not attract any elite to support their welfare interests, were excluded from the state provision of welfare (Ferge, in Ferge and Kolberg 1992). Thus far, social insurance remained

limited solely to the salaried, offering modest benefits and leaving unemployment insurance out of the picture.

The first decades of the new nation state (in the 1920s and 1930s) brought
nothing substantially new to what was already in operation in neighbouring
countries. Apart from this, the number of poor people living in urban areas
increased. These people became more visible than the poor in rural areas, but
since the state did not improve the traditional Poor Laws, the poor were left to
the mercy of the Church and private charity.

After 1945, welfare provision and social security continued targeting the
state employees primarily, while private insurance schemes were abolished,
leaving many outside welfare. Charity organisations, which were organised
either by the Church or voluntarily, were made illegal, meaning that more than
half of the population lived in poverty and had no free access to health care.
The social security system was used mainly for the purposes of the supreme and
centralised state power, for state-owned enterprises, and lastly, for the
employees in this state sector. Social policy became part of a centrally planned
economy and remained largely unchanged during the whole post-war period
(Ferge, in Ferge and Kolberg 1992). Social security schemes were being increasingly regarded as an extension of their income. Such circumstances created
room for state-owned enterprises to manoeuvre in, enabling them to use wage
and employment policies in particular as 'buffers' which protected them against
direct state intervention. The planning of social security relating to maternity
leave, child care grants and sick leave became an integral part of employment
and income policy at the micro level of enterprises. Besides, low level welfare
and a poor standard of living forced people to 'invent' their own strategies for
transcending meagre welfare and the low well-being 'trap'. They began to work
in the grey, secondary economy to improve their well-being. Close relations
between employment and social security opened new channels for labour force
mobility, but on the other hand, activities of the second economy imposed
limitations on more efficient work in the first economy (Szalai and Orosz, in
Deacon 1992: 151–4).

Slovenia: farmers and the self-employed without political support

Some scholars of Yugoslav social policy claim that it was non-existent during
the first decades of the common state, in the period between 1918 and 1941.
Although some initiatives were taken by influential intellectuals, turbulent
political conditions, economic liberalism, a socially irresponsible political elite,
and an authoritarian government prevented the country from consistently
developing any approach to solving the problem of social austerities. Under
socialism, the Bolshevist welfare model was supposed to be established (Ruzica,
in Dixon and Macarov 1992: 210).

A thorough analysis of historical literature (Kidric 1996, Kresal 1996) leads
us to reject this simplified and limited perspective. As far as Slovene society is
concerned at least, an almost perfect timing and insertion of the social insur-

ance concept, as it was pioneered by the German and the Austro-Hungarian government on the eve of the twentieth century, can be observed. The Slovene economy was a late-comer to industrialisation, but it was anything but late in implementing the Bismarckian concept of social insurance. In this sector, as a dominion in the Austro-Hungarian Empire, Slovenia followed the initiatives from the centre concurrently and applied them without ignoring the tradition of charity.

As in the neighbouring countries of the Austro-Hungarian Empire, a consistent set of social legislation started to be established in the 1880s in order to fight against the dysfunctions of rapidly proliferating industrialism and related exploitation of the labour force. Improvement of working conditions (1885) on the one hand, and the implementation of accident (1887) and sickness (1888) insurance on the other hand was also on the local political agenda. Amongst wage workers, those from the metallurgic branch, mining and railway transport had the best insurance conditions, though established in highly fragmented schemes. Before the end of the century, a provisional pension scheme was also implemented. Further, workers' representatives from the above branches participated in the management boards of various enterprises, although without voting rights. In this respect, they were more advanced than those involved in similar schedules in neighbouring regions.

Joining the new nation state in 1918 slowed down the pace of improvement of welfare schemes on the Slovene territory, while the adjustment of this pace in other regions had higher priority. Despite this slow-down, similar welfare trends to those in neighbouring regions can be observed, proving that the wheel of welfare regime change, once put in motion, could hardly be stopped. That meant that workers were paid on an equal basis, regardless of gender but, where necessary, they also benefited from family allowances, income maintenance allowances, and additional pay for working overtime. In the beginning of the 1920s, the unemployed benefited from state allowances, but at the end of the decade, they were left to rely on 'self-help' funds, initiated by employers and employees. Although the Ministry for Social Affairs remained solely concerned with wage and salaried workers, its establishment in 1929 represented a crowning achievement of federal state intervention into welfare, coping with the social hardships facing the rest of the population was left to the auspices of local authorities. The poor depended on poor relief, which was substantially linked to the local budget. This relief included benefits in cash and in commodities, such as food, clothing, coal and wood, shelter and communal flats.

Even though they were the largest category in the population, farmers remained excluded from welfare schemes. Charity and solidarity of social networks had to cater to their needs. Two attempts were made to include this category in the welfare system, but both failed. The first was made by the Austro-Hungarian Government in 1909, while the second was instigated by the Agricultural Chamber at the end of the 1930s. Farmers represented the vast majority of the population in both Yugoslavia and Slovenia, but their economic capacities were low. They had few opportunities to turn agriculture into a productive and competitive sector, but as small-holders they were financially incapable of bearing the burden of social insurance. Further they lacked the support of other political elites (Kresal 1996).

Summing up, during the first two decades of the new nation state up to World War II, the state launched and implemented a complex social legislation, including the following strategies:

1   Reduction of the working day to eight hours, introduction of workers' representatives in enterprise management bodies, and implementation of self-help for the unemployed in 1918,
2   Establishment of the Workers' Chamber for wage and salaried employees in 1921,
3   Housing protection in the 1920s, and
4   Old age insurance for all workers, a minimum wage, intervention in collective bargaining, and negotiations between employers and employees (1937).

After taking over political control in the country, the Communist regime inherited the welfare and social insurance legacy and left it, in principle, largely untouched. At the beginning of its rule, in 1947, social security was declared a constitutional right and has remained so until the present day, stressing equal payment for equal work regardless of gender. Minor improvements were implemented to protect maternity and children, and enabling universal access to health care. In the 1960s, the whole welfare system was unified at the level of the federal state by establishing a national social insurance scheme for health care, accidents, and old age to which employers, i.e. enterprises, and employees contributed on an equal basis. Welfare was also guaranteed to the families of the employed, but special attention was paid to mothers, children and the disabled. A separate social insurance scheme for farmers and other self-employed persons was also launched (1967), and some years later incorporated into the national insurance scheme, largely on a universal basis. In 1974, certain decentralised tendencies in social policy took place by delegating social protection to enterprises and municipalities (Kidric 1996).

The early 1960s heralded the coming crisis in financing welfare, while expenditure matched funds. The development of the crisis was postponed to the late 1980s, when the numbers of the unemployed and retired started to 'stampede' and, by contrast, the number of employed persons harshly decreased. These events paved the way for demands for a new wave of social policy reforms, also encompassing various international agencies who played a significant role in backing these reforming steps (Novak 1996).

Findings: commonality and divergence

What new insights can be gained from the analysis of the development of welfare state regimes in former socialist Central Europe? A very condensed review would offer the following response. Particularly in the Czech territory and in Hungary, welfare, having been provided by the state, was launched under conditions of enlightened absolutist rule. State employees were the first who were served by these schemes. On the eve of the twentieth century, social insurance schemes which targeted industrial workers accompanied those aimed at the security of state employees, adopting a fragmented shape. During the 1920s and the 1930s, Czechoslovakia and Slovenia reveal the most evident collaboration between employers and employees, focusing primarily on a class-coalition between the industrial bourgeoisie and industrial workers. Particularly in Slovenia, the welfare system underwent an additional fragmentation. Firstly, industrial workers from different branches had access to welfare under different conditions. Secondly, in the new nation state, a clear distinction between the competences of federal and local authorities was established. While the federal state administration steered and serviced a class-coalition between employers and employees (by means of law and the Ministry of Social Affairs in 1929), farmers and the self-employed were left to the market provision of welfare at large. If they failed in this venture, they had to depend on local authorities and charity. Hence, although representing the largest social category, the self-employed such as farmers, artisans and entrepreneurs, were excluded from welfare, being left to its market provision or social network solidarity, as was also the case in Hungary. Interestingly enough, particularly the poorest groups from this category failed to attract any political elite to represent and bargain for their welfare interests. Conversely, politically well-organised industrial workers presented a substantial threat to the state, that assumed a negotiating role and initiated a class-coalition to support employers against them. In the socialist period, the corporatist-rooted welfare system persisted with minor changes only. Close relations between social security and employment were merely a renewed strategy, which reflected the centre-piece position of civil servants and industrial workers from the pre-socialist period. These relations were, however, emphasised for political and ideological reasons.

Conclusions

With the perspective of a century, the Czech territory, Hungary and Slovenia underwent substantial shifts of political regimes. The dominance of Austro-Hungarian rule turned to the reign of a largely conservative political elite in sovereign national states, to be later terminated by communist rule. In socialism, welfare regimes managed to preserve their main properties, characteristic of the pre-socialist stage of their development. The close relation between employment in the state sector and social security was accompanied by the state being the major welfare provider. This gave certain groups, such as party allies and state employees, a privileged status, while the self-employed remained out of this domain. Furthermore, as discussed above, class-coalitions count. Although weak in number, industrial workers and civil servants largely attracted the political elite. While the first presented a political threat at the turn of the nineteenth century and their political strength needed to be muted, the latter used the state to serve their interests. Regardless of the difference in character, none of the newly established communist regimes changed this pattern significantly.

Reviewing these major welfare fabrics in a European perspective, some interesting trends can be observed. Large strata of marginal social classes such as small-holding farmers and other self-employed of similar economic incapacity gained varying levels of political success across Europe. In the early decades of the twentieth century, they managed to attract the political support of the Swedish agrarian aristocracy in implementing their social security scheme on all taxpayers' cost. This brought the first universal scheme in operation. Conversely, in Germany, a social security scheme for farmers was not adopted until the late 1950s (Baldwin 1990), which happened to be a decade earlier than in neighbouring socialist countries. It can be concluded that regardless of the political regime in power, the corporatist welfare regime proved to be insensible for the self-employed in general for a much longer time than the redistributive welfare regime. In contrast to German practice, socialist welfare regimes terminated social insurance fragmentation between industrial workers and civil servants by implementing the universal scheme for both social strata.

A concerted history of welfare state development also reveals that tradition is important. Political turmoil can be nationally and internationally significant and exerts pressure on welfare provisions, while welfare regimes manage to preserve their major properties more frequently by extending the set of rights in operation rather than by transforming and severely reducing them. In this respect, the Communist rule brought nothing essentially new to the welfare provision. Although severely criticised for the fusion of employment and social security, and privileged position of the state employees in this system but particularly of the bureaucracy, the socialist welfare regime proved largely to adopt the pre-socialist welfare institutions. Implementation of the universal social security scheme for the working class and civil servants can be perceived as the major welfare measure that was launched.

What can we learn from the past for the future? Over their history, welfare regimes in the countries concerned at least, repeatedly proved to be a 'solid' social fabric, which remained a formidable bastion against any major disturbance and intervention. In another pattern of development than that characterizing industrialisation, indigenous and exogenous factors combined in a compatible way, presenting no harsh discontinuity with traditional structures. From the middle of the first millennium, Europe experienced frequent cleavages which divided it into central and peripheral zones. Conversely, dissemination of the welfare state idea could be seen as a mechanism that has the capacities to bridge these gaps. Many international agencies recently swamped post-socialist countries, consulting governments that the welfare is beyond the performance of the economy. Lowering of standards and a reduction of state provision is a frequently suggested strategy that should be implemented to make more space for a market provision of welfare. Such suggestions, proposed by these agencies, provoke a mighty and persisting structure of welfare regimes which have already undergone numerous limitations and restrictions. In spite of this, they have managed to preserve their basic character.

Acknowledgement

The first draft of this analysis was elaborated during the author's stay in Wassenaar, at the Netherlands Institute for Advanced Study in the Humanities and Social Sciences (NIAS) of the Royal Academy of Art and Science in 1997.

Bibliography

Baldwin, P. (1990) *The Politics of Social Solidarity: Class Bases of the European Welfare State 1875–1975.* Cambridge: Cambridge University Press.

Deacon, B. (ed.) (1992) *The New Eastern Europe: Social Policy Past, Present, Future.* London: Sage.

De Swaan, A. (1988) *In Care of the State. Health Care, Education and Welfare in Europe and the USA in the Modern Era.* Cambridge: Polity Press.

Dixon, J. and Macarov, D. (1992) *Social Welfare in Socialist Countries.* London: Routledge.

Esping-Andersen, G. (1990) *The Three Worlds of Welfare Capitalism.* Cambridge: Polity Press.

Esping-Andersen, G. (ed.) (1996) *Welfare States in Transition.* London: Sage.

Ferge, Z. (1991) 'Marginalisation, poverty and social institutions', *Labour and Society* 16, 4: 415–38.

Ferge, Z. (1996) 'Social citizenship in the new democracies. The difficulties in reviving citizens' rights in Hungary', *International Journal of Urban and Regional Research* 20, 1: 89–115.

Ferge, Z. and Kolberg, J.E. (eds) (1992) *Social Policy in a Changing Europe.* Frankfurt/M.: Campus Verlag.

Flora, P. (ed.) (1986) *Growth to Limits*, Volume I, II, Berlin: Walter de Gruyter.

Goldthorpe, J. (ed.) (1984) *Order and Conflict in Contemporary Capitalism.* Oxford: Clarendon Press.

Jones, C. (ed.) (1993) *New Perspectives on the Welfare State in Europe.* London: Routledge.

Kidric, D. (1996) 'Socialna politika v Sloveniji po letu 1945' ('Social policy in Slovenia from 1945') in *Prevrati in slovensko gospodarstvo v XX.stoletju 1918–1945–1991 (Shifts and the Slovene Economy in the Twentieth Century 1918–1945–1991)*, N. Borak and Z. Lazarevic. Ljubljana: Cankarjeva zalozba.

Kresal, F. (1996) 'Socialna politika v Sloveniji do druge svetovne vojne' ('Social policy in Slovenia up to World War II') in *Prevrati in slovensko gospodarstvo v XX.stoletju 1918–1945–1991 (Shifts and the Slovene Economy in the Twentieth Century 1918–1945–1991)*, N. Borak and Z. Lazarevic. Ljubljana: Cankarjeva zalozba.

Leibfried, S. (1991) 'Towards a European welfare state? On integrating poverty regimes in the European Community', Working Paper.

Marklund, S. (1993) 'Social policy and poverty in post-totalitarian Europe', *Scandinavian Journal of Social Welfare* 2, 3: 104–14.

Novak, M. (1991) *Zamudniski vzorci industrializacije; Slovenija na obrobju Evrope*

(Late-coming Pattern Mix of Industrialization: Slovenia at the European Periphery). Ljubljana: Znanstveno in publicisticno sredisce.

Novak, M. (1996) 'Razvoj slovenske drzave blaginje v evropski perspektivi' ('Development of the Slovene welfare state in European perspective'), *Teorija in praksa* 33, 6: 922–39.

Roebroek, J.M. (1992) *The Imprisoned State: The Paradoxical Relationship Between State and Society*. Tilburg: Department of Social Security Studies, Tilburg University.

Szalai, J. (1992) 'Poverty in Hungary during the period of economic crisis', Working paper.

8 If class is dead, why won't it lie down?

John Scott

Researchers into social stratification and social exclusion might be forgiven if they feel that current debates in their area sound rather like a new version of the Monty Python parrot sketch. Faced with a series of persistent complaints from its intellectual consumers that 'class is dead', class analysts have replied that it may appear to be dead but is, in fact, resting. The processes of stratification that lead to social exclusion, they argue, cannot be understood in terms of gender, race and age alone: class remains a central explanatory factor. It may be less visible and less obvious than in the past, but it is certainly not dead. Indeed, class analysts often suggest that class relations are, after a short period in abeyance, once again growing in importance and will continue to do so in the future. Class theory retains its relevance. Just look at the beautiful plumage.

Indeed, there would appear to be an obvious paradox in the arguments of the critics of class analysis. If class is dead – if it is irrelevant to contemporary social life and unworthy of intellectual comment – then why do its critics find it necessary to issue its death certificate with such regularity? If class were really dead, class analysts might be expected to fade away. Instead, it is one of the fastest growing areas in sociology and appears regularly in series of books on 'key concepts' (Scase 1992, Edgell 1997, Milner 1999). Like Mark Twain, class analysts could be forgiven if they felt that reports of the death of their central concept had been much exaggerated.

It has to be admitted that class analysts may have brought their fate upon themselves by making inflated claims about the importance of class. Investigations into social inequality tended to reduce all social phenomena to divisions of class, denying any independent explanatory power to other sources of social division. Class was all-important. The rejection of class was, perhaps, a natural reaction on the part of those who could produce evidence that gender or ethnicity, say, play a critical role in generating inequalities and exclusions. It was a short step from showing that class did not explain everything, to asserting that it could explain nothing.

It is my contention that a more balanced assessment is needed. Of course class does not explain everything. Any exploration of concrete patterns of social inclusion and exclusion will require the use of a large number of analytically distinct concepts, each of which points to social mechanisms with their own, quite distinct, causal powers. The task of sociology is to assess the relative importance of each of these mechanisms and to trace changes in their importance over time. Class is one such mechanism, and a proper understanding of class can help us to understand the contribution that it makes to social exclusion today and how this compares with its significance in other places and at other times.

Pre-modern class and post-modern fragmentation

Intimations of the apparent death of class first appeared in reflections on the significance of economic growth, affluence and embourgeoisement during the 1950s and 1960s (Zweig 1961). Contemporary societies, it was widely held, were becoming more open, more individualistic and more meritocratic. The old class identities that were tied to traditional communities and to divisions in the sphere of production were in decay. They were being replaced by new identities that owed more to consumption differences and lifestyles in the fluid suburban neighbourhoods (Packard 1959). The traditional working and middle classes were on the wane in the era of high mass consumption. The slogan of the times for many was 'we are all middle class now'. And if everyone is able to enjoy what were formerly enjoyed only by the middle class, then – in a very real sense – there are *no* classes. A middle-class society, then, is a mass society (Geiger 1949, Reisman *et al.* 1953).

The first, and most forthright, statement of the implications of these alleged changes for class analysis was that of Nisbet:

> The essential argument of this paper may be stated briefly. It is that the term social class is by now useful in historical sociology, in comparative or folk sociology, but that it is nearly valueless for the clarification of the data of wealth, power, and social status in the contemporary United States and much of Western society in general.
>
> (Nisbet 1959: 126)

The classes of nineteenth-century Europe, Nisbet held, were not a product of modernity but of the persistence of certain elements of their pre-modern stratification systems. The values and the entrenched interests of the landed class that ruled pre-modern Europe perpetuated old inequalities and clothed the new inequalities of industrialism in a mask of tradition and hierarchy that gave them the appearance of solidity and fixity. They defined social strata as cohesive and self-contained groups that might – perhaps inevitably – come into conflict with each other.

In fact, argued Nisbet, there have been massive changes since the nineteenth century, and these have tended to erode the pre-modern survivals. A separation of ownership from control in modern businesses in the first half of the twentieth century (Berle and Means 1932) broke the link between property and inequality, a shift from primary and secondary sector occupations to tertiary sector occupations led to an expansion of the middle levels of the occupational hierarchy, and an increase in social mobility broke down apparently-fixed social boundaries. At the same time, modern democracies were becoming pluralistic, and each incorporated an ever-larger proportion of their population into a cohesive national society. Drawing on Marshall (1956, see also Marshall 1949), Nisbet argued that these changes meant that 'Behind the modern state lies the whole development of political, civil and social rights which have made class rule as difficult as local or sectional tyranny' (1959: 131–2).

Though many societies in 'the underdeveloped areas of the world' (Nisbet 1959: 131) could still be regarded as class societies, contemporary industrial societies could not. These societies, Nisbet held, are consumption-based, and consumption differences are neither as extreme nor as polarised as they had been in the past. As a result, 'class lines are exceedingly difficult to discover in modern economic society except in the backwater areas' (Nisbet 1959: 133). This decomposition of class, Nisbet argued, was most advanced in the United States, but it was making itself felt in all the leading industrial nations. The forces of industrialism were driving a process of convergence that would ensure the eventual demise of class across the whole of Europe as well (Kerr *et al.* 1960).

The thesis of industrialism and post-industrialism that underpinned these arguments had a great appeal, and many saw it as marking the end of class and class conflict as a factor in social development. Many European sociologists remained committed to a historically grounded class analysis of contemporary realities, though not necessarily in its classical Marxist form (Dahrendorf 1957, Aron 1964). Even those who rejected the theory of embourgeoisement and industrial convergence recognised deep-rooted transformations in the class structure (Goldthorpe *et al.* 1969, Archer and Giner 1971).

Research on social stratification during the 1970s and 1980s became increasingly focused on the analysis of social mobility (Erikson *et al.* 1979, Goldthorpe 1980, Erikson and Goldthorpe 1993) and technical questions of defining class schema and allocating individuals to class categories (Wright 1989, 1997). While some of this work retained a commitment to a theoretical framework of class analysis (Wright 1985), there was little concern with using the concept of class to explain social divisions and processes of social exclusion. In the mainstream of class analysis, class became, to all intents and purposes, an empirical indicator of occupational position that – all too often – failed to yield the predictive power expected of it. In political sociology, where class analysis had always had a strong appeal, commentators began to see class as having a declining significance and posited a process of 'class dealignment' (Sarlvik and Crewe 1983).

Given this retreat from class, the arguments of Nisbet took on a renewed appeal. An influential article by Clark and Lipset (1991) re-examined the idea of post-industrialism – which many writers were now describing as post-modernism – and pronounced the death of class. They argued that there had been a continuing erosion of the marks of inferiority and superiority that had formerly made class relations visible and distinct. Hierarchical divisions had become less marked, and class conflict had diminished. They explored the consequences of this in the three 'situses' in which class relations had operated: politics, economics and kinship.

In the sphere of politics, they pointed to the decline in class voting that had taken place between the 1940s and the 1980s – a change that was highlighted in the differences between the first and second editions of Lipset's *Political Man* (1960, 1980). The left-right division, they argued, had been transformed by the rise of a 'second left' or 'new politics' concerned not with ownership and control of the means of production but with broader social questions and with issues of lifestyle and identity. This rise of new social movements challenged the paradigm of class politics. In the economy, they highlighted the effects that economic growth and affluence had had on established hierarchies and forms of collective action. Here they saw a strengthening of individualism, instrumentalism and the direct effects of market relations on the distribution of incomes. Within business enterprises, traditional authority and hierarchy had declined and there had been a corresponding increase in the autonomy of professional managers and the extent of service sector occupations. Finally, in the area of kinship, they pointed to the crumbling of the 'authoritarian paternalistic' family. They saw this as having given way to more egalitarian family and household forms that have far less of an impact on ownership, education and recruitment to jobs.

Clark and Lipset saw these changes as bringing about a 'fragmentation of stratification'. Class relations were not completely disappearing, but they were becoming less corporate, less collective and less communal in character. There is now, they argue, a plurality of class-differentiated lifestyles, not simply a dichotomous polarisation of whole societies into opposing classes. Class relations persist, but their impact on life chances is weakening and they are no longer the principal bases of social identity.

Pakulski and Waters drew out these conclusions in the context of an emphasis on the 'postmodernisation' of contemporary industrial societies (Pakulski and Waters 1996; see also Crook *et al.* 1992). The demise of class, they held, is paralleled by the rise of new cultural differences that create 'status-conventional' divisions. The following of lifestyles based around consumption patterns and value preferences produces a shifting and unstable kaleidoscope of status groupings. Each aspect of status differentiation follows its own cultural logic and so there is an 'autonomisation' of status dimensions. This fluidity creates the space within which individuals are more freely able to *choose* their lifestyles, and so they are no longer fixed within constraining class conditions. People choose to exclude others from the lifestyles that they and their intimates have chosen. Though they recognise that the possibility of pursuing a particular lifestyle is limited by 'inequality of sumptuary capacity' (Pakulski and Waters 1996: 157), they hold that these are not the material differences of class.

How are these empirical claims to be assessed? And how might it be possible to argue for the continuing relevance of class analysis? An answer to this question requires conceptual work as much as it does empirical work. The problem with the arguments of the anti-class critics lies not simply in their empirical claims, but is embedded in the concepts and methodological assumptions that they bring to bear in interpreting these facts.

Reconceptualising class analysis

The first step is to take one step back from the empirical arguments in order to re-examine the meaning of the concept of class itself. The need to do this was first broached in an influential article by Pahl (1989), which was particularly concerned with the theoretical inadequacy that he found in the work of Goldthorpe and his colleagues at Nuffield College (Goldthorpe 1980: see also Marshall *et al.* 1988). The Nuffield programme was, arguably, the most influential approach to social stratification in Britain, and it formed the basis for a series of cross-national comparative studies (Erikson and Goldthorpe 1993, Jonsson 1993, Evans 1996, Haller 1996) and a more recent investigation into the structure of social justice in western and eastern Europe (Marshall *et al.* 1997). Indeed, for many sociologists the Nuffield programme was regarded as equivalent to class analysis *per se*. If the Nuffield programme could not be sustained, Pahl felt, then class analysis itself must fall. This resulted in a protracted skirmish in the leading British journal (see Goldthorpe and Marshall 1992, Pahl 1993, Scott 1994), and had a large impact on international debates.

Central to Pahl's argument was the question of how it is possible to evaluate competing conceptions of class and how they can be compared with non-class explanations. This is impossible in Goldthorpe's work, he argued, because it 'make[s] no commitment to any theory of class'. The programme leads Goldthorpe to 'simply construct certain demographic categories, find that these categories work well ... and then, retrospectively claim that the correlation or continuities constitute a theory' (Pahl 1993: 255–6). This nominalist strategy has been justified by a methodological opposition to what are seen as 'essentialist' definitions of class. In the words of Marshall and his colleagues, the only important question is:

> Which conception of social class best illuminates the nature of collective action, shared life-style and beliefs, and patterns of association?
>
> (Marshall *et al.* 1988: 26)

Similarly, Goldthorpe claimed that the choice between two conceptualisations of class was to be made simply on the grounds of their predictive power. This is, of course, an odd defence of any explanatory concept. While it is true that there can be no scientifically acceptable grounds for asserting the absolute necessity of a particular concept of class, it is equally implausible to abandon any theoretical concerns and simply pursue predictive power. If, for example, a measure of height proved a better predictor of spending patterns than did income, this would not be a reason for renaming the height measure as a measure of 'income'. Similarly, the addition of more and more variables to a basic class measure (for example, adding education, gender and ethnicity) would not warrant calling the combined measure 'class', even if its predictive power was superior to that of the original measure. The Nuffield programme is in danger of trying to defend the concept of class on wholly spurious grounds. Sociologists should not be choosing between competing concepts of class simply on the basis of their predictive power. The task of sociology is to arrive at theoretically grounded concepts and then to assess their explanatory power relative to other theoretically derived concepts.

The need to combine class variables with variables measuring gender, race and age has been powerfully recognised by Bradley (1996), who builds an exciting model of the interdependence of these causal dynamics. Crompton (1998) has taken a more pragmatic view that recognises the potential value of a number of different measures of class, and she seeks to incorporate equally pragmatic measures of status, gender and race into these. My own strategy is different, though it is compatible with the spirit of what these writers have argued (see Crompton and Scott 2000).

The way forward, I hold, is to retain a concept of class that is rooted in the works of Weber and Marx – the originators and popularisers of class analysis – but that is refined in the light of the changing theoretical understandings of property and market relations produced since their days. If such a concept can be shown to have a high predictive capacity, then so much the better for class analysis. If, on the other hand, its predictive capacity is low, then class analysis must be supplemented with other analytical concepts (gender, race and age, for example) if we are to yield a better explanation of observed research results. Only if we find that a concept of class has no predictive power whatsoever is it necessary to consider whether, for the time being, class analysis should be allowed to rest.

To this end, we must return to the key ideas of Weber, from whom Goldthorpe derived his initial concepts and to whom the researchers associated with the Nuffield programme and other programmes of class analysis continue to pay occasional lip service. These ideas, as I articulate them, are compatible with the aspirations that lie behind the Nuffield programme, but they do not involve a commitment to all of its specific empirical claims (see, for example, Goldthorpe 1983).

Weber recognised the intellectual power that lay behind Marx's conceptualisation of class in economic terms, but he rejected the determinism and inevitability with which it had come to be associated in the hands of Engels and Orthodox Marxism. He sought to develop it into a concept that could be tested for its relevance in particular historical circumstances. To this end, he tried to distinguish analytically many of the things that he felt Marx had combined into the single, all-encompassing concept of 'class'. These ideas were set out in his justly famous delineation of 'class', 'status' and 'party' (Weber 1914, 1920). This has been widely regarded as the basis of a three-dimensional approach to stratification, generally seen as involving the three dimensions of class, status and power (Bendix and Lipset 1953, Runciman 1968). There is much in this view with which I agree, though it is clear from Weber's discussions that he saw 'power' as a much more general phenomenon than this implies. Both class and status were aspects of the social distribution of power. It is also important to recognise that he did not see 'party' as constituting the third dimension of stratification. Party relations – collectively organised actions – occur at a totally different level of analysis, as, again, is clear from what Weber actually says. The third dimension of stratification in Weber's work is, I argue, authority or command, which he analysed in other parts of *Economy and Society*.[1]

'Class', in Weber's usage, was narrowed down to the economic sphere of property and the market, taking it close to Marx's own core usage. 'Status', on the other hand, designated the differentiation of groups in the 'social' sphere of community and cultural relations. His distinction between 'class' and 'status' helped to shape the whole structure of classical German sociology (see, for example, Schumpeter 1926, Tönnies 1931). Each is an aspect of the social distribution of power in a society, and power has to be seen as the essential basis of social stratification.

Weber also made a distinction between the 'situations' through which power is organised and the 'strata' into which individuals are formed. Individuals occupy particular situations or locations in relation to the various sources of power in a society, and they may also become grouped into demographically-constituted strata through their circulation among these situations (through association and mobility). Class relations, for example, were analysed in terms of the specific 'class situations' that form the determinants of individual life chances, and in terms of the 'social classes' that are the actual social strata formed from these class situations. Class situations comprise the property and market situations through which economic resources are distributed. Similarly, status relations were seen in terms of the 'status situations' that individuals occupy and the 'social estates' that arise as social strata from these status situations. Status situations comprise the specific lifestyles and identities through which 'social honour' or prestige is attributed to individuals. Social 'estates' (*Stände*) are divided by their relative social standing in a hierarchy of strata, and may differ very greatly from social classes.

Weber can also be read as making the case for seeing authority relations as the basis of a third dimension of social stratification (see Scott 1996). What can be called 'command situations' are analytically independent determinants of life chances, and the social strata that I have called 'social blocs' (such as 'elites') are formed around command situations. Command situations arise in organisations of all kinds, most particularly states, but also business enterprises and churches. This dimension of social stratification is far less well developed than were those of class and status, but its implications were thoroughly explored in the attempts of Mosca (1896, 1923) and Pareto (1916) to develop a framework of elite analysis.

These arguments are summarised in Table 8.1. The three types of power situation must be understood as *analytical* dimensions of social stratification. They are what Weber called distinct 'causal components' in life chances, and they operate, to a greater or lesser extent, in all societies. An individual's life chances

Table 8.1 Class, status and command

Social spheres	Power situations	Social strata
Economic	Class situations	Social classes
Communal	Status situations	Social estates
Authoritarian	Command situations	Social blocs

depend upon their property ownership and their position in the labour market (class situation), their lifestyle and the evaluations made by others (status situation), and their position in a hierarchy of authority (command situations). No one of these can be reduced to the other; each must be recognised as having a causal effect of its own. Nevertheless, they always operate together in concrete situations, and sociologists must uncover and explore both their separate and their joint effects. The nature of these effects vary quite considerably from one society to another, with the relative importance of the three causal components being always a matter for empirical investigation. On the basis of the differences in life chances that these power situations generate, individuals may also be formed into social strata of various kinds. These are the actual, historically observable collectivities of which people are members.

Where class situation is the most important determinant of life chances, and where it has a great degree of autonomy from status and command situations, Weber sees the strata as social classes and he describes the society as a 'class society'. Capitalism he sees as corresponding closely to such an ideal type. In analogous terms, he recognises the possibility of status societies, such as many of the societies of the pre-modern world. To this I would add the category of command societies, such as the state socialist societies that formerly existed in eastern Europe and Russia. It must be emphasised that these are conceptual distinctions – ideal types. All three dimensions operate, to a greater or lesser extent, in any particular society, and few will correspond perfectly to the ideal type. Concrete patterns of stratification, and their associated patterns of inclusion and exclusion, must be understood as the outcome of specific *combinations* of causal factors, and it is simply the dominant element that defines the overall character of the system of stratification.

In these terms, it is possible to see a class society as one in which class situations and social classes are the most significant element in the interplay of the three dimensions. In the strongest case of such a society, two conditions will hold. First, class situations will be the most important factors in the determination of life chances, affecting the ways in which status and command situations exert their independent influence. Secondly, people will be formed into strata that have the principal characteristics of social classes. Their consciousness, their identity, and their 'party' actions will all reflect this.

A research programme for class analysis

A central problem in the whole debate over the relevance of class analysis is that the framework of class analysis has been interpreted too narrowly, by its supporters and critics alike. Class analysis has, to all intents and purposes, been equated with the construction of broad occupational or employment categories for use, principally, in large scale survey research (Crompton 1998). Such concerns have been at the heart of the debate over the relative merits of, for example, the Wright (1997), Goldthorpe and Cambridge (Prandy 1991) schemes. This kind of research, however, generally fails to take account of the part that status and command relations continue to play in contemporary class societies. Only Wright explores these at all systematically, and Wright sees exploitative class relations, defined by property and employment relations, as operating alongside cultural forms of expertise and credentialism and the hierarchically structured 'organisational assets' of authority. Despite this recognition, however, Wright refuses to conceptualise them as independent aspects of stratification, seeing this as a 'Weberian' deviation from his Marxism. He does, nevertheless, provide a basis for exploring the impact of political authority on social stratification and the effects of gender and race on status divisions.

At the same time, all of these schemes have concentrated on technical issues of classification, and they have largely abandoned any attempt to investigate the links that exist between the *structure* of social stratification and forms of *consciousness* and collective *action*. They leave these latter issues of consciousness and action open to investigation by others. The question of the continuing relevance of class analysis, therefore, is decided by default, as class analysts, for the most part, have simply not addressed the relevant issues. The theoretical framework that I propose here is intended to provide a basis for a re-orientation of class analysis towards these issues, and a more fruitful dialogue with those employing other paradigms of analysis.

From theory to research practice

To convert this conceptual framework into a useful research paradigm, the central issues that I have discussed must be unpacked more comprehensively. This can be done by recognising five questions that need to be asked about any system of stratification. The more of these questions that are answered in the affirmative, the stronger is the claim that we are dealing with a class society. These questions are as follows:

- Are class situations the most significant causal component in life chances?
- Can class situations be clustered into economically homogeneous categories?
- Are class situations demographically clustered into social strata through patterns of association and mobility?
- Do the members of social classes have a shared awareness of their social position?
- Do social classes form the basis of political and social movements?

These questions need to be answered in sequence, as the possibility of asking the later questions depends, to a considerable extent, on whether affirmative answers have been given to the earlier questions. On this basis, we may say that the weakest case of a class society – but a class society nevertheless – exists where only question one can be answered with a definitive 'yes'. The strongest case of a class society – one that corresponds, perhaps, to the image painted by Marx and Engels in the *Communist Manifesto* (1848) – is that where affirmative answers can unambiguously be given to all five questions.[2]

Question one, of course, is fundamental, as all else hinges on it. An answer to the question depends on a researcher being able to identify the class situations that exist in a society and to assess their impact on the life chances of the individuals who occupy them. Much research that goes under the name of class analysis has, in recent years, been concerned simply with mapping the class situations on which the answering of this question depends (Goldthorpe 1980, Wright 1997). Such mappings have tended to define class situations, operationally, as occupations or narrowly defined occupational categories, seeing occupation as a proxy for property and employment relations. In Britain, for example, the detailed coding schemes produced for the analysis of Census and employment data have been the most widely used.[3] The major limitation of this kind of research is not any overemphasis on class situation, but a failure to consider class situations broadly enough. An exclusive focus on occupational differences and employment relations, while it is perfectly adequate for many people, fails to give any proper attention to those differences of property ownership that are still of considerable importance in the determination of life chances. Even the work of Wright, which incorporates a property dimension, looks only at small-scale business property. Ignoring property is generally justified on the pragmatic grounds that it is difficult to study or is not included in official, government-produced schemes. However justifiable these claims may be in the abstract, it is undoubtedly the case that it makes the job of the critics of class analysis even easier. If class analysts will not properly consider property divisions, then who will (see Scott 1991, 1997: Chapter 9)?

The mappings produced in answer to question one have generally been undertaken alongside the attempt to construct economically homogeneous occupational categories for use in mobility studies and more broad-grained investigations of life chances. For all their differences, virtually all the so-called social class schemes that have been produced in recent years have been concerned with this issue. The Registrar General's Classification and its intended replacement in Britain (Rose and O'Reilly 1997), as well as the various convolutions of Erik Olin Wright (see, for example, Wright 1976, 1985, 1997), have been oriented towards the attempt to construct homogeneous categories that seem, according to the sociological observer, to have a homogeneity in terms of their economic characteristics. The work of Goldthorpe (Erikson and Goldthorpe 1993), for example, has largely centred around precisely this issue. The original attempt to map demographically-constituted groupings (question three) has been all-but abandoned as the Nuffield programme – especially as used in comparative research – has been limited to the building of purely nominal schemes for predicting observable variables (Morris and Scott 1996).

It has often been assumed that these kinds of nominal economic categories are, or correspond precisely to, social classes in the sense referred to in question three. This question, however, highlights the crucially important question of whether the 'classes' identified are merely nominal categories or real social groups (Aron 1964). Marx approached this question when discussing the relationship between what he called a class in-itself and a class for-itself. A class such as the peasantry, he argued, might exist as a mere category or aggregate, much as potatoes are collected together in a sack of potatoes, but it exists only as a real social group if it achieves a degree of social interconnection and communication. For classes to be regarded as real social groups – actual social strata – there must be, as Weber said, frequent and easy mobility among the constituent class situations.

What he means by this is that the class situations that make up a social class are not separate and discrete units, they are connected through regular and frequent paths of inter-generational and intra-generational mobility, intermarriage, informal association and other demographic processes that form people into households, neighbourhoods and other communal structures. If carpenters, electricians and bus drivers typically associate frequently with one another and there are high levels of mobility among these occupations, while associating less frequently and showing less mobility into the occupations of doctors, teachers and architects, then the demographic relations show evidence of a real boundary of social closure – of inclusion and exclusion – between the two categories of occupation. For Weber, this demographic formation of boundaries and social closure was central to what it is to be a social class. These demographic processes of social class formation are one aspect of the wider process of morphogenesis that Margaret Archer explored (1997).

Attempts to answer the question of whether and how class situations are demographically clustered must, ideally, make direct use of mobility and associational data in the derivation of the classes. Only rarely has this been the case. Most typically, analysts have used only the nominal categories or, at best, have simply used mobility and associational data to test whether the boundaries between the nominal categories also have a real significance. This raises particular problems for comparative research. It may, indeed, be possible to devise nominal economic categories that can be used, with only minor modifications, in a large number of societies – as, for example, Erikson and Goldthorpe (1993) did in their comparative investigation. However, it is quite another matter to conclude that these economic categories are separated by identical social boundaries in all countries and, therefore, constitute the 'same' social classes. Mobility, intermarriage and informal interaction patterns between, say, doctors and engineers may be quite different in Germany than they are in, say, Britain or France. Boundaries between social classes – and, therefore, the overall shape of the class structure – are likely to be quite variable from one country to another. They may all be class societies, but the structure of class relations will differ from one to another.

The idea that all industrial societies are converging towards a common structural pattern (Kerr *et al.* 1960) has long been abandoned, and Goldthorpe (1964) was one of its most vociferous critics. The work of Esping-Andersen (1993) has focused on the ways in which mass education, welfare regimes and institutions of collective bargaining have introduced new social divisions and social closures that criss-cross older class divisions and produce quite divergent patterns of development. Britain, Germany, Norway and Sweden show great differences among themselves, and are also divergent from the United States. As Mayer shows in his contribution to this book, the available evidence suggests strongly that societies follow path-dependent patterns of divergence rather than becoming ever more similar. Generic, global processes make themselves felt in institutionally specific ways in different societies.

Marx's discussion of the class for-itself highlighted the further aspects of class analysis that are covered by questions four and five in my list. Social classes achieve a greater solidity and fixity when their patterns of association and mobility are reinforced by a shared class awareness. Mann (1973) has usefully suggested that the level of any class awareness might vary from mere *mutual awareness*, through a sense of common *identity* and a conception of *opposition* to other social classes, to a *revolutionary* concern for total change in the structure of class relations. The degree of class solidarity and the potential for class conflict in a class society varies according to the level along this four-point scale that class awareness has reached in the various social classes. The fifth question partly overlaps with this and asks whether social classes are also the basis of political and social movements that enter into patterns of collective action. A class with a 'revolutionary' awareness will, of course, tend to be formed into some kind of social movement, however loose. Classes with lower levels of class awareness may, nevertheless, also have a degree of social and political organisation into trades unions, professional associations and class-specific political parties.

At its most basic, question five raises the issue of whether class members identify with particular political parties and movements, as reflected, for example, in electoral support for them. For this reason, voting studies have always been central to class analysis. Stronger levels of social class formation exist where voting or generalised support is merged into larger patterns of collective action in pursuit of common goals. Identification and active support with, for example, a labour movement and a socialist party, might be taken as a very strong indication of the existence of a cohesive and solidaristic working class. A working class can exist without such collective mobilisation, but it would be a weaker example of one.

What is to be done?

My purpose in raising these questions is to highlight the tasks of class analysis and how it can contribute to studies of social inclusion and exclusion. There is a pressing need to find answers to the questions in new research and, equally importantly, in the re-assessment of existing evidence. Contrary to the suggestions of Nisbet, of Clark and Lipset, and of Pakulski and Waters, I would suggest that there is very strong evidence that we do indeed still live in class societies (see the collection of studies in Part 3 of Lee and Turner 1996). These class societies may not be as strongly structured into social classes as was the case through the first half of the twentieth century, but they are, nevertheless, class societies all the same.

The critics of class analysis have got this wrong for two reasons. First, they have not distinguished the various questions that I have asked. In particular, they have held that negative or weak answers to questions four and five are sufficient to refute the idea that class has any relevance at all. Secondly, they have not made the Weberian distinction between class, status and command. This is apparent at two levels. They have tended to see class itself in 'status' terms – as a matter of cultural norms and values and of lifestyles rather than of economic divisions. This allows them to focus on the implications of certain very obvious changes in the sphere of consumption for social status, and to claim that these presage the disappearance of traditional 'class' divisions. If people no longer *see* themselves as members of classes, it is argued, then there *are* no classes.

Beverley Skeggs (1997), however, has shown that class awareness is apparent in the meanings that people employ, not in the precise words that they use. She shows that the women she interviewed had a very acute awareness and sensitivity to matters of class, but they articulated these through ideas of what it is to be 'rough' or 'respectable'. Their identities and their everyday struggles reflected their classifying practices, and were closely associated with their economic positions, but they eschewed such words as 'class'. In a different context, Klaus Eder (1995) has shown that new social movements that define themselves in relation to issues and non-class identities are, nevertheless, rooted in class relations. They involve antagonistic and often incompatible interests and values that are shaped by cultural constructs that mediate between structure and consciousness.

The critics are correct to point out, however, that it is precisely in terms of questions four and five that the evidence for the existence of social classes is at its weakest. However, it is a fundamental error to assume that the absence of a strong consciousness of class means that there is no material reality to social classes and class situations. This crucial point was recognised by Richard Tawney almost three-quarters of a century ago. Tawney pointed out that this error

> is to confuse the fact of class with the consciousness of class, which is a different phenomenon. The fact creates the consciousness, not the consciousness the fact. The former may exist without the latter, and the group may be marked by common characteristics, and occupy a distinctive position *vis-à-vis* other groups, without, except at moments of exceptional tension, being aware that it does so.
>
> (Tawney 1931: 58)

That is, changes in the sphere of consciousness and collective action do not, in themselves, mean that class does not exist at the morphological level of demographic clustering and unequal life chances. Questions one, two, and three are concerned with precisely these issues of the 'facts' of class.

It is here that much of the research into nominalist categories of occupation and employment – and, I would add, property – have a real importance and significance. The work of those who have attempted to construct such schemes for class analysis highlights the ways in which life chances are unequally distributed and are shared by certain broad categories of the population. The problem with much of this research, however, is that its proponents have tended to assume that they are actually describing social classes. That is, they have confused answers to question two about the homogeneity of economic categories with answers to question three on demographic formation. Those who have come to see that these are not the same thing have tended to fall into the opposite error of denying *any* theoretical importance whatsoever to their class schemes. Goldthorpe and Marshall (1992), for example, counter the arguments of their critics by explicitly abandoning any theoretical purposes and presenting the categories of the Goldthorpe class scheme as purely pragmatic categories. The number of 'classes' that a researcher identifies in a particular society, they say, will vary with the purposes of the research. I have tried to show that this may be the case for nominal economic categories – what Crompton (1998) calls 'employment aggregates' – but it is not a prescription that can be followed if we are searching for the existence and significance of real social classes.

Direct research into the formation of social classes (question three) is a matter of major importance, and there is a real need to construct models of social class hierarchies – incorporating also an awareness of the part played by status and command – and to investigate how these vary from one society to another and how they change over time. The articulation of stratification (class, status and command) with gender, race, and age divisions must also figure centrally in this work, as must an awareness of how these articulations are influenced by, for example, life course effects, and shaped by institutional variations in citizenship and state formation. Such models tell us critical things about the nature of particular societies, and they provide an essential framework for posing longitudinal and comparative research problems. Such research is, however, extremely difficult to undertake. The amount of data required is often beyond even the largest social survey, and the technical instruments of research are often inadequate. The measuring instruments available to us simply do not allow us, yet, to answer all the questions that are raised at this level.

This allows us to see an additional rationale for research in relation to question two on economic categories. The nominal categories constructed may, if sensibly employed, serve as indicators or proxies for social classes. They will not correspond to social classes in a one-to-one way, but they may tell us something about the actual structure of social class boundaries. At their best, of course, they may come very close to disclosing the contours of the social classes that would otherwise need to be uncovered through different forms of research. Class analysis will advance if the efforts currently being put into the construction of nominal categories are guided by an awareness of both their limitations and their great potential. This point has been powerfully put by Rosemary Crompton, who advocates a pragmatic pluralism of class schemes that recognises their role as proxies for real social class categories:

> For many purposes ... research carried out using different schemes will be broadly comparable, and in many instances, the use of a 'good enough' occupational classification will suffice – indeed, the relevant data may not be available in any other form.
>
> (Crompton 1993: 123)

Thus, nominal categories are a half-way-house on the way to real classifications, but they are a half-way-house that is likely to be with us for some time. So long as we recognise their pragmatic purpose, and appreciate that no one scheme is likely to be an all-purpose 'best buy', they will, as Crompton argues, allow us to approach the serious empirical questions raised in theories of class and stratification. The categories are not, themselves, proposing radically different *theories* of class; they are alternative devices for *reporting* (Runciman 1983) the extent of class inequalities and their consequences. Research in Britain, for example, has used such categories to document the great and growing disparities in health, mortality and other life chances that affect people in so many ways (Black 1980, Acheson 1998, Reid 1998) and for beginning to address crucial theoretical issues. There remain sharp inequalities of life chances around the distribution of property and employment opportunities. These inequalities of income and assets are reflected in a wide range of material life chances: birth weight, infant mortality, life expectancy, disability, serious illness, housing, education, victimisation in crime and many other areas are shaped, overwhelmingly, by class situation. These are not simply economic inequalities, they are socially structured differences in life chances that often have their effects 'behind the backs' of the people involved and that may not be reflected in their social awareness or the cultural meanings that they give to their lives. Class relations have a causal effect on people's lives, despite the fact that they may not articulate this in class terms.

Class analysis cannot, of course, remain only at this level of analysis. There are important issues – highlighted in my questions four and five – that also have to be addressed and that are, in fact, central to the arguments of the critics of class analysis. What they point to are changes at the level of consciousness and action that, they argue, constitute the death of class. I have already argued that these changes do not, in themselves, mean that the material aspects of class have disappeared. How then, are the implications of their arguments to be seen from the standpoint of the framework of class analysis that I have presented here?

There has, until recently, been a very close relationship between class and status. Status reinforced class relations and made them more visible. The features that Nisbet identified for the nineteenth century, and which persisted well into the twentieth, are simply one element of this. Alongside the persistence of the traditional landed, agrarian and rural values that he identified have been those features of the cohesive occupational communities, in all countries, that have defined the social position of the manual worker. A pride in manual labour, the traditions of struggle and opposition, support for localism and cooperation all helped to define the class position and class consciousness of the proletarian worker (Lockwood 1966). Occupational identity and occupational prestige reinforced one another and legitimated the material aspects of class. The material realities of class were experienced and interpreted subjectively as the consciousness of class. It was this close association of class and status that gave class relations the solidity and visibility found in study after study (see, for example, Popitz *et al.* 1957).

The changes highlighted by the critics of class analysis reveal a weakening of the cultural and political aspects of class formation, and this has been especially marked since World War II. This can be seen clearly in the case of the working class. The period from the 1880s to the 1950s, with the concentration and monopolisation that the development of organised capitalism implied, saw the consolidation of cohesive working-class communities that sustained a proletarian consciousness and form of political action. Localised kinship networks, communal forms of leisure, and local co-operatives, friendly societies, trades unions, and socialist or labour party branches all reinforced this proletarian lifestyle and gave solidity to the working class as a cultural and political formation. As researchers such as Lash (1984) and Gallie (1984) have shown, these similar processes of class formation made themselves felt in different *forms* of class consciousness and class action, the French labour movement differing quite significantly from the British, but this was class consciousness and class action nevertheless (see also Mann 1973).

Relative affluence and a general improvement in economic conditions, changes in patterns of work and employment, increased geographical mobility, and the growth of consumerism all helped to bring about a weakening of the proletarian communities. The new 'privatised' lifestyles of workers have involved the declining salience of work in their sense of personal identity and, therefore, a declining salience of class in their consciousness of their own social situation.

These changes constitute a re-alignment of the relationships between class and status. It is this re-alignment that the critics of class analysis have wrongly hailed as the 'death of class'. This re-articulation of the relations between class and status has involved the declining salience of work and employment for personal identity, which now owes a great deal to consumer identities, sexuality and lifestyle. Of particular importance has been the changing position of women in relation to paid work, which has had major implications for work organisation and household relations, 'exploding the traditional class–gender nexus' (Esping-Andersen 1993), and the autonomisation of gender and ethnic identities from their long-standing subordination to class-based identities. For all of these reasons, we must be more sensitive to the dissolution of the close link that formerly existed between class and status and the corresponding pluralisation of status divisions.

As Eder has argued,

> Class is a structure that translates inequality and power into different life chances for categories of individuals. It is therefore a structural determination of life chances. A structure which distributes chances to act, and delimits action spaces, which are often highly resistant to the attempts of social actors to change them. This structure boundedness of action is what a class theory is supposed to explain.
>
> (Eder 1995: 12)

Class operates alongside other factors that play their part in the analysis of social stratification and social exclusion. Advocates of class analysis have no need to argue that class is the only, or even the most important, causal mechanism at work. The strategy of the anti-class critics in this respect is like that of the aircraft passenger who whiles away the time by writing an academic paper on 'the death of gravity'. The fact that an aircraft flies, of course, does not mark the end of gravity, but, instead, the way in which other causal mechanisms can operate *alongside gravity* to provide the airlift that flight requires. Class, too, must be seen in this way, as one among the many tools in the sociological toolbox.

Class will not lie down because it is not dead. It remains a fact – a crucial fact – in contemporary societies. The consciousness and collective organisation of class has weakened and the material structures of life chances have, as a result, become less visible. But it is precisely the task of sociology to look for those features of societies that are hidden from view. Sociologists should not be bound by the perceptions and awareness of those they study. We must investigate the structural features of stratification alongside forms of consciousness and social identity. Far from being dead, class is merely resting. While resting, it nevertheless continues to exercise its effects on people's life chances.

Notes

1 This argument is developed at greater length in Scott (1996).
2 These same five questions can be asked, with appropriate modifications, about the structuring of status and command relations in non-class societies and will allow researchers to decide whether they are dealing with a status society or a command society.
3 These are the *Classification of Occupations* and the *Standard Occupational Classification*.

References

Acheson, D. (1998) *Independent Inquiry into Inequalities in Health*. London: HMSO.
Archer, M.S. and Giner, S. (1971) 'Social stratification in Europe', in *Contemporary*

  Europe: Class, Status and Power, M.S. Archer and S. Giner (eds). London: Weidenfeld and Nicholson.

Archer, M. (1997) Realist Social Theory. Cambridge: Cambridge University Press.

Aron, R. (1964) La Lutte de Classes. Paris: Gallimard.

Bendix, R. and Lipset, S.M. (eds) (1953) Class, Status and Power. New York: Free Press.

Berle, A.A. and Means, G.C. (1932) The Modern Corporation and Private Property. London: Macmillan.

Black, D. (1980) 'Inequalities in health' (The Black Report), in Inequalities in Health, P. Townsend and N. Davidson. Harmondsworth: Penguin, 1992.

Bradley, H. (1996) Fragmented Identities. Cambridge: Polity Press.

Clark, T.N. and Lipset, S.M. (1991) 'Are social classes dying?', International Sociology 6. Also in Class, Volume 1, J. Scott (ed.). London: Routledge, 1996.

Crompton, R. (1993) Class and Stratification. Cambridge: Polity Press.

Crompton, R. and Scott, J. (2000) 'The state of class analysis', in New Directions in Class Analysis. Sociological Review Monograph, F. Devine, et al. (eds). Oxford: Basil Blackwell.

Crook, S., Pakulski, J. and Waters, M. (1992) Postmodernization. London: Sage.

Dahrendorf, R. (1957) Class and Class Conflict in an Industrial Society. London: Routledge and Kegan Paul, 1959.

Eder, K. (1995) The New Politics of Class. London: Sage.

Edgell, S. 1997. Class. London: Routledge.

Erikson, R. and Goldthorpe, J. (1993) The Constant Flux. Oxford: Clarendon Press.

Erikson, R., Goldthorpe, J.H. and Portocarero, L. (1979) 'Intergenerational class mobility in three European countries', British Journal of Sociology 30.

Esping Andersen, G. (1993) Changing Classes. London: Sage.

Evans, G. (1996) 'Social class and interest formation in post-communist societies', in Lee and Turner (eds) 1996.

Gallie, D. (1983) Social Inequality and Class Radicalism in France and Britain. Cambridge: Cambridge University Press.

Geiger, T. (1949) Die Klassengesellschaft im Schmelztiegel. Köln: Hagen.

Goldthorpe, J.H. (1964) 'Social stratification in industrial societies', in The Development of Industrial Societies, Sociological Review Monograph, number 8, P. Halmos (ed.).

Goldthorpe, J.H. (1980) Social Mobility and Class Structure. Oxford: Clarendon Press.

Goldthorpe, J.H. (1983) 'Women and class analysis: in defence of the conventional view', Sociology 17: 465–88. Also in Class, Volume 3, J. Scott (ed.). London: Routledge, 1996.

Goldthorpe, J.H. and Marshall, G. (1992) 'The promising future of class analysis: a response to recent critics', Sociology 26.

Goldthorpe, J.H., Lockwood, D., Bechhofer, F. and Platt, J. (1969) The Affluent Worker in the Class Structure. Cambridge: Cambridge University Press.

Haller, M. (ed.) (1996) Class Structure in Europe. New York: M.E. Sharpe.

Jonsson, J.O. (1993) 'Education, social mobility, and social reproduction in Sweden: patterns and changes', in Welfare Trends in the Scandinavian Countries, E.J. Hanson et al. (eds). New York: M.E. Sharpe.

Kerr, C., Dunlop, J.T., Harbison, F. and Myers, C.A. (1960) Industrialism and Industrial Man. Cambridge, MA: Harvard University Press.

Lash, S. (1984) The Militant Worker: Class and Radicalism in France and Austria. London: Heinemann.

Lee, D. and Turner, B.S. (eds) (1996) Conflicts About Class. Harlow: Longman.

Lockwood, D. (1966) 'Sources of variation in working class images of society', in *Working Class Images of Society*, M. Bulmer (ed.). London: Routledge and Kegan Paul, 1975.

Mann, M. (1973) *Consciousness and Action Among the Western Working Class*. London: Macmillan.

Marshall, G., Rose, D., Vogler, C. and Newby, H. (1988) *Social Class in Modern Britain*. London: Hutchinson.

Marshall, G., Swift, A. and Roberts, S. (1997) *Against the Odds: Social Class and Social Justice in Industrial Societies*. Oxford: Clarendon Press.

Marshall, T.H. ([1949] 1963) 'Citizenship and social class', in *Sociology At The Crossroads*, T.H. Marshall. London: Heinemann.

Marshall, T.H. ([1956] 1963) 'Changes in social stratification in the twentieth century', in *Sociology at the Crossroads*, T.H. Marshall. London: Heinemann.

Marx, K. and Engels, F. ([1848] 1967) *The Communist Manifesto*. Harmondsworth: Penguin.

Milner, A. (1999) *Class*. London: Sage.

Morris, L. and Scott, J. (1996) 'The attenuation of class analysis', *British Journal of Sociology* 47.

Mosca, G. ([1896] 1982) 'Elementi di Scienza Politica, first edition', in *Elementi di Scienza Politica*. Edited by G. Mosca.

Mosca, G. ([1923] 1982) 'Elementi di Scienza Politica, Second Edition', in *Elementi di Scienza Politica*. Edited by G. Mosca.

Nisbet, R.A. ([1959] 1996) 'The Decline and Fall of Social Class'. *Pacific Sociological Review*, 2. Also in J. Scott (ed), *Class*, Volume 1. London: Routledge.

Packard, V. ([1959] 1961) *The Status Seekers*. Harmondsworth: Penguin.

Pahl, R.E. (1989) 'Is the emperor naked? Some questions on the adequacy of sociological theory in urban and regional research', *International Journal of Urban and Regional Research* 13: 709–20.

Pahl, R.E. (1993) 'Does class analysis without class have a future? A reply to Goldthorpe and Marshall', *Sociology* 27.

Pakulski, J. and Waters, M. (1996) *The Death of Class*. London: Sage.

Pareto, V. ([1916] 1963) *A Treatise on General Sociology*. Edited by A. Livingstone. New York: Dover, four volumes bound as two.

Popitz, H., Bahrdt, H.P., Jures, E.A. and Kesting, H. (1957) *Das Gesellschaftsbild des Arbeiters*. Tubingen: Mohr.

Prandy, K. (1991) 'The revised Cambridge scale of occupations', *Sociology* 24, 4.

Reid, I. (1998) *Class in Britain*. Cambridge: Polity Press.

Reisman, D., Glazer, N. and Denney, R. (1953) *The Lonely Crowd*. New York: Doubleday Anchor Books.

Rose, D. and O'Reilly, K. (eds) (1997) *Constructing Classes: Towards a New Social Classification of the UK*. Swindon: ESRC and Office for National Statistics.

Runciman, W.G. (1968) 'Class, status and power', in *Social Stratification*. Edited by J.A. Jackson, 25–61. Cambridge: Cambridge University Press, 1968. Also in *Class*, Volume 1, J. Scott (ed.). London: Routledge, 1996.

Runciman, W.G. (1983) *A Treatise on Social Theory, Volume 1*. Cambridge: Cambridge University Press.

Sarlvik, B. and Crewe, I. (1983) *Decade of Dealignment*. Cambridge: Cambridge University Press.

Scase, R. (1993) *Class*. Buckingham: Open University Press.

Schumpeter, J. (1926) 'Social classes in an ethnically homogeneous environment', in

Imperialism and Social Classes. Edited by J. Schumpeter. New York: Augustus M. Kelley, 1951.

Scott, J. (1991) *Who Rules Britain?* Cambridge: Polity Press.

Scott, J. (1994) 'Class analysis: back to the future', *Sociology* 28. Also in Lee and Turner (eds) 1997.

Scott, J. (1996) *Stratification and Power: Structures of Class, Status and Command.* Cambridge: Polity Press.

Scott, J. (1997) *Corporate Business and Capitalist Classes.* Oxford: Oxford University Press.

Skeggs, B. (1997) *Formations of Class and Gender.* Cambridge: Polity Press.

Tawney, R.H. (1931) *Equality.* London: George Allen and Unwin.

Tönnies, F. ([1931] 1996) 'Estates and classes', in *Class*, Volume 1, J. Scott (ed.). London: Routledge.

Weber, M. (1914) 'The distribution of power within the political community: class, status, party', in *Economy and Society.* Edited by G. Roth and C. Wittich, 926–40. New York: Bedminster Press, 1968. Also in *Class*, Volume 1, J. Scott (ed.). London: Routledge, 1996.

Weber, M. (1920) 'Status groups and classes', in *Economy and Society.* Edited by G. Roth and C. Wittich, 302–7. New York: Bedminster Press, 1968. Also in *Class*, Volume 1, J. Scott (ed.). London: Routledge, 1996.

Wright, E.O. (1976) 'Class boundaries in advanced capitalist societies', *New Left Review* 98.

Wright, E.O. (1985) *Classes.* London: Verso.

Wright, E.O. (1989) 'The comparative project on class structure and class consciousness: an overview', *Acta Sociologica* 32.

Wright, E.O. (1997) *Class Counts.* Cambridge: Cambridge University Press.

Zweig, F. (1961) *The Worker in an Affluent Society.* London: Heinemann.

9 Tackling inequality and exclusion

Towards a dimension of active citizenship participation

Carlos Machado and Jacques Vilrokx

Although Western societies have witnessed substantial developments in the achievement of equally guaranteed civil and social rights during the nineteenth and twentieth century, the idea of being a citizen – in the whole sense of the word – has been challenged by the economical and structural changes that have occurred in post-industrial countries during the last decades. In this context, and linking new visions of citizenship with new meanings of work, this chapter examines the latest socio-economic trends in European welfare states.

Indeed, one of these transformations is related to the decline of the role of work in society. It is argued in this chapter that to participate in society has nevertheless been envisaged by administrators and policy-makers as mainly labour market participation. Social exclusion in practice has thus been primarily about exclusion from the labour force. Hence, many of the social integration mechanisms observed in Europe are orientated to activation and integration via (paid-)work. Still, there is a growing body of research that demonstrates the inadequacy of social inclusion policies when they focus exclusively on employment. This chapter reflects on the findings of two recent European Commission funded comparative empirical studies on the central issue of social inclusion–exclusion – SEDEC ('Social Exclusion and the Development of European Citizenship') and INPART ('Inclusion through Participation').[1] Their results allow us to consider the nature of labour as source for social integration and, likewise, reveal the significance of citizen participation as an essential element for reducing social inequalities and exclusion.

This chapter presents new ways of addressing exclusion in order to achieve a more comprehensive model of equality and inclusion. For this, a shift from equality of opportunity to equality of participation, directly linked to the principle of active citizenship participation, is necessary. A number of initiatives undertaken by 'third system organisations' in local neighbourhoods illustrate how the notion of being a citizen can be construed as something more than entitlement to citizenship rights by way of waged employment, when other forms of work are encouraged by a more 'social approach'. Being a citizen is then tantamount to being able to participate fully in the local community and society.

The strength of the link between the individual and the state is not a magic effect of any consensual ideology but comes from a number of different bonds that bring citizenship forth. We conclude that by widening and validating other forms of social inclusion and citizen participation aside from those pertaining to the (paid-)work and market driven employment to which citizenship rights are commonly attached, we can address exclusion on a broader scale. Exclusion not only refers to exclusion from resources, but also to exclusion from social participation.

Structural transformations in a welfare state based on full employment

While welfare states are associated with the improvement in standards of living and social rights for everyone, the economic transformation initiated after the oil crisis of the 1970s had profound effects in modern society. Over the years, the pace of socio-economic transformation has accelerated as technical and technological advances, diffusion of new products, processes and methods of organisation evolve, as economies become more open and competition in world markets have been intensified. Riccardo Petrella (1998) describes the world economy as governed by rules, principles and institutions that only serve the interests of actors operating in global markets requiring less labour. This deconstructs professional categories and salaries, promotes flexibilisation, and thereby, produces precariousness of resources and devaluation of (paid-)work. The restructuring of the capital–labour relationships resulting from the information technology revolution has forced national economies and private firms to act on labour costs since the early 1980s, either by increasing productivity without employment creation (in Europe) or by lowering the cost of a plethora of new jobs (in USA) (Castells 1996: 277–8). The impact of globalisation on European welfare states is an emergent problem that has been analysed in recent studies (Castells 1996, 1997, Rhodes 1996, Hout 1997). Moreover, these changes are endangering the stability of European welfare states since laggard economic growth, unemployment and increasing public expenditure motivated by demographic patterns and the structural crisis of the social security system (with exponential national debts) limit the capacity of the governments for adopting effective economic policy actions.

As a result of these changes, the possibilities for employment in a dominant system that associates new technologies with concepts such as globalisation, liberalisation, deregulation, privatisation, competitiveness (in short, the new economy of the information society), are increasingly uneven for every one. Indeed, recent economic structuring has made life in society very difficult for the unemployed and those excluded from economic, social and cultural spheres. This has given rise to a social division and the consequently emergence of an 'exclusive society' (Lister 1990). One can observe that the process of participation in an 'employment society' unevenly involves different groups of the population. Acting as a citizen – understood in the broad sense of exercising one's rights and duties and participating fully in the occupational and social institutions of the community concerned as well as its political and cultural life – turns out to become a challenge rather than a reality. T.H. Marshall was one of the earliest to appreciate the significance of this tension when writing about the realisation of citizenship in Western democracies (Marshall [1973] 1977). Likewise, Claus Offe (1985, 1993) underlines the unmistakable signs of a crisis of the labour market and the legitimation of the state in the sustainment of the model of social progress based on full employment, economic growth and social security. The importance of this crisis lies – apart from the impossibility of working, experienced by many people – in the fact that the erosion of the traditional characteristic of work as a structuring element in the economy and society has become a direct factor in the loss of societal cohesion and poverty (see Table 9.1 below).

Although the formal recognition of any individual as a citizen can be defined in terms of access to legal rights of citizenship, widely recognised in present-day plural democracies, the resources and powers that implement and embed the very concept of citizenship are neither equally nor fairly distributed. In this sense, the strain between citizens and rights within the European Union is partly because the basis for those rights is restricted to a number of categories such as freedom of movement, production, capital, labour and services. These equate the rights of citizens with those of workers, the worker–citizen. Historically, the central issue of inequality, in the era following the golden period of the 1950s and 1960s in Western Europe, acquired a new dimension by way of high unemployment, growing marginalisation and exclusion from the labour market, and increasing numbers of people dependent on public support.

These inequalities put pressure on some segments of the population, such as women, more than on others. Feminist movements for gender equality, equality of employment opportunity and autonomy in the creation and maintenance of families and households have contributed to a restructuring of women's roles in Western societies. Societies faced a readjustment of welfare services during the

Table 9.1 Poverty rate for employed and not-employed population between 16–64 years of age (data from the beginning of 1990s)

	Employed	Total	Not-employed
Belgium	4.6	9.2	0.7
Denmark	4.0	9.8	2.8
Norway	4.4	11.5	3.2
Netherlands	6.9	12.8	3.8
Germany	6.3	13.1	3.7
Sweden	6.6	16.8	5.2
Spain	13.1	18.4	7.5
Australia	12.5	31.4	5.4
Canada	12.3	32.8	7.6
UK	14.5	38.9	4.1
USA	19.1	42.7	13.8

Source: Luxembourg Income Study (LIS), cited in De Lathouwer and Thirion 1999: 10.

1990s, and demonstrated a widespread acceptance of the necessity of providing stability to families and/or households, and their children. In this context, a basic theoretical idea is that, for women, a weakening of dependence through employment is a necessary emancipatory step, both individually and professionally speaking. Making the welfare systems of modern society more gender-equal and 'woman-friendly' presents a common challenge to European states whatever the type of welfare regime they have set up.

Currently, trends toward 'work-fare' policies and socio-demographic changes are creating common societal features and exclusionary problems to which existing European institutions are ill-adapted. Nonetheless, the socio-economic conditions generated in advanced post-industrial countries provide challenges and opportunities for which European social and economic policies need to be developed. In analysing the policies within the European Union over the central element of social inclusion/exclusion, we notice that social policy debates are driven by the assumption that unemployment is directly linked to social exclusion. Work and welfare systems tend to prioritise employment above all else and pursue social inclusion and citizenship through this means. From a sociological perspective, it is a truism, as Møller asserts, that work – understood as paid work – has been the most critical institution with regard to the integration of individuals, groups and classes in society (Møller 1997: 83). Broadly speaking, among the perspectives on the nature of work, none presents higher consensus than the one represented by the notion of employment. In the past, paid work was the major (if not sole) source of income and also the most important link between individual and society, defining one's identity and social status. Undoubtedly, from a sociological point of view, the emphasis on (paid-)work was to guarantee economic and social stability. However, considering the developments in the labour market with the flexibilisation of work, it is very doubtful that the integration mechanisms that operated in the past via waged labour will continue to have the same functional role.

Rebutting the integrative nature of paid-work: active policies on the spot

For our purpose, which is to gain insight into ways of addressing exclusion (through the concept of active citizenship), the consequences of the heterogeneisation of 'work' in terms of exclusion and inclusion of people are the object of analysis, both normatively and sociologically speaking. In the two European projects, INPART and SEDEC, we observe that (paid-)work has multiple benefits in the form of generating resources (namely via income), giving socio-economic stability and a sense to life. However, inclusion must stretch well beyond work, not only because of labour market constraints, but because of the necessity of an equilibrium between work and other inclusive facets of life.

Even if unemployment may increase the risk of social exclusion, exclusion is not necessarily an unavoidable consequence of lacking a job. This can be inferred from the above mentioned research projects. There is a whole range of complex factors that may increase rather than decrease the likelihood of both economic and social exclusion. For example, the sum of some factors increases the risks of becoming more vulnerable to being or feeling excluded, such as age, income, household composition (see the data in Table 9.2). Likewise, protective welfare systems such as Belgium, Sweden or Denmark mean that individual unemployment is not a sufficient cause for poverty or exclusion in terms of an income level.

Consequently, any discussion on social exclusion which focuses on integration through employment alone will tend to reduce the social to the economic, as Ruth Levitas stresses (Levitas 1999). Simultaneously, it will limit our understanding of work to a market activity while ignoring its importance as a social activity. In this sense, policies that pay much attention to inclusion through (paid-)work, albeit very important, may neglect the relevance of participation as a social goal. There should then be a balance – when making use of the dynamic markets – between the economic and the non-economic in the life of a society.

The view that active measures serve as a panacea for tackling exclusion is based on the assumption that exclusion and marginalisation are a consequence of an incomplete (or non-existing) individual adaptation to the social environment, and more specifically to the work environment. Participation in today's world of work is urged for the young and long-term unemployed and risk groups such as lone parents, people with disabilities, older workers and those without the basic literacy and numeracy skills. In Spain, for example, the problems have been concentrated in a high percentage of youth unemployment

Table 9.2 Incidence and risk of poverty

Country	Single-parent households		'Working poor'		Pensioner	
	Incidence (%)	Risk (%)	Incidence (%)	Risk (%)	Incidence (%)	Risk (%)
Austria	5	24	57	12	21	9
Belgium	8	25	27	6	26	10
Germany	7	38	N/A	N/A	N/A	N/A
Denmark	(2)	(5)	32	4	28	9
Spain	2	30	47	12	22	11
France	6	23	40	9	25	12
Italy	3	19	59	12	27	10
Netherlands	6	24	39	6	13	5
Portugal	4	33	40	15	48	43
United Kingdom	16	36	28	6	27	12

Source: ECHP User Database, 2nd wave (SEDEC, 1999. Report 2, Vol. 1, ch. 2).

Notes
Those findings which correspond to cells with less than 20 cases are in parenthesis.
The information dates from 1994.

(see Table 9.3 below), together with a continuous relatively high level of unemployment (15–20 per cent). In Belgium, 54 per cent of the unemployed in 1997 did not have an upper secondary school-leaving certificate (cf. MET 1997).

Paradoxically, the growing interest that social polices have shown for activation and participation through work, education and training schemes are in many cases countervened by the debates on the efficiency of their compulsory nature. To illustrate this, although European policy makers are increasingly concerned with activating unemployed onto the labour market, certain employment schemes (e.g. Social Activation Scheme in Netherlands, Job Pools in Denmark, Social Enterprises in Belgium) tend to focus on the social risks to which the majority of unemployed people might be subject – that is, lack of a job. Yet they are not particularly designed to tackle the specific needs of their recipients. Inclusion through Participation-INPART findings indicate that even if most current inclusion policies in Europe are, indeed, employment policies aiming at increased employability and labour-market integration, their main objective seems to be increasing economic independence and decreasing social benefits dependency, rather than promoting social inclusion in a wider sense (INPART, WP4: 17, 2000).

Regarding the social status supplied by a subsidised paid job, for example, Jens Lind reminds us that jobs created primarily to secure employment do not have the same status as a 'normal job'. They cannot provide the sense of having a useful social function that paid jobs tend to have. Conditioning the entitlement to unemployment benefits by being available for any vacant job clearly expresses that the status of being unemployed is subordinate to employment in any type of job (Lind 1995: 201). In some cases, the participation in subsidiary schemes may create negative effects such as stagnation and stigmatisation. In other employment policy measures, it has been revealed that leaving people confined to marginal economic resources tends to exclude them in the long run

Table 9.3 Key socio-economic indicators, INPART European countries and EU average, 1997

Country	Unemployment (%)	(%) LTU[a]	Youth unemployment (%)	Female unemployment (%)	Labour market participation rate (%)	Female labour market participation rate (%)
Belgium	9.2	58.7	6.8	11.9	57.3	47
Denmark	5.5	27.2	6	6.6	77.5	71.1
Netherlands	5.2	48	6.1	6.9	66.7	54.9
Portugal	6.8	51.5	6.2	7.8	67.5	58.6
Spain	20.8	51.9	15.9	28.3	48.6	33.9
UK	7	38.6	2.7	6	70.8	63.9
EU-average	10.7	48.6	9.8	12.4	60.5	50.5

Source: EU/DG5, *Employment Policies in the EU and in the Member States.* Joint Report 1998.

Note
a LTU = Long Term Unemployment

from the larger society. Reducing benefits to force individuals into work pushes them into de-motivating jobs and already crowded low-wage labour markets.

The LEA (Local Employment Agency) system in Belgium, Melkert-I scheme in Netherlands or the API (Work-Place Introduction) in Sweden can serve as examples. Programmes initially designed to give unemployed a means for supplementing their benefits by way of a low-threshold work experience turned into programmes creating their own employment dynamics with the subsequent promotion of a dualisation of the labour market. Consequently, linking training measures with various labour market policies may make possible different pathways to social integration (ESF 1997).

Hence, the shift from passive to active policies does not always result in a better situation for the participants in secondary labour-market schemes, either economically or professionally speaking. Other experiences rooted in community-based initiatives (e.g. 'Mutual Aid Contracts' and 'LETS system' in the UK) reveal that access to income improvement, economic independence and purchasing power can also be organised in other ways than by regular jobs (for further documentation see, for example, Williams 1996, Williams and Windebank 1997, INPART WP3 1999). Besides, limiting activation and participation to work and income do not necessarily make people contribute in a better way to society or get them involved in meaningful and useful activities. In countries like Belgium, the integrative nature of (paid-)work can be 'called into question' when looking at the nature of some labour market measures (Vilrokx *et al.* 1999). Should the function of (paid-)work be considered the most important (if not the unique) instrument for social inclusion, when certain particular government measures during the 1980s and 1990s (pre-pension schemes, career-breaks, etc.) aimed at reducing official unemployment by drawing people out of the labour market have had a notable success? These policies pose a paradox, if it is believed that only paid jobs are socially integrating.

One may dispute then whether labour market participation is the only possible road to inclusion and full citizenship. To better integrate the so-called 'socially excluded' into society, and thereby promote social cohesion, a reconceptualisation of work, activity and employment is needed. Different models of full- or part-time work may permit men and women to reconcile work and family responsibilities, alternate periods of paid activity with training or other leisure activities or reduce the propensity for the marginalisation of excluded individuals. For single mothers with children, for example, juggling school, career and childcare might sound too much like hard work to be worthwhile. Other forms of work can have a more enticing attraction than having to work all the time. In short, going beyond employment and workfare policies, other 'integrative' and 'participative' forms of work might be more desirable. If we deny the potential of one major facet of contemporary social life, that is, work and all its possibilities for greater participation in other arenas, we deny women and men the chance for a multifaceted life. Thus, activation policies may still move in different directions should they pursue other socially cohesive forms of integration away from sole 'labour market approaches'.

New models of equality and participation: beyond opportunities and work

In the search for solutions concerning the inclusion and participation of the individual in society, new dilemmas arise in relation to the way social responsibilities can be shared by the actors involved, and, as a consequence, to the scope and quality of citizenship in Europe. A society that depends exclusively on work but does not have adequate jobs for everyone is likely to produce numerous societal casualties along the way. Whenever the work identity has been lost, more than one's self-esteem is affected. Loss of a job carries further effects, the uncertainty about one's role in society and a loss of personal pride and esteem, often recognised by the kind of contribution a person makes to society in the form of organised labour (Honneth 1994: 266). Therefore, an 'inclusive society' should provide the basic needs for those who do not find a job (or are not able to work) and recognise the wider diversity of goals life has to offer, including the positive values pertaining to other forms of work (voluntary, unpaid, part-time). However, whereas 'equality of opportunities and meritocracy' have been championed for a long time, moving towards a social democratisation process for all and by all implies that social policies should combine individual choices with common social goals. This analysis bring us to a typology of equalities as depicted below (Figure 9.1).

As presented in the figure below, neoliberal proposals have stressed equality of opportunities as the only acceptable model of equality for decades, even though equality of opportunities can come along with real inequalities of outcome. Since the concept of 'equality' can be applied to a multidimensional domain, the definition of equality in one of its dimensions implies logically the causal acceptance of inequalities in other dimensions (Walzer 1983). The paradox is that the foundations of certain principles of equality lead to social inequality and exclusion. But these inequalities would be unacceptable by society if the original principle of equality of opportunities had not been respected. Following the capitalist ethic, this is acceptable if, in the economic game, there are winners and losers, provided everyone has an 'equal start'.

Principle of organisation

		Society	State
Principle of distribution	**Exclusion**	Individualistic (Meritocracy)	Liberal democracy (Equality of opportunity)
	Inclusion	Solidaristic (Equality of access and use)	Active citizenship democracy (Equality of participation)

Figure 9.1 Distribution of equalities.

Thus, the problem of legitimating equality of opportunities is not that it creates deeper inequalities of outcome but that it leads substantially to a merito-cratic system. In an individualistic society, equality and fairness can both be used to justify inequalities of outcome on the basis of hard work; the rich are entitled to more because they have earned it (meritocracy). The danger, as Taylor-Gooby points out, is that the postmodern emphasis on individualism, pluralism and choice will be a 'smokescreen' behind intended projects towards a residualised system of welfare provision. This blinds us to the significance of market liberalism and the associated trends as engine for extended inequality and lack of opportunity structures and real possibilities at the bottom of the social ladder (Taylor-Gooby 1994: 385). In this situation, driven as it is by structural ebbs, the expanding inequality flow is not so easy to combat. As Friedman puts it, the ideal of equality compatible with capitalism is not equality of outcome, which would discourage people from realising their full potential, but equality of opportunity, which encourages people to do so (in Haslett 1994: 239).

Giddens (1998) reminds us that access to work is one main context of opportunity (the way it is formulated nowadays). Whereas equality of opportun-ities is commonly interpreted in contemporary politics as the equal chance any person has or should have to get a job – 'all deserve to be given an equal chance in life' – the essence of the principle of 'equality of opportunity' although wholly egalitarian in theory is not so in effect, when it is confronted with the limits placed by the market system itself. For Atkinson (1980), the central point is not whether equality of opportunity is a good thing, but whether it is compat-ible with high levels of income and wealth inequality and poverty. Equality of opportunity (as 'fairness') is, indeed, as much a procedural as a distributional concept (Levitas, op. cit.).

This liberal model, as we have presented, is contrasted with a Western Euro-pean society whose models of equality are based on the principle of redistribu-tion and solidarity (e.g. equality of access and use) in which every citizen can participate fully on a broader basis than via the institution of work. Instead of bestowing full-fledged legitimacy on mere business with the subsequent risk of creating social cleavages and deconstructing society, one can follow principles like citizenship or citizen-based participation, individual and collective security and protection. Creating new forms of representation and social participation is also a way to prevent exclusion and to restore participative democracy.

In a period of transformation and globalisation in a new information society, equality must therefore go 'beyond the equal opportunity for all' to be placed in the sphere of the equal opportunity of participation for all. Therefore, it seems pertinent to develop a broader concept of citizenship – 'active citizenship' (as opposed to the more legalistic approach to citizenship), connected to the prin-ciple of equality of participation – in the battle against the impacts of social inequality and exclusion. From a functional perspective, participation, when applied to the sphere of labour, should not be solely understood as a formal par-ticipation in the labour market wherein every kind of job is valid, but must be extended to participation in society at large. Then every citizen – and not only those who belongs to the labour force – has a real chance of being 'socially useful'. Hence, on assuming that citizenship is a status bestowed on those who are active members of a community, all who possess that status must be equal with respect to the rights and duties with which the status is endowed. However, the legal embodiment of 'citizenship' is solely attached to sovereignty and civil and political rights. Nonetheless, the sphere of social participation and social citizenship goes beyond, for example, the simple entitlement to vote. The underpinning of this social model approach can only be found when citizenship transcends the space of right to entitlements to be placed in the sphere of active participation that social life endows. 'People should have optimal chances to societal participation in order to achieve equality of opportunities ... Active participation in society is exactly one of the essential chances each individual should acquire,' asserts Frank Vandenbroucke, Belgian Minister for Social Affairs and Pensions (in De Schampheleire and Vilrokx 2000). The development of policies and institutions that embody and deliver these new social rights, and also monitor appropriate related responsibilities, constitutes the core of 'a new social model', namely the kind of model of welfare and work which is most positively adapted to the particular needs of societies and individuals in post-industrial economic and political conditions (SEDEC 1999 – Report 4: 11).

The model of equality that needs to be imposed in the new European society is one which connects the problem of social exclusion to broad social democratic definitions of citizenship and thus to civil, political and social equality. This may fit into the perspective offered by a common construction of Europe and the Treaty of Amsterdam, aiming to reinforce the European Union's capacity to promote equality, guarantee fundamental rights, ensure that equal opportunities are mainstreamed into all relevant community policies and fight against discrimination. A broader sense of citizenship could be thus developed in which participation and social inclusion would be stimulated to respond to processes of inequality and exclusion. The key issue, however, is on what grounds European citizenship can be constituted. European participation and citizenship remain for many abstract terms. However, the commitment at local, national and supra-national levels to undertake strategies that seek the promotion and evolution of (social) rights should lead us to address the problems produced by our post-industrial societies. Indeed, the contours and the conflicts which can be expected to arise around the development of a common citizenship across European countries will be shaped by the ways in which the different nation states, and the EU itself, respond to the challenge of maintaining or rebuilding the social fabric from its lowest layer (Andersen 1996: 5). As opposed to a liberal model, in which the social relations are embedded in an economic system controlled by the market, a united Europe can offer a new kind of society wherein the economy is embedded in the social relations to the extent to which a combination of state and civil society in the provision of welfare may promote social citizenship with equal rights of participation and reduce the risk of social exclusion.

When – we argue – participation and active citizenship are seen as major tools to be used against inequality and exclusion, maximising people's involvement in their local communities can therefore be used to advance the cause of equality. From a bottom-up approach, fostering social participation in the local community might contribute to the evolution of new forms of democratic action geared to social change, with public participation in policy making and development planning at local level. Indeed, the forms of social solidarity are inextricably related to the historical contexts in which the processes of modernisation occur (Hespanha *et al.* 1997: 170). Similar to the English coffeehouses of early 1700s described in *The Structural Transformation of the Public Sphere* by Habermas (1989 [1962]), the greatest contribution to the development of a modern agency which mediates between society and state is the emergence of an institutional base and organisational structures that can allow local networks of social participation to exist. As Habermas put: 'A discursive democracy requires a continual and variegated "interplay" between a multiplicity of "public spheres" emerging across civil society and a broad spectrum of formal political institutions' (in White 1995: 13).

Hence, it is appropriate to see 'citizenship' as an ethic to be implemented by both public and private entities in their policies of recruitment, in the role of training and in the use of social benefits. Because exclusions not only threaten the excluded but annihilate the social exchange of every member of society, the (solidaristic) model of social relationships allowing members of a society to live cohesively and symbolically with each other can only be realised if the different social actors share the responsibilities for the risks taken by the civil society. This can counter-act the imbalance between winners and losers, rich and poor, included and excluded.

Cockerill, Fortis and other European enterprises have created funds and projects of 'citizenship solidarity' targeted at the insertion of low-skilled or disadvantaged people. Thus, social entrepreneurship embedded in a mixed economy may link the growth of a solidarity culture as the new arena of public life, to a new infrastructure for social participation.

Fostering citizen participation using a local approach: empirical evidence from community-based third system organisations

In the wake of the interest shown by EU authorities in facilitating people's active involvement in their local communities, some European governments have started actions fostering and promoting citizen enablement. These include bottom-up community regeneration with community development programmes that encourage human capital through long-life education, more democratic citizen participation and development of supporting local networks. In countries like Denmark or Austria, there is a long tradition in the sharing of welfare responsibilities by local authorities. When empowerment and participation are linked to the concept of social citizenship – as Andersen remarks (in Andersen and Larsen 1998) – they become an empowering extension of institutionalised universal social rights and, thus, they provide the possibility for all the citizens to take part in a new post-industrial environment and community life.

'Third system organisations' are examples of private initiatives with public support in the delivery of work and training for the local community, responding at the same time to unsatisfied social needs. Differing from the social economy, the third system includes cooperatives, mutual organisations, associations and foundations, and is distinguished not only from capitalist enterprises but also from public-sector bodies. The term 'third system' is a broader concept that embodies not only social economy activities but also a range of social and cultural activities operated by NGOs, and non-profit associations sustained by public institutions, providing new opportunities for socially-excluded people. Examples include the numerous social-cooperatives in Portugal, Italy and Spain, '*Enterprises d'Insertion*' in France, Social and Work Training Enterprises in Belgium, Heritage Associations in Sweden, and Labor foundations in Austria, to cite but a few. The inclusionary and exclusionary potential of some of them, as well as the nature and quality of participation in these activities, were analysed within the framework of the INPART and SEDEC research projects.

Maria Jepsen and Danièle Meulders launched parallel research from a gender perspective on the quality of employment created within community-based organisations (1998). They present the risks and potential effects on women's employment associated with jobs born out of these initiatives. The welfare debate stresses female adaptability and flexibility in the workplace and the provision of childcare for women. Full equality for women in job opportunity is probably impossible without freedom from housework, and the industrialisation of housework is unlikely unless women are leaving the home for jobs. In some cases, participation in community-based activities brings women more possibilities in the labour market as well as fulfilling a demand for alleviating other women's household and caring tasks. The difficulty in other cases is that the participants are entrapped in activation programmes, not so much for the lack of financial incentives they receive as for the lack of opportunities of developing their skills or re-entering the regular labour market. These approaches can stimulate inclusion but they can (re)produce exclusion at the same time. Table 9.4 illustrates the variety and likely impact of participation in local initiatives for men and women. While the first objective of most of these projects was to have been the creation of high quality, stable employment instead of unstable situations devoid of future prospects, it seems that some initiatives are more likely to be successful in this than others.

Pointing in the same direction, European Inclusion through Participation (INPART) research results indicated the necessity for social programmes to invest more in human capital by supporting people in developing themselves and by offering opportunities to meet newly-arisen needs, avoiding participation traps and strengthening career prospects. People need to be able to develop their knowledge and skills throughout their working lives and to improve their

Table 9.4 Typology and quality of the employment created by local initiatives

Type	Intensity	Effect	Quality of employment	Professional status	Stability of activity	Part-time ratio	Gender
Everyday life							
Home service	High	+	Low	Not defined	Unstable	++	Women
Child care	High	+	Low	Not defined	Unstable	++	Women
ICT	Average	+=	High	Being defined	Stable	0	Men
Help integration of young people	High	+	Average–low	Not defined	Unstable	++	Women/men
Improving the quality of life							
Improving housing	High	+=	Variable	Not defined	Variable	+	Men
Security	High	+	Average–low	Not defined	Unstable	++	Men
Local public transport	Low	=	Low	Defined	Stable	+	Men
Rehabilitation of urban spaces	High	+=	Variable	Defined	Stable	+	Men
Local shops	Low	+	Average–low	Defined	Stable	++	Women/men
Culture and leisure							
Tourism	High	+	Average	Being defined	Unstable	++	Women/men
Audio-visual	High	+	High	Being defined	Stable	+	Women/men
Cultural heritage	High	+	Variable	Defined	Variable	++	Women/men
Development of local culture	Low	+=	Variable	Not defined	Unstable	++	Women/men
Sport	High	+	Average–low	Not defined	Unstable	++	Women/men
Environment protection							
Waste management	Average	+	Variable	Not defined	Stable	0	Men
Water management	Low	+	Variable	Defined	Stable	0	Men
Protection of natural habitat	Average	+	Variable	Being defined	Unstable	0	Men
Regulation of pollution	Low	+	High	Defined	Stable	0	Men
Saving of energy	High	+=	Variable	Not defined	Stable	0	Men

Source: Adapted from Jepsen and Meulders (1998: 451).

employability in a changing labour market. For example, 'Creasol' (Work training enterprise – *'Enterprise de Formation par le Travail'* – in the region of Liège,
Belgium), is an employment-oriented activity which fights social exclusion by
elaborating specific integration programmes according to the history, profile and
needs of the participant. The regular use of the social spaces provided by these
local initiatives allows the participants to get know-how, working experience,
access to new social practices and often leads to the reconstruction of lost social
and professional identities. For this reason, the concept of 'one participant, one
project', an article of faith for many reinsertion programmes' managers, stresses
the importance of underlying tailor-made approaches and socio-professional
guidance on individual basis. 'Our major concern is to offer every stagiaire
better prospects than the case of her non-participation, even if one cannot
predict how long the effects of participation will be upheld,' states Godelieve
Rulmont-Ugeux, General Manager and creator of 'Creasol' (in Rulmont-Ugeux
1999).

By improving the effectiveness of social policy measures (e.g. matching
recipients' needs with labour demand), third system organisations can generate
positive impacts on the problem of unemployment, poverty and social exclusion, in some cases through a multidimensional approach but in others by a
more specific targeted strategy. Certainly, there is increasing awareness at EU
level that these organisations are a source of latent job creation and neighbourhood services and, therefore, a key component of European employment policies for generating local employment and tackling social exclusion through
bottom-up, community-based initiatives. Many of these activities should be
encouraged, not only because of their potential for creating employment and
work experience but, from a broader inclusionary side, because of their capabil-
ity to enable people to help themselves, through education and training.
Obtaining employment may be the end goal of many non-profit activities, but it
may not be the beginning. It is absolutely necessary to help people without
basic skills or qualifications to acquire them in order to be employable, to help
people whose skills are out of date to update them, and to raise confidence
caused by long-term unemployment. The best way of protecting employment is
to guarantee the capacity of people to adapt to the new needs of a society that
undergoes a very fast speed of technological change. Citizenship, thus, should
turn into a concrete expression in which every citizen realises – or is able to
realise – their full potential as such.

Therefore, prevention (and activation) implies that the fight against social
exclusion is not limited to specific labour market programmes, but has to be
integrated into a multifaceted approach. Particularly, activities analysed by
INPART, such as Creasol – which was specifically devoted to socially disadvantaged women – try to reorientate unemployment, social exclusion and an inadequate sense of citizenship in a positive inclusionary way through effective
actions that allow its participants to have equal rights, equal access to exercise
their rights and equal opportunities to participate and contribute in the activity
and society. For its director, equality is not only seen as the reduction of the

symbolic distance of power, as the recognition of the difference of resources and skills that question the strategical axes of influence, but as the equality of rights, respect and participation (Rulmont-Ugeux 1999). Promoting active participation and citizenship requires efforts to remove a number of obstacles that hinder the construction of a coherent society.

Adequate integration programmes require an approach in which social services are provided in a harmonised and coordinated way. Yet, one of the main criticisms to the process of policy delivery in the involvement of third system organisations is the frequent lack of adequate coordination between local, regional and national authorities that forces some of these organisations 'to coordinate what is not coordinated elsewhere' and to unload responsibilities to the local level without a clear management framework. Some forms of local development raise particular questions concerning 'a democratic deficit', in the sense that collective local action is enhanced, but with a lack of involvement of the target/excluded groups themselves (Geddes 1998: 47). In many European cities there are people – or groups – who are acknowledged to be an active part of a community, contributing to it even when they do not enjoy political citizenship ('ausländische arrbeitnehmers' in Germany; ethnic minorities in the United Kingdom, etc.). Even if, for these groups, exclusion from the political realm may accompany other forms of exclusion, it does not *per se* imply exclusion from the local community or denial of those rights attached to the membership of that society. Our welfare systems need to be reoriented as a key component of economic effectiveness that maximises the participation and empowerment of those who experience social exclusion and support the voice of the excluded in the political debate if we are to fulfil a vision of a Europe which is 'L'Europe sera l'Europe de tous, de tous ses citoyens, ou ne sera pas' (Comité des Sages 1996).

Evidence from comparative investigation of inclusion policies in the empirical INPART and SEDEC research has shown that, when the objective of social inclusion policies is to combat social exclusion by enabling people to become more involved in social and societal participation, other forms of work than mainstream employment need to be taken into account. Other types of work and participation have an inclusionary potential that should not be ignored. Compared to regular labour market participation, voluntary or unpaid work, for example, may offer lower income resources. Nevertheless, these other non-standard forms of work do offer participation and resources that may be important for people's social integration. People are looking for both meaningful employment and opportunities for commitment outside of work. If society can upgrade and reward such commitment and put it on a level of gainful employment, it can create both individual identity and social cohesion (Beck 1997: 106).

Unfettering the shackles of work: from activation to citizen participation

This chapter has focused on the links between changing welfare states, the transformation of the role of (paid-)work and social inequality and exclusion. In

Europe, these issues are closely related. Given the realities of the employment arena in Europe, an important policy issue for those interested in extending the objectives of social inclusion policies is that of how to increase participation in a wider sense rather than in the narrow meaning that labour-market policies impose. For that, social policies should be based on a broader concept of participation than most of them are now. In more general terms, a conclusion from comparative sociological research is that social policies should be based on an engagement concept of society rather than an employment concept (INPART, WP4: 64).

A much greater variety of arrangements surrounding work exists in our world than the one conceded by the official marketplace. The notion that modern workers increasingly turn to activities outside the sphere of regular (paid-)work for a sense of meaning and identity appears regularly in most sociological thinking about the nature of participation in work. Lessons can be drawn from the studies of participation in underground and informal economies (see for example, Pahl 1984, Redcliffe and Mingione 1985, Ferman 1990, Williams and Windebank 1998, Williams *et al.* 1999). For some groups, participation in voluntary and/or unpaid activities might match their ambitions and capacities better than labour market participation. In a study on the informal sector in the European Union, Williams and Windebank (1997) show that unpaid activities or activities that take place in the context of non-monetary exchange systems are a resource for full participation as well.

Acknowledging that unemployed or poor people are able to develop informal strategies to counter exclusion and manage their own inclusion and participation, should encourage social policies aiming at inclusion to recognise and support these strategies (INPART, WP4: 65). Thus, the lack of alternative forms in the attribution of work would expose those men and women without standard employment's mantel of identity and social status (whether due to unemployment or poverty) to the unfair and unequal effects emanating from labour market exclusion. Activities that operate outside of the regular circuit – secondary or tertiary – are useful for members of society and deserve a decent remuneration, as well.

From the conclusions of the INPART research, compulsory measures are not necessary to stimulate people to contribute to society and to get them involved in meaningful and useful activities. Many people want to be socially included and want to contribute to society themselves (ibid. WP4: 21). It is primary then to unravel stigmatising clichés attached to the participants of certain activities. Not only is it necessary to remunerate and compensate these participants for their efforts, but it is also important to understand unemployment benefits – or social assistance – as the means that allows them to invest in themselves and contribute to society (ibid. 85).

It does not seem far-fetched to us to conclude that fighting poverty and exclusion requires an injection of economic resources, perhaps best applied to support local initiatives that foster social participation and integration. The path that brings us to this recommendation is intensely sociological, based on a reconsideration of the consequences of twentieth-century developments for the kinds of visions we want and are able to achieve (new models of citizenship via social participation and stimulation of community-based third system organisations), and also of the consequences of twentieth-century development that are dysfunctional (such new forms of exclusions due to the transformation of the role of (paid-)work for both men and women). John Andersen correctly points out that the important and still unanswered questions are what new institutional formations and what new processes of societal dynamics (mainly based at local community level) can further supply the larger social cohesion and the more flexible means to solidarity and integration, together with a redistribution of power and resources that offer people closer control over the decisions that affect their lives (Andersen op. cit. 6–7)?

Enhancing the development of local communities, combining more democratic and decentralised approaches that allow citizens to feel part of their community and bestowing the right to a modicum of welfare and security should be a goal attainable by an active inclusionary society. This can offer citizens the right to fully share the social heritage and to live the life of a civilised being according to the standards prevailing in society while diminishing inequalities that are specifically grounded in the market relations of a capitalist order. Poor citizens will no longer be regarded as recipients in a culture of dependency, but as citizens that can contribute to the local community and thereby to social life.

In short, the concern of much of the research on which this chapter is based is not only about the parts of life that involves us deeply – work, family and community – but also about the superficial interaction of the different social actors in public spheres. In the attempt to foster community renewal and development within the sphere of civil society between public and private agencies, there is a complex process. It requires a move to an integrating multidimensional approach, combining 'bottom-up' initiatives with 'top-down' support and facilities in order to combat social exclusion as well as to acknowledge other forms of integrative participation in the local community that allow women and men to combine family, social life and work. The real value of a new conceptualisation of citizenship lies therefore in its social activation.

Note

1 On the one hand, against the background of an analysis of active social policies in Europe, INPART set itself the objective of investigating the inclusionary–exclusionary potentials of participation into various types of work, using both 'objective' and 'subjective' approaches in researching inclusion and exclusion. On the other hand, SEDEC introduces some of the key normative and analytical concepts needed for a cross-national analysis of 'social inclusion' and 'social inclusion policies', connected to the development of citizenship and social rights in European societies both at national and supra-national EU level.

Bibliography

Andersen, J. (1996) 'Solidarity and social citizenship in post-industrial welfare models', in *Re-conceptualizing the Welfare State* – Proceedings from symposium in connection with Maastricht II'. Danish Center for Human Rights, 1996. Reprinted for CID (Center for Integration and Differentiation).

Andersen, J. and Larsen, J.E. (1998) *From Social Class to Social Exclusion.* CID Studies, 21.

Atkinson, A.B. (ed.) (1980) *Wealth, Income and Inequality.* Oxford: Oxford University Press.

Beck, U. (1997) 'Capitalism without work', *Dissent* Winter, 51–6.

Castells, M. (1996) *The Rise of the Network Society.* Oxford: Blackwells.

Castells, M. (1997) *The Power of Identity.* Oxford: Blackwells.

Coenen, H. and Leisink, P. (1993) *Work and Citizenship in the New Europe.* London: Edward Elgar.

(Comité des Sages, 1996) European Commission (1996) 'For a Europe of civic and social rights'. Luxembourg: Office of the Official Publications of the European Communities.

De Lathouwer, L. and Thirion, A. (1999) 'Unemployment traps in Belgium', Paper for the IUAP workshop, 10 June 1999. Centrum voor Sociaal Beleid, UFSIA, Antwerpen.

De Schampheleire, J. and Vilrokx, J. (2000) 'Belgian social policy inspired by new active welfare state approach', in *Eiroline,* European Foundation for the Improvement of Living and Working Conditions, Jan 2000. *http://www.eiro.eurofound.ie*

Erikson, K. and Vallas, S.P. (eds) (1990) *The Nature of Work.* New Haven: American Sociological Association Presidential Series and Yale University Press.

ESF (1997) 'Pathways to integration', *European Social Fund.* Bruges, October.

Ferman, L.A. (1990) 'Participation in the irregular economy', in *The Nature of Work,* K. Erikson and S.P. Vallas (eds). New Haven: American Sociological Association Presidential Series and Yale University Press.

Fitoussi, J.P. and Rosanvallon, P. (1996) *Le Nouvel Age des Inégalités.* Paris: Editions Seuil.

Geddes, M. (1998) 'Local partnership: a successful strategy for social cohesion?' *European Foundation for the Improvement of Living and Working Conditions.* Luxembourg: Office for Official Publication of the European Communities.

Goldthorpe, J.H. (ed.) (1984) *Order and Conflict in Contemporary Capitalism.* Oxford: Clarendon Press.

Gough, I. (1979) *The Political Economy of the Welfare State.* London, Basingstoke: Macmillan.

Giddens, A. (1998) *The Third Way.* Cambridge: Polity Press.

Habermas, J. (1962) *The Structural Transformation of the Public Sphere: An inquiry into a category of bourgeois society.* Trans. Thomas Burger [1989]. London: Polity Press.

Haslett, H.W. (1994) *Capitalism with Morality.* Oxford: Clarendon Press.

Hespanha, P., Ferreira, C. and Portugal, S. (1997) 'The welfare society and the welfare state. The Portuguese experience', in M. Roche and R. Van Berkel (eds).

Honneth, A. (1994) 'The social dynamics of disrespect: on the location of critical theory today', *Constellations* 1, 2, 254–69.

Hout, W. (1997) 'Globalisation and European welfare states', paper presented at COST A7. Final Conference: London.

INPART (1999) *Inclusion through participation. The Case studies, National Reports and Comparative Report. Work Package 3,* Coordinator Rik van Berkel, Utrecht University. December.

INPART (2000) *Inclusion through participation. Final Report Work Package 4*, Coordinator Rik van Berkel, Utrecht University. January.

Javeau, C., Lambert, M. and Lemaire, J. (1998) *Excluant . . . Exclu*. Brussels: Editions de l'Université de Bruxelles.

Jepsen, M. and Meulders, D. (1998) 'Quality of employment and gender in local employment activities', *Transfer: European Review of Labour and Research* 4, 3(Autumn), 444–62.

Levitas, R. (1999) *The Inclusive Society? Social exclusion and New Labour*. London: Macmillan.

Lister, R. (1990) *The Exclusive Society: Citizenship and the Poor*. London: CPAG.

Lind, J. (1995) 'Unemployment policy and social integration', in N. Mortensen (ed.) op. cit.

Machado, C., De Schampheleire, J. and Vilrokx, J. (2000) 'Actief sociaal beleid: een nieuw "El Dorado" voor werklozen en uitgeslotenen op de arbeidsmarkt?', in *Tijsdshrift voor Arbeid en Participatie* 21, January, 109–26.

Marshall, G. (1997) *Repositioning Class. Social Inequality in Industrial Societies*. London: SAGE.

Marshall, T.H. ([1973] 1977) *Class, Citizenship and Social Development*. Chicago and London: The University of Chicago Press.

Ministerie van Tewerkstelling en Arbeid (1998) 'Het federal werkgelegenheidsbeleid. Evaluatie rapport 1997'. Brussels: Federal Ministerie van Tewerkstelling en Arbeid.

Møller, I.H. (1997) 'Social integration and labour market marginalization. The Scandinavian experience', in M. Roche and R. Van Berkel (eds) op. cit.

Mortensen, N. (ed.) (1995) *Social Integration and Marginalisation* Copenhagen: Samfundslitteratur.

Offe, C. (1985) *Disorganized Capitalism*. Cambridge: Polity Press.

Offe, C. (1993) 'A non-productivist design for social policies', in *Work and Citizenship in the New Europe*, H. Coenen, H. & P. Leisink (eds). London: Edward Elgar.

Pahl, R.E. (1984) *Divisions of Labour*. New York: Basil Blackwell.

Petrella, R. (1998) 'Competivité à tout prix?', in Javeau *et al*. op. cit., 151–7.

Pixley, J. (1993) *Citizenship and Employment. Investigating Post-Industrial Options*. Cambridge: Cambridge University Press.

Redcliffe, N. and Mingione, E. (1985) *Beyond Employment*. Oxford: Basil Blackwell.

Rhodes, M. (1996) 'Globalisation and West European welfare states: a critical review of recent debates', *Journal of European Social Policy* 6, 4, 305–27.

Roche, M. and Van Berkel, R. (eds) (1997) *Social Exclusion and European Citizenship*. Aldershot: Ashgate.

Rulmont-Ugeux, G. (1999) *L'économie sociale au féminin pluriel*. Liège: Editions Luc Pire.

SEDEC (1998) *Developing the European Social Model: Researching Social Inclusion Policies in Europe. Report 1*. Coordinator Maurice Roche, Sheffield University.

SEDEC (1999) *Developing the European Social Model: Researching Social Inclusion Policies in Europe. Final Report*, Coordinator Maurice Roche, Sheffield University, December.

Sen, A. (1992) *Inequality Reexamined*. Oxford: Clarendon Press.

Taylor-Gooby, P. (1994) 'Post-modernism and social policy: a great leap backwards', in *Journal of Social Policy* 23, 3, 385–404.

Vilrokx, J., Oste, J., Machado, C., De Schampheleire, J. and Ranson, D. (1999) 'Tussen Arbeid en Inkomen', Werkgelegenheid Arbeid Vorming. *Niewsbrief van het Steunpunt WAV* 9, 3, Aug, 178–82.

Vranken, J., Geldof, D. and Van Menxel, G. (1999) *Armoede & Sociale Uitsluiting*. Jaarboek. Acco, Leuven, Amersfoort.

Walzer, M. (1983) *Spheres of Justice. A defense of pluralism and equality*. New York: Basic Books.

White, S.K. (1995) *The Cambridge Companion to Habermas*. Cambridge: Cambridge University Press.

Williams, C.C. (1996) 'Informal sector responses to unemployment: an evaluation of the LETS', *Work, Employment and Society* 10: 341–59.

Williams, C.C. and Windebank, J. (1997) 'The informal sector in the European Union. Mitigating or reinforcing social exclusion?', in M. Roche and R. Van Berkel (eds) op. cit.

Williams, C.C. and Windebank, J. (1998) *Informal employment in the advanced economies: Implications for work and welfare*. London: Routledge.

Williams, C.C., Cook, J., Roche, M. and Windebank, J. (1999) 'Participation in informal economy and part-time employment and experiences and exclusion', INPART WP3, UK Report.

Part III

Inclusions and exclusions beyond the nation state

Europe and the world

10 Conceptualizing the process of globalization

Zdravko Mlinar

Introduction

The issues of inclusion/exclusion tend to be discussed as changes within a given, usually national, context that is assumed to be constant. Globalization presents the challenge of examining these same issues as part of the transformation of territorial social organization encompassing the entire range of units and levels, from the local to the global. This can contribute to understanding of the processes of inclusion/exclusion, both on the geographical (horizontal) and hierarchical (vertical) dimension, even though globalization itself still needs to be conceptualized and embedded theoretically. It has been shown (Mlinar 1995) that growing accessibility entails both 'expanding territories' and 'flattening hierarchies'.

Europe is undergoing radical transformation. National societies are opening up and recognizing more and more the de-legitimization of territorially exclusive criteria. Even 'Fortress Europe' is but a moving target. Globalization implies a trend of change towards maximization of territorial inclusiveness; staying out (de-linking, de-coupling), or excluding outsiders will no longer be an option.

In the Simmelian sense, expanding territories entail widening the circle of actors upon whom one depends, but also a diminishing dependence on any one of them. This erodes the hierarchical order and the mutual exclusivity of the different levels of territorial organization, something that is still poorly understood both in theory and in policy making. For example, the 'Europe of Regions' is often taken to be an alternative instead of a complement to the 'Europe of Nations States', and treated separately from the 'Europe of Citizens', and the like.

Consequently, an attempt is made here to identify the regularities of cross-level dynamics, particularly in terms of the shift from domination/subordination to multi-level power-sharing. Yet, does global inclusion entail local exclusion in some sense? This is not merely a matter of policy and values, as EU representatives (J. Monnet, J. Delors and others) have suggested. It may be rather independent of intentions and policies. Jacques Delors (1996: 17) argued 'people need gradually to become *world citizens* without losing their roots and while continuing to play an active part in the life of their *national* and *local* community' (my italics). But what is actually happening today is still a challenge to researchers.

The most common notion that crops up in discussions of globalization is that the growing interconnectedness and interdependencies between people over increasing distances, beyond national and continental frameworks, is conducive to the emergent world society. Although this is already a truism of sorts, many questions immediately arise which remain unanswered, are answered in divergent ways or are wrongly posed and cannot be answered properly.

An illustration of the last case is the question whether territorial diversity decreases or increases in the process of globalization. It shall be shown that this question can be answered either way.[1] Further more, however easily we may speak of globalization, the empirical evidence for countries around the world indicates that the *primary* bond for people in the 'global times' or 'global age' is that of *the local*, eventually national, community, and that hardly anyone identifies with the world as a whole (Jacob, Ostrowski and Teune 1993, Mlinar 1994).

The movement of people is still predominantly limited to the local–national frameworks and movement of goods to supra-national regions. Even with open borders, migration between the EU countries is relatively limited. Why did intra-EU trade in the previous decade grow while that with the rest of the world decreased relatively (Park 1994)?

Actually much evidence (e.g. Clark and Hoffman-Martinot 1999) points to a historically significant transformation of society towards the empowerment of sub-national actors such as regions, minorities and individuals. *For the first time in history* the individual can exercise his or her rights at the supra-national level, for example at the European Court. National sovereignty, expressed through the right of the state to non-interference in internal affairs, is becoming less important than protection of universal human rights and minorities. But how can the following incongruity be explained: proscription of discrimination according to *territorial provenance* is becoming a civilizational norm within Europe, at the very time that the Fortress Europe is being erected?

These are only some of the challenges in the European context which require more systematic research and a more comprehensive sociological interpretation from the standpoint of possible regularities in a wider time and space. One feasible approach is to conceptualize socio-spatial changes on the basis of the unity of opposites of individualization (autonomization, diversification) and globalization (interconnectedness, homogenization).

Difficulty in understanding the dialectics, i.e. the opposition and interdependency of these two processes, is one of the main reasons for perplexity and disorientation both in theory and in practice.

Sociologists are facing the co-presence of two world orders. One was built from above, through an *expansionistic* drive based on power and force, while the other is emerging from below in the form of *emancipatory strivings*. The first is tending to weaken, the latter to strengthen. But what are the prospects for the one and the other in the short and the long run? It may well be that the predominant paradigm of today may not be the same tomorrow.

Globalization and sociology

From exemplification to sociological conceptualization

Sociology is one of the last of the social sciences – with some exceptions like world system theory or some general notions of classics – to take up the subject of the globalization of society, although (given the inclusive nature of its subject matter) it could have been the first. As a general and generalizing social science which encompasses all spheres of social life in all periods of time (and as such comes in the category of the nomothetic as distinct from idiographic sciences)[2] it offers the most suitable starting-point for study of an emerging world society with the highest ever level of complexity. To date, sociological study of social change has mainly remained within the national state framework[3] and has not advanced as far as political science with its 'international relations' and then 'world politics', or economists and their 'integrated global political economy' (Gill and Law 1988).

The literature on globalization is dominated by exemplificatory and fragmentary descriptions of supposedly indicative changes. However, it is precisely at the highest level of complexity that it becomes obvious that we will not arrive at the 'whole' merely by listing and adding innumerable particularities or fragments.[4] Even the most widely accepted World Systems Theory, which however did not go beyond its sectoral (economic) bounds, is more a *perspective* encompassing great blocks of aggregated particularities, than a groundwork for a high degree of organized complexity in the cognitive process. What we need is not simply an extension to the world as a whole, to a world system with a crude internal structure (core, semi-periphery, periphery) as understood by Wallerstein (1979), which cannot account for much of its internal complexity. Rather what is needed is both more holistic and individualistic analytical approaches together, as well as study of the changing relationships between the two spheres.

It is becoming plain that globalization is not an 'out there' phenomenon 'far removed from the concerns of everyday life', that 'might appear *as another field of study* ... globalization is an "in here" matter which affects or rather is *dialectically related* to even the most intimate aspects of our lives' (Giddens, in Beck, Giddens and Lash 1994: 95 – my italics). This also presents a challenge to the established (sub)disciplinary fields to reinterpret their subject from the standpoint of the newly-emerging society and contribute to the enrichment of sociology by the analysis from a cross-level perspective.

Globalization as déjà vu?

One of the reasons for the present void is the attitude towards the past. Is globalization really something so new that we have to start from the beginning? Irrespective of which of the numerous explanations of the beginning of this process we adopt, sociology still has to reassess its own heritage from the new point of view. Globalization cannot be discussed in isolation; it has to be placed in the context of sociology's tradition of Grand Theories which wrestled with the questions of long-term development processes and regularities (Mlinar 2001). There is often a sense of déjà vu even though the new terminology creates an impression of discontinuity. Today ideological swings and simplifications are creating distance from the past. So it may not seem appropriate to apply Marxist interpretations of 'societalization' on a world scale, for example, because praxis in the former 'socialist states' failed to confirm it.

But Marx had already pointed out the global tendencies of the capitalist system (Fiamengo 1959, Marx and Engels 1980). Local and national self-sufficiency and limitations are now giving way to all-round transportation links and the interdependence of nations, as well as the declining role of nations. Capital and goods know no borders, homeland or nation and presuppose the growing role of the world market. A world literature is arising from the multiple national and local literatures. Marx saw man's emancipation in 'societalized mankind', as a pan-human community in which people become citizens of the world, no longer bound to class, nation or state.

The paradox is that at the very time Marxism is being discarded, at least in the previous socialist countries, some of the ideas rejected are only just attaining their proper significance in the emerging situation. An example is the idea of the withering-away of the nation state, which has become a central preoccupation. Then, the idea of societalization (*Vergesellschaftung*), which in the 'socialist' countries was reduced to and equated with nationalization, is actually only now being realised on a world scale through the process of globalization.

Consequently, globalization presents a whole series of issues that classical sociological theory had already raised in connection with the long-term development of society, its antinomies, developmental stages, its 'driving forces', the relations between the micro and macro spheres of society, and so forth. Today's changes are, to a great extent already implied in Spencer's interpretation of the differentiation of the homogeneous and assimilation of the heterogeneous (Spencer 1975). Even in his forgotten work in rural sociology between the World Wars, Sorokin pointed to a transition from territorial, 'cumulative communities' to the networked interlinking of actors ('functional associations') which today is becoming the fundamental model of interconnectedness on a world scale (Sorokin et al. 1930). A great deal of this has been transcended today; but it may help, at least as a challenge, to more easily establish what the *differentia specifica* of the globalization process is.

Globalization as a process or epoch?

The prospects of the process of globalization which disembed and free actors from predetermined structures of narrow territorial communities and their participation (inclusion) in a wider social context are being challenged from the point of view of post-modernity. Albrow (1996) questions whether globalization constitutes a continuation of social evolution to date, or whether a new type of society is arising that he labels the Global Age.[5] But even if it is a qualitatively different type of society, the emerging global society is not necessarily beyond the explanatory framework of the theory of social development. Rather it may be that their common features have to be sought at a more general level of analysis.[6]

In connection with this, another debate has been evolving already in the 1960s and 1970s which is related to the present discussions of globalization and is continued in various ways. This is the controversy over neoevolutionism (Nisbet 1969, Lenski 1976, Becker 1979). The objection to neoevolutionism is that it gives too little room for the multitude of essentially indeterminate developments – 'random events', 'unique occurrences', 'the purely fortuitous', the 'wilful' and the 'adventitious' (Nisbet 1969: 171).[7] Lenski argued that, in sociology, evolutionary theory has moved from deterministic to probabilistic interpretations. Thus he rebutted the thesis that the future course of events is necessary and predetermined and hence quite predictable, as well as the thesis that no predictions whatsoever are possible. The probabilistic viewpoint is that not all possible future developments are equally probable.

But what is overlooked here is that the answer differs with respect to the level of development, particularly from the standpoint of the autonomization of subsystems and individuals (to be dealt with later in this chapter).

Albrow (1996) objects to treating globalization as a process, the way urbanization and other '-ization' terms associated with modernity have been for decades. 'Using the term "process" for historical change elides the difference between open-ended transformations and repeatable, predictable sequences.' Consequently he introduces the concept of the 'Global Age' as an age of globality, that is, a new level of organization 'to which any agent can relate, but which has no organizing agent ... Yet the lack of central organization is not disintegration' (121).

It has to be borne in mind here that not all processes have the same time span; emancipation (individualization, autonomization), for example, is not restricted to a certain historical epoch and the empirical evidence shows its continuation in the Global Age (leaving aside for the moment ecological finites). The 'end of the Grand Narratives' does not mean the end of the (meaningfulness) of seeking regularities in general, since understanding why this (disorder) comes about may also be related to the process of individualization in the context of globalization.

One of the main reasons for the numerous misunderstandings and a certain disorientation amongst sociologists is that 'developmental logic' is not distinguished sufficiently from concrete experiential reality, which in some parts of the world reveals the most diverse 'admixtures' of different stages of social development. The assumption underlying ideal types is precisely that they are never fully realised; but this does not diminish their heuristic value.

Generalizing past experience

The foregoing also leads to the question: to what extent can we draw on the wealth of experience that is available, with regard to changes within national societies, in view of all the dilemmas and great divergence in forecasts of the outcome of present changes on a world scale? Will national homogenization at the expense of local particularities, such as the adoption of a standardized literary language and the parallel extinction of dialects, be the pattern that is repeated at the level of national languages and the 'global language' that English is now becoming? Or are circumstances different now, and such generalizations impermissible? Besides empirical research, this question calls above all for a general explication of the relationships between levels of territorial organization of society, which shall be dealt with in particular later in this chapter.

In principle the greater complexity of society at the global level also constitutes its greater capacity to absorb territorial particularities that have already become established at 'lower' levels.[8] Precisely the most popular metaphor, 'the global village' (McLuhan 1962), shows how misleading and sociologically unfounded mechanical comparisons between global society and traditional local communities can be (see Mlinar 1997b: 6).

If the 'global village' metaphor was intended to contribute to understanding the emerging world-scale society by means of the familiar village community, it has to be noted that this analogy actually does the opposite. Namely, in many respects it conceals essential differences (Mlinar 1997b) which are presented in the following table:

Inasmuch as the term 'global village' or 'global neighbourhood' (The Commission on Global Governance 1995) is used to mainly stress the drawing nearer that occurs through 'time–space compression', this neglects the on-going fundamental structural transformation from a community based on relative internal homogeneity, and the subordination of the individual within it, to a global society which can only arise through the autonomous interlinking of a great diversity of groups and individuals.[9]

Some conceptual and theoretical dimensions

Globalization and individualization

Some further cognitive structuring of the subject matter is necessary to make the move from exemplification to sociological conceptualization of globalization and to understand the socio-spatial context of inclusion/exclusion. Two general

Table 10.1 Instead of McLuhan

Village community	Global society
contiguity	dispersion
homogeneity	heterogeneity
predetermination	choice
spatial aggregation	selective association
predominant loyalty	multiple loyalties
rigidity	fluidity

analytical dimensions must be introduced here and the changes in both of them are interpreted in the light of the contradictory relationship between globalization and individualization.

Two analytical dimensions

First, the issue of distinctions between *distributions* of people, goods and ideas world-wide, including the comparison of their attributes (similarities, differences) is important. Secondly, their *interconnectedness* on a world scale in terms of the growing probability that change in one unit will produce change in the others is relevant. The first dimension of distributions is relevant to the controversial issues of *homogenization* and *diversification*. The second dealing with interconnectedness relates to the issues surrounding *autonomy* and *dependency*. Both also represent dimensions of individualization, namely the strengthening of autonomous and unique actors (world citizens) in the context of the emerging world society. But as we will see, *uniqueness* and *autonomy* are not alternatives to *uniformity* and *dependency*. Individualization is not an alternative to globalization. They represent a *unity of opposites* in the course of socio-spatial change.

Unity of opposites

While the predominant preoccupations with globalization today are still one-sided, there are also some attempts to deal with the contradictory and simultaneously interdependent changes such as the strengthening of both ever-larger and ever-smaller units (e.g. Naisbitt's popular version of 'Global Paradox', 1994) or globalization and fragmentation (Clark 1997), or issues of subnational autonomy and supra-national integration.

Although homogenization of the world at first seems to contradict diversification, it is actually a condition for it. To understand this, two kinds of diversity have to be distinguished:

a   diversity based on *exclusion* (separation) and
b   diversity based on *inclusion* (communication).

Territorial diversity formed through exclusion or separation (such as different dialects) contradicts increasing connectedness and diminishes it inasmuch as it limits the free flow of people, goods and ideas. This free flow requires a certain underlying homogenization or harmonization, as can be seen in Europe and world-wide (Mlinar 1992a). On the other hand, greater connectedness entails wider access to variety and the creation of new combinations, thus contributing to diversification. Thus the result is both more standardization (or harmonization) and an increasing number of unique phenomena.[10]

The great variety of discrete, 'peacefully coexisting' observations of opposite trends of change may thus be understood more easily, such as, for example, 'community decline' and 'new localism', 'the destruction of regional cultures' and 'revival of regionalism', 'the loss of national identity' and 'new nationalism', etc. (Mlinar 1992b). The old identities took shape on the basis of isolation, the new ones are based on selective communication.

Diversity, which arose in the form of territorial exclusivities (and was a result of limited communication), is declining but at the same time it is being deliberately and selectively incorporated into global society to enrich the total fund of diversity.[11]

With regard to interconnectedness, the autonomy of the actors/individuals is both rising and falling. There is no simple shift from autonomy to dependency (as implied by 'dependistas' in Latin America) or vice versa. The two are not alternatives. Globalization implies both increasing autonomy of actors in terms of their expanding range of choice as well as increasing dependency on society as a whole. The autonomy of actors increases as their independence decreases. In other words, the process of globalization implies a transition from autonomy with exclusion (autarchy) to autonomy with inclusion.[12] The zero sum logic which applied well to empires, great powers, power politics, economic and cultural imperialism, 'independent state' etc.[13] is losing its explanatory power.

In today's globalizing world, political decisions on frontal separation (secession) are less and less important and increasingly illusionary. Discretionary power in this sense is more and more restricted,[14] as is discretion concerning universal human rights.

Globalization and internationalization

There is quite a bit of confusion and inconsistency in the use of the terms globalization and internationalization. In the disciplinary field of 'international relations' especially, we witness a highly redundant repetition of the debate between the advocates of the 'realistic' and 'idealistic' schools, and a long line of critics trying to scupper both. The former reflect the hitherto and the latter the prospective, declining, role of the nation state (see, e.g. Shaw 1994, Clark 1997). A possible rapprochement of the two is indicated, for the strengthening of the global does not entail the simple demise of the nation state but rather its changing role. It is also becoming clear that not only relations between nations are involved but that a growing diversity of territorial and non-territorial actors (regions, cities, municipalities, economic actors, etc.) have become autonomous and are linking up on a world scale. It is quite wrong then to assume that internationalization preserves the internally homogeneous structure of society, as exemplified by the 'billiard ball' metaphor in international relations theory. Internationalization refers to relations between nations, and hence assumes a lower level of differentiation and individualization than globalization.

Globalization and universalism

While the concept of globalization has temporal and spatial parameters, universalism is a characteristic of principles which are applicable irrespective of time and place. However, even universal principles are manifested and observable only in concretely defined times and places. 'Globalization is an extension of the application of universal principles everywhere.... But, the spread of universal principles, does not mean homogenization, everything the same everywhere. Rather they can appear in practically limitless unique combination' (Teune and Mlinar, forthcoming).

Consequently it is mistaken to call for 'abandoning universalism for true indigenisation' (Park 1981: 161). For this incorrectly presupposes that these two are alternatives, mutually exclusive states. In fact what is involved are the differences in approach by nomothetic and idiographic sciences. It has to be asked how much a generalization is based on limited evidence from the developed world, e.g. is 'Eurocentric'.

Territorial inclusiveness and selectiveness of actors: a question of scale

'Local' and 'global' are usually synonyms for the small and the large. But this parallel is true primarily in terms of the geographical, territorial inclusiveness. Typically it overlooks the fact that expanding accessibility both necessitates and enables increasing selectivity which results in the formation of various (sub-)groups, organizations or networks made up of a small number of actors. These groups have no necessary territorial base nor do they discriminate on the basis of territorial provenance.

It may be concluded then that the size of a group, the number of its members, does not necessarily indicate the progression of the globalization process. Even the territorial dimension has to be understood more as potential world accessibility than actual, complete territorial 'coverage'. Before us, then, is not only a society with ever-larger groupings as with the territorial expansion of integration processes (e.g. EU, NAFTA, etc.) but also a society made up of increasingly smaller or diverse groups and individuals, linked-up on a world scale.

'Globalization' by sectors and beyond

A convenient way of presenting the issues of globalization is by sectors (functional, issue areas). A large part of the sociological discussion on globalization focuses either on individual sectors (e.g. Wallerstein (1979) on economy, Robertson (1992) on culture etc.), or considers several of them simultaneously (Sklair (1992): economy, polity, culture – ideology).

While this may suit more pragmatic or short-term preoccupations, it bypasses the basic long-term restructuring and 'de-structuring' resulting from individualization/globalization. The sectoral approach assumes the structure to be constant and focuses on changes within it. This is inconsistent both conceptually with the holistic nature of globalization and with the empirical evidence on 'melting structures' (e.g. Lash and Urry 1994: 94, 97, the melting economy and culture when the production process is basically a design process; Delors *et al.* 1996 on education in the sense of 'learning by interacting'; Castells (1985) on reintegration of education and production, etc.). The sectoral model will increasingly tend to hide rather than reveal the actual process of globalization. The trends toward high diversity and unique actors operating in the 'space of flows' increasingly departs from the notion of a segmentalized society.

Cross-level dynamics

Many of the unsettled issues of globalization and especially the issues of inclusion/exclusion of territorial and non-territorial, and of collective and individual actors, may be clarified by placing them in the context of the interdependencies and interaction between levels of societal territorial organization. This opens up a much neglected sphere of sociological inquiry which has hardly been touched by the simplified debate on the micro/macro sociology division and interrelationships.

The range of levels and their relationships

A crude distinction between micro and macro cannot suffice for identifying possible regularities in these 'cross-level dynamics'. Only a more finely differentiated scale of levels of territorial organization can begin to reveal any regularities in the dynamics. However, it must be noted that for both society and the social sciences the situation is changing. For society it is relevant that the system of states, which constituted an important barrier between the local and the global, is now weakening. In the social sciences, the establishment of several (sub)disciplinary fields has brought a *division of labour* in which each still concentrates on just *one level* of territorial organization of society (Alger and Mendlowitz 1985, Alger 1988: 336).

Besides the existence and *inclusivity* of a whole range of levels, the interrelationships between these levels and changes in them over the course of time have to be borne in mind. A quite divergent set of viewpoints is found in the literature. One attempt to systematize them might be as follows.

1   The argument that there is a kind of 'peaceful coexistence' of social reality at different levels, and each has its niche and does not interfere with the others (Solar 1987).
2   Another typical argument indicates or presumes that there is a *complementary* relationship, with the levels interlinking to mutual benefit on a win/win type of model. Jean Monnet showed that national sovereignty diminishes when it is locked in obsolescent forms and only isolated 'pockets' attempt to assert it. In order to be efficient, it has to be translated to broader spheres where it can blend with the sovereignty of others. No-one loses in this process; on the contrary, all gain new powers (Monnet, cited by Fontaine and Monnet 1988: 31, my italics).

3 A third approach argues in favour of mutual competition or even incompatibility, which fits the zero sum game model. This is more common amongst Marxist writers who tend to see a zero sum game relationship between levels of territorial organization, as with social classes. Wallerstein argues that the *world level* is not just one of the levels but the *fundamental, decisive one*, which then in some way replaces the national level.[15]

Each of these arguments may rest on particular elements of reality. But their main flaw is that they are static and do not explain how relationships between levels change with time and how much they differ according to the levels involved.

In general there seems to be a paradox in that *the range of levels is expanding* on the one hand (besides the national there is also the supra-national and the global) while on the other hand there is a *rapprochement between levels*.

The regularities of inter-level relationships

The following regularities of inter-level relationships can be hypothetically specified.

1 The first proposition: relations between levels vary according to their positions on the whole scale from local (if we stay with territorial units, otherwise it starts with the individual) to the global according to their proximity/distance on the scale; the closer the two levels are, the more competitive their interrelationships; the further apart they are on the scale, the more complementary and mutually supportive their relations. Thus relations between the national and supra-national are more competitive while there is greater mutuality between the regional and the supra-national levels.[16]

2 The second proposition: relations between levels change over time, but these are not a) coincidental changes; nor b) linear changes in relations between the levels of territorial organization of society. It may be observed empirically that as linkages at the level of supra-national regions (Europe) have strengthened, trade flows on a global scale have been declining for a decade (Park 1994). This may be interpreted in terms of a higher degree of diversity in an expanded territorial framework requiring a certain amount of time for integration before the process can continue again at a higher level. A different case again is represented by some newly-formed states which have reduced their previous external links and, at the same time, reduced the autonomy of their subnational units, but there are indications that this is only temporary.

3 The third proposition: there is a general tendency for a unit at a certain level to seek an interlinking (integration) with units at the same or higher levels by itself without allowing any simultaneous internal differentiation and autonomization. This implies a deviation from the general trend of 'the

penetration of differentiation into the substructures' (Blau 1977) and has no chance of enduring for any length of time. This is a striking contradiction in the European context especially where nation states typically tend to join broader continental frameworks, although as relatively homogenous units.[17]

4   The fourth proposition: with the increase in accessibility (interlinking) between levels, their mutually-exclusive character and their hierarchic nature diminishes. In place of the alternatives: centralization or decentralization, relations become more and more partner relations with multi-level power sharing in dealing with particular matters. A typical example is the Phare programmes of the European Union, the design and implementation of which require cooperation by supra-national, national and regional and/or local levels. The same is the case with certain UNESCO programmes on a world scale.

5   The fifth proposition: as interlinking at a higher level intensifies, there is a rising trend towards homogenization (for example, the 300 harmonization measures of the European Union) which reduces the mutual exclusivity (standards) of territorial units at a lower level. This applies not just to technical standards but also pressures from above for cooperativeness in resolving conflicting territorial claims. The resulting heightened accessibility becomes a basis for possible increases in diversity. However this is no longer the diversity that stems from frontal territorial separation; rather, it stems from more selective interlinkings.

All the propositions presented above have to be considered in the broader context of expanding territories and flattening hierarchies (Mlinar 1995) and of tendencies toward deterritorialization. This involves the local–global convergence: strengthening direct linkages and weakening intermediaries.

These propositions about cross-level dynamics as a whole are intended to provide a conceptual and theoretical (re-)orientation as well as specification of the regularities which have not been considered in research until now. They either directly or indirectly touch the issues of inclusion/exclusion and present a challenge for operationalization and more focussed empirical research, which are tasks beyond the scope of this text.

A return to a closed system paradigm

In conclusion we must note that globalization as a process is a very different 'narrative' from global society. It entails expansion in space, both in terms of economic/corporatist forms as well as having an emancipatory drive. It involves enlargement of scale as well as the freeing of actors from predetermined structures within narrow territorial units. However, the more rapid this expansion beyond the traditional boundedness in space is, the more it approaches the opposite; namely, the ecological finites of the world. Ultimately limits to growth mean limits to freedom.

The highest level of territorial *inclusiveness* socially implies the loss of the outside world and thus a shift *from the open to the closed system* paradigm. The world is becoming socially a total system, without 'exit' and thus with less efficient 'voice', to use Hirschman's terminology (1970). There will be no external alternatives either to *free oneself* from this totality or to escape from one's responsibility (as the middle class escapes from downtown). Neither will there be a way to transfer the undesirable effects, e.g. ecological ones, to others without being affected oneself. A widening divergence between living in *physically restricting* and *informationally expanding* space will gain in importance. While inclusion expands in the virtual space of global information society, the finites of the physical world will necessarily require the come-back of zero sum logic. This will mean more restrictions on the autonomy of actors in space, more control and more conflicts.

Conclusions and challenges for the research agenda

The above discussion attempts to disclose both some conceptual dimensions of the process of globalization as well as their relevance for understanding the issues of inclusion/exclusion, particularly from the point of view of the on-going socio-spatial transformation both horizontally and vertically. Globalization represents a maximization of territorial (geographic) inclusiveness which is – in the long run but not linearly – providing an extending range of choice. However, at the same time, it means losing the option of exclusion from the world as a 'total system'.

Globalization involves changes which have to be studied simultaneously in the sense of multi-level analysis and cross-level dynamics both in terms of autonomy and dependence as well as homogenization and diversification. The vision of global society includes actors who have a lot in common and at the same time represent a unique combination of characteristics of the various territorial provenance.

The interpretation presented departs from the ones claiming a general decline of territorial diversity and autonomy, as well as from the others, arguing simply for the continuation of the existing territorial structures and identities. Thus globalization is often understood (e.g. by Wallerstein, but also, in a way, R. Dahl) as a succession from the local to national and world level in which the 'higher' level replaces the power of lower ones. In other words global inclusion is understood as suppression (exclusion) of the national and subnational powers.

Rather than following such one-sided interpretations of globalization as successive replacement of lower with higher levels, so that in the end world level becomes decisive, the author here outlines a more dialectically conceived understanding of socio-spatial changes, which considers empowerment of ever-smaller units within an ever-larger territorial context. This is the emancipatory vision of freeing of actors from predetermined, rigid structures within narrower territorial units and their participation (inclusion) in the ever-larger context.

In general, inclusion into the global society less and less implies exclusion from the 'lower' levels. But these relationships are still far from being clear and deserve to be a subject of the research agenda. An attempt to make a step forward in this direction and particularly to identify regularities of cross-level dynamics, at least in a hypothetical form, was presented above. But more empirical research as well as further theoretical examination is needed in order to answer questions like: in how much of what is happening within nation states – e.g. in the relationship between local and national level (exclusion of local particularities, like dialects and standardization of the literary national language) – is there a pattern which will be repeated in the relationship between national and supra-national (European) levels? To what degree is the present experience of European integration generalizable in terms of globalization (where the concept of integration is less applicable), and so forth? Globalization is not a linear and unidirectional process, but rather one side of the oscillatory dynamics of the unity of opposites of globalization and autonomization/diversification.

The issues of inclusion/exclusion are closely connected with the logic of zero sum which tends to be present in social thought, even if it is losing ground in social reality. Extending accessibility and connectedness both horizontally in space as well as vertically, hierarchically, makes the old understanding of mutual exclusiveness obsolete. The logic of win/lose was the common denominator of territorial expansionism, of power politics, of economic and cultural imperialism, of the (world) core and periphery, of 'Americanization', of centralization and decentralization, etc. This zero sum logic is less and less able to explain the present social change in European societies. That can be better understood in terms of interpenetration, mixing, (multi-level power) sharing, glocalization, partnership, hybridization, multiple loyalties, etc.

What takes place is both the tendency toward inclusion of the territorial diversity which is compatible in (more) global combinations, as well as the tendency toward exclusion of diversity which arose on the basis of territorial separation (isolation) and is incompatible with the territorial extension of connectedness. We can observe in Europe both empowerment of actors based on the universalistic criteria as well as the widening of delegitimization of territorially exclusionary criteria.

Investigations are carried out under the pressure of the predominant social values and policies which tend to protect the traditionally understood territorial identities, particularly the national ones. There is a lot of simplistic commitment to the continuity of the heritage of territorial cultures without awareness of their exclusionary nature and awareness of the implications of this for other values like autonomy/identity of human personality, which are gaining importance. Continuity cannot be absolutized, but should always be considered together and in a dialogue with discontinuity. There is a general shift from identities based on territorial separation ('identity as island') to the identities formed on the basis of selectivity and choice ('identity as crossroad'). What is not distinguished is the following: territorial diversity in the context of globalization is actually declining as far as this diversity is based on the frontal territorial separation, but it is at the same time increasing, if it is based on the autonomy and selectivity of actors in the context of widening access to the world's variety. This is a challenge for further examination.

Notes

1 Depending on whether we have in mind differences that have come about through the isolation of primordial communities; or differences that stem precisely from greater connectedness and combinations of foreign and indigenous elements.

2 The features of postmodernity require a different understanding of sociology as well; more in terms of oscillation between the two. For a broader discussion of nomothetic and idiographic sciences see the Gulbenkian Commission on the Restructuring of the Social Sciences, 1996; the Commission was chaired by the sociologist I. Wallerstein.

3 Apart from inertia, some sociologists have also been critical of the rather loose debate on global social problems characteristic to date of certain international organizations.

4 This is evident from the discussions of 'the New Europe' and is only magnified when the world as a whole is concerned. Insofar as research in the tradition of Area Studies is involved, again, the treatment is descriptive with great aggregation of superfluous data.

5 In relation to this Brethertoem and Poutom (1996, cited in Clark 1997: 18–19) take the view that globalization is qualitatively distinct from earlier integrations in international relations.

6 Henry Teune and I attempted this in the book *Developmental Logic of Social Systems* (1978) from the standpoint of the dynamics of the inter-dependence of growing diversity and integration. A logically-founded sequence of three types of social systems are presented: coaction, interaction and transaction systems. The transaction system, as a conceptual–logical construct of a particular stage in development includes certain basic features which are today taken as the distinguishing features of the emerging global information society.

7 Nisbet (1969) critically examined what he considered the fundamental premise of the classical theory of social evolution: change is normal, directional, immanent, continuous and cumulative, necessary and proceeds from unitary causes. Lenski (1976, AJS, 84, 5, 1244) rebutted his argument and concluded the debate with 'a plea for an end to the quarrel between humanistic historians, with their focus on unique events and unique personalities, and evolutionists, with their focus on the regularities and patterned trends which emerge from the study of the historical record. There is need for both in today's world. Humanistic history is a valuable antidote to fatalism, just as evolutionism is a check on utopianism.' The discussion today continues in several ways, like in the mentioned Gulbenkian Report (1996), or as a challenge to the Eurocentric and thus exclusionary 'universalism' in sociology (Park 1981), etc.

8 In connection with globalization as an 'emergent reality' the literature contains only a warning for caution in 'ascribing to it forms which have characterised previous societies and draw attention to its historically specific features' (Shaw 1994: 18).

9 This is not an attempt to describe the actual situation today, but rather the developmental logic which holds insofar as ecological constraints are abstracted at least for analytical purposes.

10 Standardization, and uniformity as well, are generally seen in a negative light and little attention has been paid to them by sociologists.

11 Paradoxically, the results of human *incapacity* to overcome spatial barriers in the past has become *a value*, i.e. a particular territorial culture, *threatened* today by the increased *capacity* of people as technology provides wider accessibility in space.

12 See also discussion on the 'logic of sets, networks and systems' by Jan Makarovič (1995).
13 The 'socialist' states pretended to eliminate the contradictions of social development by simply ignoring or repressing the autonomy of (sub)groups and individuals.
14 The dependency theory saw the solution of dependency from the world core in self-sufficiency (de-linking, de-coupling) and dis-engagement from the world capitalist system. However such exclusion from the world system is no longer a matter of choice.
15 But also Dahl and Tufte (1973) stress that smaller, local units yield their autonomy to the next bigger units in a kind of sequence, so that upon joining a supra-national organization the sovereignty of the nation state also begins to diminish. Thus, in the future, the nation state could become a kind of 'local government'.
16 For example, the European Union gives even direct support to transnational inter-linking of regions through numerous programmes, but typically this interlinking is often curbed at the national level by various means because it reduces its control (Bučar, 1993).
17 Some French statesmen have stood up for France's 'right to be different' in the face of the strong trends towards Americanization, but not for analogous rights inside France.

References

Albrow, M. (1996) *Global Age*. Cambridge: Polity Press.
Alger, C. (1988) 'Perceiving, analysing and coping with the local-global nexus', *International Social Science Journal* 40, August, 321–41.
Alger, C. and Mendlowitz, H. (1985) *Approaches to Global Issues by Local Activists in the United States*. Washington, DC: International Studies Association Convention.
Axtmann, R. (ed.) (1998) *Globalization and Europe: Theoretical and Empirical Investigations*. London: Pinter.
Beck, U., Giddens, A. and Lash, S. (1994) *Reflexive Modernisation*. Cambridge: Polity Press.
Becker, G. (1979) 'Comment on Lenski's history and social change', *American Journal of Sociology* 84, 5, March, 1238–42.
Blau, P. (1977) *Inequality and Heterogeneity*. New York: Free Press.
Bučar, B. (1993) *Mednarodni regionalizem* (International Regionalism). Ljubljana: FDV.
Castells, M. (1985) *High Technology, Space and Society*. London: Sage.
Clark, I. (1997) *Globalization and Fragmentation*. Oxford: Oxford University Press.
Clark, T.N. and Hoffman-Martinot, V. (eds) (1999) *The New Political Culture: Urban Policy Challenges*. Boulder CO: Westview Press.
The Commission on Global Governance (1995) *Our Global Neighbourhood*. Oxford: Oxford University Press.
Dahl, R.A. and Tufte, E. (1973) *Size and Democracy*. Stanford: Stanford University Press.
Delors, J. *et al.* (1996) *Learning: The Treasure Within*, Report to UNESCO. Paris: UNESCO.
Fiamengo, A. (1959) *Kozmopolitizam i proletarski internacionalizam* (Cosmopolitism and proletarian internationalism). Sarajevo: Veselin Masleša.
Fontaine, P. and Monnet, J. (1988) *A Grand Design for Europe*. Luxemburg: Office for Official Publication of the EC.
Giddens, A. (1994) 'Living in a post-traditional society' in *Reflexive Modernization*, U. Beck, A. Giddens and S. Lash (eds). Cambridge: Polity Press.

Gill, S. and Law, D. (1988) *The Global Political Economy*. London: Harvester.

Gulbenkian Commission on the Restructuring of the Social Sciences (1996) *Open the Social Sciences: Report of the Gulbenkian Commission on the Restructuring of the Social Sciences*. Stanford: Stanford University Press.

Hirschman, A. (1970) *Exit, Voice and Loyalty*. Harvard University Press.

Jacob, B.M., Ostrowski, K. and Teune, H. (1993) *Democracy and Local Governance: Ten Empirical Studies*. Honolulu: Matsunaga Institute for Peace, University of Hawaii.

Landeck, M. (ed.) (1994) *International Trade: Regional and Global Issues*. New York: St. Martin Press.

Lash, S. and Urry, J. (1994) *Economies of Signs and Space*. London: SAGE Publications.

Lenski, G. (1976) 'History and social change', *American Journal of Sociology* 82, 3, November, 548–64.

Makarovič, J. (1995) 'Od avtarkije k avtonomiji, od homogenosti k enkratnosti (From Autarchy to Autonomy, from Homogeneity to Uniqueness)', in *Osamosvajanje in povezovanje v evropskem prostoru* (Autonomy and Connectedness in the European Space), Mlinar, Z. (ed.). Ljubljana: FDV.

Marx, K. and Engels, F. (1980) *On the Means of Communication*. Bagnolet, France: International Mass Media Research Center..

McLuhan, M. (1962) *The Gutenberg Galaxy*. Toronto: Toronto University Press.

Mlinar, Z. (1992a) 'European integration and socio-spatial restructuring: actual changes and theoretical response', in *International Journal of Sociology and Social Policy* 12, 8, 33–58.

Mlinar, Z. (ed.) (1992b) *Globalization and Territorial Identities*. Aldershot: Avebury.

Mlinar, Z. (1994) *Individuacija in globalizacija v prostoru* (Individuation and Globalization in Space). Ljubljana: SAZU.

Mlinar, Z. (1995) 'Territorial dehierarchization in the emerging new Europe', in *Small States in the Emerging New Europe*, J. Langer and W. Pöllauer (eds). Eisenstadt: Verlag für Soziologie und Humanethologie.

Mlinar, Z. (1997a) 'Territorial diversification and/or homogenization? From identities as islands to identities as crossroads', in *Cultural Crossroads in Europe*, T. Forsgren, (ed.). FRN, Stockholm: Swedish Council for Planning and Coordination of Research. 163–77.

Mlinar, Z. (1997b) *The Process of Globalization and Social Transformation in Central and Eastern Europe*, European Science Foundation Conference: 'The transnational processes and dependencies in the transformation of Central and Eastern European societies', Praha, 14–16 February, Institute of Sociology, Academy of Sciences of the Czech Republic.

Mlinar, Z. (2001) 'The developmental logic of globalization' (co-authored with H. Teune), in *The Art of the Feud: Reconceptualizing International Relations*, J.V. Ciprut (ed.). Westport, CT and London: Praeger.

Mlinar, Z. and Trček F. (1998) 'Territorial cultures and global impacts', in *Globalization and Europe: Theoretical and Empirical Investigations*, R. Axtmann (ed.). London: Pinter, 77–92.

Naisbitt, J. (1994) *Global Paradox*. New York: William Morrow and Co.

Nisbet, R. (1969) *Social Change and History: Aspects of the Western Theory of Development*. Oxford: Oxford University Press.

Park, J.H. (1994) 'Trading blocks and US–Japan relations in pacific trade and cooperation', in: *International Trade: Regional and Global Issues*, M. Landeck (ed.). New York: St. Martin Press.

Park, P. (1981) 'Toward an emancipatory sociology: abandoning universalism for true indigenisation', *International Sociology* 3, 2, 161–70.

Robertson, R. (1992) *Globalization: Social Theory and Global Culture.* London: Sage.

Shaw, M. (1994) *Global society and international relations: sociological concepts and political perspectives.* Cambridge: Polity Press.

Sklar, L. *Sociology of the Global System.* London: Harvester Wheatsheaf.

Solar, M. (1987) 'Kulturni pluralizam u Jugoslaviji', *Kulturni radnik* 40, 2.

Sorokin, P. *et al.* (1930) 'Systematic source book', in *Rural Sociology.* Minneapolis: The University of Minnesota.

Spencer, H. (1975) *The Principles of Sociology.* Connecticut: Greenwood Press.

Teune, H. and Mlinar, Z. (1978) *The Developmental Logic of Social Systems.* London: SAGE Publications.

Wallerstein, I. (1979) *The Capitalist World Economy.* Cambridge: Cambridge University Press.

11 European processes and the state of the European Union

Volker Bornschier

Framing the question

The issue of inclusion and exclusion has a long history in European modernity. Social movements that advanced the various manifestations of liberalism and of nation-building represented the more inclusive drive, whereas the fact that citizen rights and entitlements always remained fragmented in a multitude of exclusive European states put a brake on inclusion. These two sides of European modernity are clearly present in Europe's recent institutional innovation – the state of the European Union – some aspects of which will be discussed in this chapter.[1]

The relaunch of European integration since the 1980s was set in motion by the Single European Act of 1987 with its Single Market project, the new technology policy, and social and economic convergence measures. In the wake of this thrust the integration dynamic continued: the Maastricht Treaty on European Union of 1993 in addition institutionalized the Economic and Monetary Union project and the Amsterdam Treaty started the institutional and financial reforms for the Community's enlargement to the east.

There is hardly disagreement that the events of these dozen years changed statehood in Europe considerably. But what kind of new and additional state level did emerge? We suggest that the curious nature of the form of state called the European Union can be explained as a manifestation of the two conflicting social movements and processes characteristic of European development – past and present. More precisely, the puzzling nature of the governance structures embodied in the institutions of the European Union is due to a renewed compromise between two old European processes – which have become manifest in different forms of nationalism and liberalism.

What exactly is 'odd' about the form of state called the European Union?

The European Union which emerged as a new state level remains a somewhat strange hermaphrodite – something between a confederation of states and a federal state. One important difference between the two is that a federal state unites several states within the framework of a single state in a single nation and is the exclusive subject of international law. By contrast, a confederation of states does not constitute a subject of international law on its own (Scholz 1995: 116f). The latter is formally the case of the EU insofar as its Member States have remained sovereign in terms of international law. But even *de jure* the status of the EU is beyond a confederation, since the sovereignty that the Member States retain is substantially truncated by the self-binding treaties to which they have agreed. Community law – the *acquis communautaire* – is indeed supra-national, binding all Member States in the sense that the regulation is directly applicable.

Yet despite these ambiguities, the EU *de facto* represents a respected and powerful actor on international stage. For example, during the renegotiations of the General Agreement on Tariffs and Trade (GATT), which led to the foundation of the World Trade Organization (WTO) in 1993, the EU was an accepted party to the fierce bargaining that took place with the USA. Furthermore, the EU is regularly represented by the president of the European Commission when the famous Group of Seven gathers.

We used the metaphor of a hermaphrodite to indicate that conventional social science categories fail to come to terms with what the EU actually is. This view is shared by scholars studying the nature of the state in the European Union, regardless of their theoretical approach (see, for example, Münch 1993: 133–81). Klaus Dieter Wolf (1996: 3) stated it concisely: 'The governance structure embodied in the institutions of the European Union is of a puzzling nature, no matter which theoretical perspective is applied to it.' Beverly Springer (1996: 274), reflecting on the 'March toward Monetary Integration,' concluded that the EU is neither an international organization nor a fully sovereign state.

It was Raymond Vernon (1994, see Springer 1996: 273) who poetically described the European Union as 'an historical aberration smuggled into the family of nations.' While poetic, this is an ultimately inaccurate characterization. The European Union is indeed a strange novelty when compared to other products of mainstream state formation, which culminated in the full establishment of nation states in the nineteenth century. But in historical perspective, the EU represents something that was rare but not uncommon in the history of European state-building, and the EU has at least one very influential and eminent European forerunner (see p. 199). However, in its present form, the EU represents a reconciliation between two mighty European forces that was seldom achieved in mainstream European development.

The compromise and its price

It is obvious that for its Member States, the EU restricts their sovereignty and preserves their jointly-exercised sovereignty. Keohane and Hoffmann (1991: 7f, 16f) describe it aptly as the 'pooling and sharing of sovereignty' rather than the transfer of sovereignty to a higher level. Indeed – as all scholars of EU affairs acknowledge – the Council and the European Council represent the real political power in the Union. Member States wield ultimate authority through these Councils: they negotiate and agree on treaties and their amendments, extensions or modifications, which then become law in the Union.

In this context, Klaus Dieter Wolf (1996) has drawn our attention to yet another puzzle. The Member States – normally very proud of the democratic achievements and forms of political participation in their respective nation states – obviously refuse to allow similarly strong forms of democracy to develop at the level of the Union. They are the only formally authorized actors who could jointly agree to let such forms arise. Obviously, the nation states do not want to do so or cannot do so due to restrictions placed upon them by their electorates.

This leads to what is commonly referred to as a deficit of democracy at the level of the Union (see, for example, Lepsius 1991, Bach 1993, Buchmann 1999). Fully democratic procedures at the Union level would certainly legitimate that supra-national governance structure, which then would gain power at the expense of the Member States. Faced with this prospect, the Member States have preferred to supply the Union only with indirect democratic legitimation since they – as democratically-elected and controlled governments – have the last say on treaty matters.

The so-called deficit of democracy, although often referred to in both public as well as academic discourse, is not always fully understood. There are several dimensions to this problem which need to be distinguished.

First, democratic governance requires not only that majorities legitimately decide on political action but that, at the same time, minorities are protected against the arrogance of majorities. In the latter respect the EU's track record is not bad, provided of course that the interests of minorities find a way to be represented by a nation state.

Second, an important criterion of the degree of democratic governance is the equality of each individual vote. However, the quota system through which the assembly of the European Parliament is constituted poses a severe problem in this respect since it violates the principle of equality in franchise (see also Scholz 1995: 120): the number of seats for a country is not directly proportional to the size of its population. A vote for a representative of the European Parliament, for example, in Ireland or Greece has more impact on the distribution of seats in the assembly than a vote in France or even more so in Germany.

Third, the lack of separation of powers is also a serious drawback. Since only the Council can create Community law by amending, extending and renegotiating the treaties binding on all Member States, this body simultaneously also creates supra-national law. In this way, the Council forces the national parliaments to automatically ratify changes in Union law, i.e., by incorporating it into their national laws. This, however, clearly violates the democratic principle that only legitimized parliaments have the power to legislate (see also Vaubel 1995: 131).

Fourth, the EU is characterized by a lack of democratically constituted control. The Commission wields *de facto* executive power rather extensively in the sense that it transforms Union law into decrees and specific regulations that affect the lives of many if not all Union citizens (see also Bach 1992), something that is, of course, the very intention of the treaties. Under strictly democratic conditions, such executive power should be responsible to parliamentary control and parliamentary investigating committees, which, as noted above, are not available in a legitimized form at the Union level.

These are several relevant aspects of what is called the democracy deficit. Since the democratically constituted governments of the nation states have reserved for themselves the right to legislate Union matters, the trade-off between the sovereignty of Member States and democracy at the Union level has been resolved in favor of joint implementation of national sovereignty at the expense of democracy at the highest level of European statehood. Partialized citizenship – coexisting elements of inclusion and exclusion – is a consequence. As economic actors, the people in the states of the Community have become fully integrated citizens of the European Community, whereas most of the political rights and social entitlements remain in the domain of the fragmented nation states.

Nationalism meets liberalism

Despite the nationalist element present in the governance of the European Union discussed above, liberalization in the form of deregulation of formerly quite heavily segmented national economies was successfully implemented through the program of completing the Internal Market. The so-called four freedoms – capital, labor, trade and services – and the establishment of a common governance structure for economic matters through harmonization and/or mutual recognition of regulations correspond to a liberal economic program advocating the removal of barriers to trade and a homogenized market as a basis for and benefit to prosperity and growth. There is no doubt that the transition of formerly nationally regulated and thus quite substantially segmented markets into a single market represents an important step in institutionalizing economic liberalism throughout Europe. Indeed, it is the largest and most far-reaching deregulation project in economic history.

We can thus conclude that the form of state in the European Union represents a compromise between nationalism and liberalism. This conclusion is hardly novel; Wolfgang Streeck (1996: 305) has already described this state as an 'alliance of nationalism and neoliberalism.' Nevertheless, we would like to add that this compromise between divergent forces present throughout European history should be acknowledged as a reconciliation of forces that – to the detriment of Europe – has been quite rare.

Elsewhere we reflect on state-building in Europe (Bornschier 1988, 1996, 2000, see p. 200). Here we would like to acknowledge the two key social forces which acted on this process throughout European history. During the first phase of modernity, i.e., until the beginning of the nineteenth century, European states became more dissimilar. On the one hand, the absolutist state projects accentuated war, while on the other hand, decentralized social systems emphasized trade. Important predecessors of the latter included Venice, the Hanseatic League, the United Provinces of North Holland, and later England and the United States. Over centuries, this polarization in state-building was accompanied by a dramatic process of concentration, reducing the number of states from about 500 to twenty-five (Tilly 1975: 27).

The historical roots of contemporary processes

Which exactly were the forces acting on state formation over these centuries? They consisted primarily of two quite contradictory forces that emerged following the dissolution of the medieval world of Catholic European society. Each represented a new 'absolutism,' albeit in ways that were diametrically opposed to one another. One emphasized collectivism, while the other promoted individualism (see also Coleman 1974). The first was expressed in the theory of the absolute power of the state, the second through a theory of individualism in which the individual is of paramount importance.

Absolute power of the state and individual pre-eminence clashed not only with each other but also with the medieval idea of a fixed position for each social agent within the whole. Power exercised on the basis of the absolutist claim of the state or the individual claim to pre-eminence thus needed new justifications to convince the public that order beyond collective and individual egoism was possible. In collectivism the exercise of power was legitimated over time through the claim that this power was deployed 'for the people.' This justification remained inherently problematic since power exercised in favor of one group of people easily clashes with the claims of other people, and thus engendered belligerent competition between the emerging states of Europe. In the end, attempts at creating order through mutual recognition of the territorial power base of others and the promise of non-intervention in the internal affairs of sovereign states were only a kind of temporary truce.

In the case of individualism, the prescribed form of legitimation seemed much more elegant. Adam Smith provided the well-known justification of individualism: while egoistically pursuing their own ends, humans are led by an invisible hand in such a way as to promote an end that was never part of their intentions. The mysterious alchemy of the market thus transforms individual egoism into a social good – if and only if the market is given free rein. Thus, laissez-faire, i.e., restricting the state to a minimal role, is an integral part of this alchemy. This evolved into the doctrine of economic liberalism, which assumed – just as in the case of the other absolutism – a quasi-religious status.

Yet, liberalism has always been more than that. While it is true that the ideology of liberalism started to spread throughout Europe after the French Revolution, the central ideas and social movements that became liberalism are, in fact, much older. A very early example that demonstrates the roots of liberalism as a manifestation of individualism is the preamble of a law promulgated in Florence in the year 1289 (!) which proclaimed:

> Because liberty as the basis of will cannot be conditional upon alien criteria but must be based on self-determination; because personal freedom derives from natural right – the same that protects people from oppression, that protects and elevates their rights – we are determined to preserve and enhance it.
>
> (quoted in Raith 1979: 29, our translation)

Thus, declarations of human rights came into being long before the Dutch, English, American and French revolutions. They are manifestations of an old and powerful European social movement and theory – individualism – that became elaborated in European Enlightenment with its program of self-empowerment and nourished diverse forms of liberalism – in economic, political and everyday life. The term 'liberalism' as such, however, appeared late; first it came into use in the political sphere at the beginning of the nineteenth century (i.e., *los liberales* in the Spanish Cortes) and signified a plea for the liberty of the individual and his/her right to self-expression.

Each of two aforementioned 'absolutisms' – collectivism and individualism – became manifest in diverse and even conflicting movements. With respect to individualism, we mention here only three of its often conflicting manifestations: in economic, political and everyday life. Collectivism was an emerging consequence of the claim to absolute power by the state. The expansion of state power in Europe ultimately created a most powerful ideology – nationalism, a mixture of primordial and invented collective bonds of belonging, and distinctiveness – in order to both legitimate and to limit through democratization the exercise of this absolute power of the state. At the same time, the territorial expansion of state power produced its own collective enemy, based also on collective bonds, i.e., regionalism. Regionalism, which can be seen as a lower level nationalism, opposed the centralization implied by modern state-building, which abolished or restricted older identities that included patriotism and the right to self-governance at the regional level. This opposition between regionalism and the central state is a consequence of the key feature of European state-building, i.e., the aforementioned shrinking of 500 state-like entities to only twenty-five over the last 500 years of European history.

Socialism, although in theory an internationalist movement, is collectivist in orientation but also oriented toward a strong state. The program of revolutionary socialism was to conquer state power and exercise a new and more just rule prior to the withering away of the state. Even when the reformist, social democratic version of the movement triumphed, socialism was still interested in a strong state with an extended role in economic and social matters whose purpose was to improve the destiny of the people. In this respect socialism and nationalism had a common interest; although in severe conflict with each other, they both were hostile toward liberalism.

The two conflicting historical movements (collectivism and individualism) are still found today in the rather different notions of the state present in political science (Wolf 1996: 8). In the realist approach, the state is mystified as a single unitary rational actor trying to maximize its autonomy within a system of states. By contrast, the liberal perspective on the state sees it as a subsystem of national or international society, which reflects societal needs based on people's preferences and which produces a public good. Here the state is seen as the problem-solver instead of a mystified, glorious, and autonomous actor.

Both currents of thought have been influential in terms of political practice as well as political theory. Thus, the two opposing theories were also embedded as conflicting principles in the Charter of the United Nations, which establishes both the rights of nations (along with a non-intervention clause) and the human rights of the individual. Today, the clash between the principle of territoriality, established on the basis of social groups within a certain area, and the capitalist logic of the free use of economic opportunities in markets, which are fundamentally trans-territorial, has become clearly evident. To some observers this appears to be a *new* feature of global capitalism. But the battle between these principles has been going on in Europe for centuries. Unlike today, these forces were rather represented in conflicting state projects prior to the convergence that began in the nineteenth century.

An early form of reconciling the two conflicting forces was the United Provinces of North Holland, which developed at the end of the sixteenth century. This state was highly atypical for its time but seems very up-to-date when we compare it with the European Union (see Bornschier 1996: 350f). In the provinces of North Holland, the most fully-urbanized area at that time, civilian rule had created for the first time in European history a state structure that was also able to dominate its territory, which became the home of civil liberalism. The balance between the patriotic forces of the sovereign provinces and the newly-emerging liberalism sheds new light on what has been called the curious form of state that is the present-day European Union.

To conclude this section, let us make the following points. *First*, the conflictive compromise between nationalist claims of sovereignty and economic liberalism, which we observe in present-day Europe at the level of the Union, is not as new as it might seem. *Second*, during the process of reconciling nationalism and liberalism in the competitive setting that was Europe, the modern state was ultimately more strongly influenced by the 'trade and economic state' as a 'contract of association' than by the colossal, rapacious states founded on domination and military power that represent the European tradition of war. The formation of the European Union is consistent with this trend toward peace. This aspect of European cooperation is not simply a recent occurrence, but was intended from the beginning, when, on the fifth anniversary of the end of World War II (May 9, 1950), French Minister of Foreign Affairs Robert Schuman proposed a common organization in Europe.

Shifts in the composition of nationalism and liberalism

Compromise – even if conflictive – is not such a bad thing. More often in European history, the supremacy of collectivism was imposed at the expense of liberalism. To be sure, the forerunners of the capitalist project in Europe, which over time were situated in very different places (Venice, the Hanseatic League, North Holland and Britain), were always more liberal than their historical counterparts. But apart from this, the composition of nationalism and liberalism in Europe as a whole shifted in considerable waves which mark distinct phases.

In order to understand the different phases in our century we must briefly turn to the nineteenth century, which started with an initial surge and ended with a resurgence of nationalism. Nevertheless, it was also the century in which liberalism triumphed for the first time in large parts of Western Europe. Liberalism then began to lose strength during the 1880s, both within as well as between countries (Mommsen 1969). The new nationalism after 1870 was an attempt at ideologically mending societal ruptures without having to undertake more fundamental reforms. European imperialism from 1885 until the end of World War I can be seen as an extreme form of nationalist thinking, not only in the continental countries, but also under liberal imperialism in England.

Extreme nationalism, popular arrogance, and accompanying racism and xenophobia were reactions to an insufficient compromise in the class-polarized societal model around the turn of the century. Once again, during the 1920s and the 1930s, such attitudes could be observed in many European countries (and something similar, although much weaker, took place during the 1980s and the 1990s). These ideologies were used to divert attention from domestic conflicts. In this respect Hitler's race hatred and lust for conquest are directly related to this imperialist phase.

The various Europes in the twentieth century

The *first phase* of the composition of nationalism and liberalism in Europe in the twentieth century is actually the continuation of the resurgence of nationalism in the last third of the nineteenth century which ends in the Thirty Years War of this century, 1914–45. In the course of this phase, hyper-nationalism and imperialism triggered the World Wars of this century, in the course of which dramatic changes in economic and political positions within Western core society became evident. By the end, Europe had lost its leadership position to the United States. After 1945, in the *second phase*, Europe, under the hegemony of liberal Keynesianism and US liberalism, recovered. But liberalism remained restricted – 'The state is the solution' was the key phrase to characterize the societal model – and national alliances of the state, business, and the laboring classes for recovery and growth kept a tight rein on liberalism. The *third phase* started with the decay of the Keynesian societal model.

As the 1960s drew to a close, liberalism experienced a resurgence. In one respect, this was obviously evidenced by the renewed absolutism of neoliberalist doctrine, which became hegemonic during the 1970s. But in important respects there was more to it than that. Political liberalism was strengthened, as evidenced by the anti-authoritarian youth movements and the subsequent broad wave of progressive political and social movements which, in addition to their specific themes, had a strong and common focus on basic democratic procedures. It was not only the anti-authoritarian and autonomous movements that evidenced a fresh and radical claim to freedom throughout the Western world; wider segments of society were also increasingly affected. The greater desire of citizens to assume responsibility to organize their own lives was clearly evident. These citizens demanded a society of multiple choices that makes an individualized lifestyle possible. 'Individualization' is the term sociologists have created for this concept. Even those who do not like the quasi-religious nature of economic neoliberalism have been forced to admit that it is only part of a broad current of resurgent individualism.

In sociology and political science this remarkable shift, which altered both the themes of political discourse and the forms of interest articulation, has been labeled by Ronald Inglehart as 'The Silent Revolution.' But this term does not tell the whole story. When institutionalized value priorities and those manifest at the level of citizens begin to diverge, society is on the move. Political potentials can be defined as value priorities among the citizens which – given appropriate political opportunity structures and framing through theories – feed oppositional movements expressing discontent and opposition (Sacchi 1998). The decay of the Keynesian compromise triggered, however, not only one new political potential (the so-called new social movements) but two. Since the beginning of the 1970s, these two emerging political potentials were becoming increasingly polarized in Western countries. This is shown by the detailed empirical research of Stefan Sacchi (1998) covering the past quarter of a century. Indeed the 'silent revolution' represented both the rebirth of oppositional (and universalist) liberalism and the rebirth of a regressive and authoritarian political potential that nourished the renewed identification with forms of 'nationalisms' at the regional and nation state level.

The move toward political union: did liberalism eventually beat nationalism?

The modern push toward European integration, which started as early as the beginning of the 1950s, persisted through two phases of Europe in the twentieth century – the above-mentioned Keynesian era and the resurgence of liberalism (Ziltener 1999). But it was only the revitalization of the Community in the 1980s that changed the very nature of integration by adding a considerably extended political dimension to it, one that was continued but in no way fundamentally altered by the Treaty on European Union, ratified in 1993.

Elsewhere we have argued based on research that the European transnational corporations represented by informal but indeed influential Roundtables were – together with the Commission – the ultimately decisive protagonists behind the thrust of the 1980s without which the move toward European Union would not have happened (Bornschier 1996, 2000). The fact that the transnational economic elite of Western Europe were pushing core elements of the Single European Act in the mid-1980s could be falsely interpreted as a triumph of deregulationist philosophy over the state, but this is, in fact, not the case. Even for the European transnational corporations themselves, a compromise between protective nationalism and economic liberalism is evident. To be sure, this new type of nationalism is a social force that transcends the established nation states. It seems less emotional and more instrumental in kind, and its frame of reference is competition in the world system. The European business elite and the political elite in Brussels were and are the early, influential spokesmen of this Euro-nationalism. Among the latter, the political Euro-entrepreneur Jacques Delors has always been a strong advocate of this new form of Euro-nationalism and one willing to project European brilliance into the future.

But Euro-nationalism was in no way restricted to the elite who managed the integration thrust of the mid-1980s. A significant minority of Community citizens belongs to this group, too. Unfortunately, despite the continuing efforts at monitoring European public opinion, we cannot say whether this group has increased in size over time. At least we know that in 1982 – before the push for integration – a bit more than twenty percent of the Community's citizens could be classified as Euro-nationalists, i.e., often self-identifying as 'Europeans' and expressing mistrust against extra-European powers (Krummenacher 1997).

We now must acknowledge the varieties of 'nationalism' in Europe. At present, nationalism as a powerful historical manifestation of a collective ideology assumes different and opposing forms: regionalism, nationalism, and Euro-nationalism. Patriotism rooted in local or regional bonds may easily reactivate resentments against the nation state, since the victory of that very nation state originally put an end to their forms of self-government. Therefore, this kind of nationalism is most often opposed to classical nationalism, although it might well seek alliances with Euro-nationalist forces against the nation state in order to regain more independence. Classical nationalism is rooted in historically-constructed bonds which are based on entitlements, political and social rights that became institutionalized at the level of the nation state during the last two centuries. It may regard regional bonds as forms of backwardness while at the same time perceiving Euro-nationalism as threatening established political and social rights. Euro-nationalism is progressive in a historical sense insofar as it seeks protection at a level beyond the nation state, a collectivity large enough to provide competitive advantages in a world system in which smaller political units increasingly feel the threat of falling behind.

Unfortunately, we have little empirical evidence on the shifts in size of the different kinds of collective identities over time and on their exclusiveness. Even if we have little information on changes over time, we can say that up to 30 percent of EU citizens can be classified as distinct nationalists, and about twenty percent can be termed marked Euro-nationalists in the above mentioned sense (Krummenacher 1997). Another finding for two time points at the beginning of the 1990s suggest that about fifty-five percent of EU citizens feel very attached to their region (Rothenbühler 1997). The latter study suggests that nationalist and regionalist identification are of about the same size, whereas the identification with Europe or the EU is clearly lower and declining between 1991 and 1995 (note that identification with Europe or the EU is not identical with Euro-nationalist attitudes, see p. 196).

From recent research we can conclude that distinct nationalist orientation does not represent a serious threat to European integration. The expression of national pride and support for European integration are not mutually exclusive alternatives. Less spectacular is the finding that Euro-nationalists on the average are more favorable toward integration than the rest of the population and would regret it more if it failed (Krummenacher 1997). The citizens of the EU seem to be increasingly attached to smaller units like the region or city while the corresponding figures for feelings of attachment to the European Union slide down. But there is no hint at all that identification with their own region is affecting the attitude toward European integration (Rothenbühler 1997).

A compromise – no victory of liberalism

Interpreting the form of the state in the European Union as a compromise between nationalism and liberalism must acknowledge not only the tensions between the underlying forces of collectivism and individualism, but also the fact that European reality is a bit more complex than that. Indeed – in the case of different forms of nationalism – it is a multi-level compromise. Modern day liberalism quarrels with nationalism, but different forms of collective identity also quarrel among themselves: regionalism, classical nationalism and Euro-nationalism. The same is true for the various manifestations of liberalism, although to a lesser extent. While economic liberalism is quite well established at the Union level, the key claims of political liberalism are not – as evidenced by the democracy deficit to which we referred.

Looking back at European history, the various manifestations of collective identity have changed considerably in terms of their impact. Regionalism has always been opposed to the centralization implied by state-building, which restricted or abolished older rights and forms of self-government of smaller political units. Nationalism and the creation of a nation became a strategy to legitimate the authority of the nation state. This in turn triggered the extension of citizens' rights (see Marshall [1950] 1965). At the Union level this process is repeated. Nationalism now seems to be playing the role of an oppositional force with respect to the Union project much as regionalism once did vis-à-vis the emerging nation states. However – and this is quite important – contemporary regionalism has not become weakened by the process of European integration; quite the contrary. Thus regionalism and nationalism have become two distinct forces in opposition to the centralization of authority, while at the same time both are in opposition to each other.

The European nation state has thus come under pressure to compromise from two sides: from the quest for more regional autonomy, and from being forced to give away regulatory authority to the supra-national body of the Union. The European nation states reacted to these pressures by maintaining ultimate control over the matters of the Union. However, the binding nature of the Union treaty is, at the same time, significant and transfers considerable executive power from the nation states to the new supra-national European state. The price of this overall compromise is the aforementioned and not insignificant deficit of democracy in European politics. Given the complicated forces behind the compromise this deficit will not be easy to overcome. Empirical evidence for the compromise is suggested by the mentioned findings: contrary to general opinion classical nationalism as well as regionalism – in their present forms at least – are not endangering European integration, although they do help to shape it.

Given the weight of the multi-level compromise of collective identities embodied in the overall governance structures of European institutions, one can hardly say that liberalism took over in Europe. Yet, it increased its impact at the same time. Without question, the deregulation project in Europe is of a historic dimension and was pushed by a forceful ideology. We should, however, not make neoliberalism a comic figure. This is only one aspect of the resurgence of liberalism, which has become accepted by wider segments of the population in the realm of politics (grassroots democracy, referenda) and everyday life (individualization). Thus we have to accept, even if we do not admire, that European citizens have become more liberal and seek to democratize their freedom. This is why opposition to economic liberalism has been limited.

The European state of nations – model for the world society?

The heading of this concluding section is not a product of arrogance or eurocentrism; it is quite obvious that previous European social innovations have been models for the world. The cultural legacy of the Atlantic West – the roots of which lie in Europe – shaped those institutions which incontrovertibly determine core status in world society: the market, social egalitarianism, the rule of law along with the sharing of power and political checks and balances, economic enterprise and modern schools. To be sure, within that globally dominant social practice Europe does not play the role it once did. But it is far from being on the decline, as evidenced by its revitalization of the 1980s with the continuing integration dynamic in the 1990s, and its proven ability to again contribute innovatively to the future shape of world society – the supranational state level being the case in point here.

At present, two quite different kinds of state alliances prepare for leadership in the next century: the United States of America as a federal nation state and the European State of Nations. Even if different, the two are actually not independent, a point made obvious by the NATO alliance linking the Atlantic West under American leadership and military might. Despite this joint leadership, which is facilitated by a strong common cultural heritage, the differences in the two forms of state are important and will not wither away soon.

It has become clear from what we and others have already said (see Lepsius 1991) that there will not be a United States of Europe in the foreseeable future, since that would be implying a melting pot of nations – although admittedly this was an admirable historical accomplishment in case of the USA. Contrary to this, the European state project rests for the time being on the acknowledgment of its constituent nations, which have developed in the course of history. What the Union contributes to this is an increasingly European identity – not as a replacement for, but as an addition to, national, regional and local bonds. Such an over-arching European identity has existed for long in Europe's history, albeit to varying degrees and restricted to elites.

Does the specific type of alliance of state power that recently developed in Europe imply that the resulting state will be a comparatively weak one? What is a strong state and what is a weak one? A strong state is one that is also able to institutionalize solidarity – an obvious strength of recent European state-building – and can reconcile the different forces, nationalism and liberalism, in a productive compromise that represents more than a stalemate. This does not seem impossible in case of the EU – for efforts see 'target cohesion' and 'social and economic convergence' in Bornschier (2000). But will such a state configuration also be successful in taking part in peaceful world economic competition? This remains to be seen (cf. Bornschier and Chase-Dunn 1999), but the history of Europe suggests that pessimism is not appropriate. The example of the state of North Holland seems to be relevant for the debate. Here we recall Fernand Braudel's (1984: 193) question: Can the United Provinces of North Holland be called a 'state'? No matter how that question is answered for the 'Dutch Century', there is no doubt that during its time the novel system of governance in North Holland achieved pre-eminence in the emerging world economy for a century and that this societal system was astonishingly liberal compared to its contemporary rivals.

Thus, what has been termed the 'odd nature' of the form of state represented by the European Union and what has even been called 'a historical aberration' must be re-interpreted in a rather different light. The present-day uniqueness of this European social innovation – which follows that earlier European innovation, the nation state – may become a model to the world for reconciling the different manifestations of nationalism and liberalism in a multi-level system of governance.

Note

1 This chapter is based on the author's talk, opening the sessions on 'European Processes, Boundaries and Institutions' at the Third European Sociological Association Conference, University of Essex (UK) 27–30 August 1997. For the sake of brevity many aspects relevant for the European integration process and for the EU in the triad had to be omitted.

200   *Volker Bornschier*

References

Bach, M. (1992) 'Eine leise Revolution durch Verwaltungsverfahren. Bürokratische Integrationsprozesse in der Europäischen Gemeinschaft', *Zeitschrift für Soziologie* 21, 1: 16–30.

Bach, M. (1993) 'Vom Zweckverband zum technokratischen Regime: Politische Legitimation und institutionelle Verselbständigung in der Europäischen Gemeinschaft', in *Nationalismus, Nationalitäten, Supranationalität*, A.H. Winkler and H. Kaelble (eds). Stuttgart: Klett-Cotta, pp. 288–308.

Bornschier, V. (1988) *Westliche Gessellschaft im Wandel*. Frankfurt/Main and New York: Campus.

Bornschier, V. (1996) *Western Society in Transition*. New Brunswick and London: Transaction Publishers.

Bornschier, V. (ed.) (2000) *Statebuilding in Europe. The Revitalization of Western European Integration*. Cambridge: Cambridge University Press.

Bornschier, V. and Chase-Dunn, C. (1999) 'Technological change, globalization and hegemonic rivalry', in *The Future of Global Conflict*, V. Bornschier and C. Chase-Dunn (eds). London: Sage, chapter 14.

Braudel, F. (1984) *The Perspective of the World*. Vol. 3 of *Civilization and Capitalism 15th–18th Century*. New York: Harper and Row.

Buchmann, M. (1999) 'European integration: disparate dynamics of bureaucratic control and communicative participation', in *European Societies: Fusion or Fission?*, T.P. Boje, B. van Steenbergen and S. Walby (eds). London: Routledge, pp. 53–65.

Coleman, J.S. (1974) *Power and the Structure of Society*. New York: Norton.

Keohane, R.O. and Hoffmann, S. (1991) 'Institutional change in Europe in the 1980s', in *The New European Community. Decisionmaking and Institutional Change*, Keohane and Hoffmann (eds). Boulder CO: Westview, pp. 1–39.

Krummenacher, F. (1997) *Nationalismus und europäische Einigung*. MA thesis, University of Zurich, Sociological Institute.

Lepsius, R.M. (1991) 'Nationalstaat oder Nationalitätenstaat als Modell für die Weiterentwicklung der Europäischen Gemeinschaft', in *Staatswerdung Europas? Optionen für eine Europäische Union*, R. Wildenmann (ed.). Baden-Baden: Nomos, pp. 19–40.

Marshall, T.H. ([1950] 1965) *Class, Citizenship and Social Development*. Garden City: Anchor Books.

Mommsen, W.J. (1969) *Das Zeitalter des Imperialismus*. Frankfurt Main: Fischer.

Münch, R. (1993) *Das Projekt Europa. Zwischen Nationalstaat, regionaler Autonomie und Weltgesellschaft*. Frankfurt Main: Suhrkamp.

Raith, W. (1979) *Florenz vor der Renaissance. Der Weg einer Stadt aus dem Mittelalter*. Frankfurt Main: Campus.

Rokkan, S. (1975) 'Dimensions of state formation and nation-building', in *The Formation of National States in Western Europe*, C. Tilly (ed.). Princeton, NJ: Princeton University Press, pp. 562–600.

Rothenbühler, A. (1997) *Regionale Indentität und europäische Integration*. MA thesis, University of Zurich, Sociological Institute.

Sacchi, S. (1998) *Politische Potentiale in modernen Gesellschaften. Zur Formierung linksgrüner und neokonservativer Bewegungen in Europa und den USA*. Frankfurt Main: Campus.

Scholz, R. (1995) 'Europäische Union – Voraussetzung einer institutionellen Verfassungsordnung', in *Europa zwischen Ordnungswettbewerb und Harmonisierung*, L. Gerken (ed.). Berlin: Springer, pp. 113–27.

Springer, B. (1996) 'The march toward monetary integration: Europe and the Maastricht Treaty', in *International Political Economy. State–Market Relations in the Changing Global Order*, C. R. Goddard, J.T. Passé-Smith and J.G. Conklin (eds). Boulder CO: Lynne Rienner, pp. 272–87.

Streeck, W. (1996) 'Public power beyond the nation-state. the case of the European community', in *States Against Markets. The Limits of Globalization*, R. Boyer and D. Drache (eds). London: Routledge, pp. 299–315.

Tilly, C. (1975) *The Formation of National States in Western Europe*. Princeton, NJ: Princeton University Press.

Vaubel, R. (1995) 'Diskussionsbeitrag', in *Europa zwischen Ordnungswettbewerb und Harmonisierung*, L. Gerken (ed.). Berlin: Springer, pp. 129–34.

Vernon, R. (1994) Speech to the Academy of International Business Conference. Boston, November 4.

Wolf, K.D. (1996) 'Defending state autonomy. Intergovernmental governance in the European Union', Working Paper no. 5, World Society Research Group, University of Darmstadt and University of Frankfurt.

Ziltener, P. (1999) *Strukturwandel der europäischen Integration. Die Europäische Union und die Veraenderung von Staatlichkeit*. Münster: Westfälisches Dampfboot.

Index

206   *Index*

interconnectedness 170;
interdependencies 170;
internationalization 176; intimacy 171;
life courses 97–8; process/epoch 172–3,
181–2; sectors 177–8; sociology 171–4;
universalism 176–7; welfare states 148
Goldthorpe, J. 117, 131–2, 135, 136–7,
138, 140
Goodin, R.E. 2
Gramsci, A. 60
grey economy 120
group rights 67–8

Habermas, Jürgen 40, 157
Habsburg Empire 116
Hall, Stuart 59, 63, 64
Hammar, Tomas 42
Hareven, T.K. 93
harmonization, European Union 180
Harris, D. 66
health care 122
health inequalities 141
Held, T. 93
Heritage Associations, Sweden 158
Hill-Collins, Patricia 68
Hirschman, A. 181
Hoffmann, S. 188
Holland, North 193, 199
homogenization 76–7, 174, 175, 180
housing policy 118
human rights 66, 192
Hungary: social security 120; welfare state
116, 119–20, 123

identity: class 128; construction 72;
culture 59; difference 73; discourse 59;
ethnicity 61–2; Europe 199; regionalism
197; territory 75; work 161
identity, types: communal 73; forced 64;
hybrid 64; Jewish 62–3, 65; nomadic 64;
postmodern 74; post-national 74;
symbolic 65
identity narratives 61–2
identity politics 11–12
immigration: *see* migration
imperialism, European 194
inclusion: civic 8; economic 6–8;
employment 8; global 169–70;
integration 10; political 4–6; systems
theory 4; territory 177, 181
inclusion/exclusion 1, 5, 10–11, 21–3,
78–82, 169, 175, 187
income inequalities 103
individual: autonomy 71, 73; modernity

71–2; postmodernism 155; society 4, 22,
25–8; state 147–8
individualism 191, 192
individualization: autonomy 4; Beck 31;
citizenship 195; generality 22, 30–1, 35;
globalization 14, 170, 174–6
industrialism, class 129
inequalities: class 3, 141; gender 105, 149;
health 141; income 103; increasing 98;
life chances 71–2
information technology 90
Inglehart, Ronald 195
INPART (Inclusion through
Participation) 147, 150, 152, 158, 160,
161, 163n1
institutions: life courses 12, 95, 96, 99;
mediation 34
integration: employment 150, 151;
European Union 14, 147, 187, 195, 197;
functionalism 9; inclusion 10; planetary
society 78–9; social services 161;
training schemes 153
interconnectedness 170, 175, 176
interdependencies 170
intermediation 34–5
international human rights 66
international markets 90
international relations theory 176
internationalization/globalization 176
intimacy/globalization 171
Islamic fundamentalism 63
isolation 3
Italy: feminism 68; social cooperatives
158
ius sanguinis 47–8, 55n24
ius soli 48, 55n19, 55n29

Jellinek, Georg 42
Jepsen, Maria 158
Jewish identity 62–3, 65
Job Pools, Denmark 152
job schemes, stigmatization 152

Keohane, R.O. 188
Keynesianism 194
Kidric, D. 120, 122
kinship networks 142
Kohli, M. 6, 93
Kresal, F. 120, 122
Krummenacher, F. 196
Kurdish immigrants 38
Kymlicka, Will 67

labor: age 6; exclusion 107, 147; gender
97; migration 6; trade unions 90; *see also*